FAVORITE

from a Treasury of
Country Inns and Lodges

Compiled by
Lucille Carloftis

The Overmountain Press

JOHNSON CITY, TENNESSEE

Notes from original publication by the author in 1988

My special thanks for the encouragement to finish this book goes to my husband Carlos, my daughters carcille, Koula, and Betsy - and my sons Buzz, Dusty, and Jon.

To my grandchildren, Laura Whitney, Koula Verda, Carly Rae, John Zachary, and Betsy Lucille.

For my friends Clara Mitchell Hinton, Latisha Jones, Julia Stacy, and Darlene Rains who worked on this project — many thanks. Thanks also to the travel writers and artists.

Cover photograph of the Bailey House used by permission from Tom and Diane Hay, Innkeepers.

Map design by Julia Stacy.

To the innkeepers and chefs
who are helping to preserve
these treasures of America and
for graciously contributing their recipes,
I dedicate this book.

Whoe'er has traveled
life's dull round,
Whate'er his various
tour has been,
May sigh to think
how oft he found
His warmest welcome
at an inn.

William Shakespeare

With the publication of this book it is acknowledged by all parties concerned that changes occur from time to time. . .even the innkeepers themselves. Therefore, it is suggested the traveler call in advance for further information regarding current services, amenities and availability.

The Abbey is an opulent seaside villa located right in the heart of historic Cape May, New Jersey. The old structure is remarkably built and measured drawings of it are recorded in the Library of Congress.

Elegant accommodations and warm hospitality define this beautiful structure with its imposing sixty-foot tower, stenciled ruby glass arched windows and shaded verandas. The building was completed in 1869 as the summer home of wealthy Pennsylvania coal baron and politician, John B. McCreary.

Inside, the inn has been meticulously restored, and the large comfortable rooms are furnished with Victorian antiques, chandeliers, 12-foot mirrors, and ornate gas fixtures. The guest rooms have tall walnut beds and marble topped dressers.

A "community" home-prepared breakfast is served every morning.

Must-Go-Quiche

1 lb. Havarte cheese, grated	1 doz eggs
1 lb bacon, cooked & crumbled	4 cups light cream
1 med zucchini, grated	1 cup Bisquick
2 tomatoes, cut into wedges	3 finely chopped scallions

Place cheese in bottom of 2 x 10 pie plates. Top with cooked, crumbled bacon and grated zucchini. Arrange tomato wedges on top and sprinkle with chopped scallions. In large bowl, lightly beat eggs, add cream and Bisquick and mix thoroughly. Pour over cheese mixture and bake at 350 degrees for 45 - 50 minutes.

Columbia Avenue and Gurney Streets
Cape May, NJ 08204
Tel (609) 884-4506

NORTHEAST

Adirondak Loj

Adirondak Loj enjoys an unparalleled setting that includes 27-acre Heart Lake and the Adirondak peak, Mt. Jo. The rustic resort is eight miles south of Lake Placid with hundreds of miles of marked trails leading from the front door and with most of New York's highest peaks within easy reach.

Outdoor activities abound, and the Adirondak's wilderness education program provides workshops for those who wish to learn a new skill or to sharpen an old one. Instructors are available from natural history to ice climbing.

The comfortable lounge is typical with a huge stone fireplace, making it an ideal spot for get-togethers with other guests or just plain relaxing. Accommodations are provided for up to 48 guests in private rooms or small bunkrooms.

Tasty homecooked meals are served family-style in the pine panelled dining room.

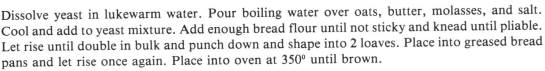

Rolled Oats Molasses Bread

2 cups oats	**1 3/4 tsp salt**
1/2 cup molasses	**1 tbs butter**
2 cups boiling water	**1 tbs yeast**
1/4 cup lukewarm water	**bread flour**

Dissolve yeast in lukewarm water. Pour boiling water over oats, butter, molasses, and salt. Cool and add to yeast mixture. Add enough bread flour until not sticky and knead until pliable. Let rise until double in bulk and punch down and shape into 2 loaves. Place into greased bread pans and let rise once again. Place into oven at 350° until brown.

Box 867
Lake Placid, NY 12946
Tel (518) 523-3441

NORTHEAST

olive Metcalf

ANDOVER INN

Andover Inn serves both European and Indonesian specialities in the warm atmosphere of a Georgian brick structure located in the middle of Andover's academic community: the campus of Phillip's Academy. Near major highways, Andover Inn is an ideal stopover for traveling businessmen as well as visiting alumni and parents of students. The lounge is filled with colorful colonial furniture and a warming fireplace. Guest rooms are very comfortable with views of the garden, pond, and campus.

Meals are prepared and served in a dining room with richly polished wood, beamed ceilings, shimmering chandeliers, lofty windows, and white linens. During the evening, guests enjoy light classical music played on the grand piano.

Mushroom en Croute

1 lb mushrooms
4 oz creme fraiche
1/2 oz dry white wine
4 slices trimmed wheat toast

1/2 small shallot

1 oz clarified butter
4 oz freshly grated Swiss cheese

Saute mushrooms and shallots in butter and wine until tender. Place toast on baking sheet and divide equally prepared mushrooms (do not include any liquid). Top each with equal portions of creme fraiche, then cheese. Place under broiler until cheese has melted but not browned. Serves 4.

Chapel Avenue
Andover, MA 01810
Tel (508) 475-5903

NORTHEAST

Asa Ransom House

Asa Ransom House stands on a land grant issued in 1799 by the Holland Land Company. Although several additions have been made, portions of the original building are still intact and date back to 1853.

The cozy library is a favorite gathering place with board games, books, and periodicals. Guest rooms are attractive and furnished with antiques. These include canopied and brass beds and period reproductions. We are a full service Village Inn with nine guestrooms, most with fireplaces and porches or balconies. The porch has intimate tables for two for alfresco lunch or dinner in season. The inn is entirely non-smoking, and in the Ransom Room a jacket is still expected; however, in the Clarence Hollow, jackets are optional. Our country gourmet menu changes with the seasons, four times a year. Soup is still served from the kettle tableside, and everybody "ODs" on our homemade rolls and muffins. Our specialties include Pretzel & Ale Chicken, Smoked Corned Beef with Apple Raisin Sauce, and Country Veal Shanks.

Chicken Corn Chowder

3-1/2 cups chicken stock	1 cup med. diced carrots
salt & pepper to taste	1 cup med. diced celery
1-3/4 cups med. diced onions	2 tbs chicken fat
1/2 cup corn (raw or cooked)	1/3 cup flour
1-1/2 cups chef's med. diced potatoes	1-1/2 cups med. diced cooked chicken

In a separate sauce pot heat chicken stock, then using a 3-qt sauce pot sauté onions, celery, and carrots in chicken fat. Season lightly with salt and pepper. Cook until onions are transparent in color. Reduce heat and add flour to absorb fat, stirring so it will not scorch. Cook 5-8 minutes. To this add half hot chicken stock and stir well to dissolve flour. Add remaining stock. Turn up heat and bring to boil. Add potatoes and corn and simmer until potatoes are tender. Season to taste and add chopped parsley for garnish. Makes 2-1/2 qts.

10529 Main Street
Clarence, NY 14031
Tel (716) 759-2315
Fax (716) 759-2791
http://www.asaransom.com

NORTHEAST

The Balsam House

The Balsam House is Victorian in style and sits among a grove of trees above the sparkling waters of Friends Lake. It was built as a home in 1845 and expanded in 1891 to accommodate summer boarders. Wicker chairs on the front porch and breezes from paddle fans invite easy conversation and relaxation.

Elegant furnishings tastefully range from bold, rich colors and voluptuous sofas to the intricate details of lace...reminders of her Victorian past. All guest rooms are comfortable and pleasantly decorated with grandmother spreads, feather pillows, and interesting old pieces. Each room is quite different with recessed windows and little nooks and crannies.

Dinner is served in an elegant dining room that blends soft peach and navy colors with a large marble fireplace. The menu includes Adirondack Trout, Duckling Chambertin, Sauteed Veal Kidneys, Steak, Veal, and Rack of Lamb that has been described by an internationally-known writer as "the best I've had on four continents." This never-before-published specialty Sweetbreads Balsam House is prepared by Master Chef Ernest Doffe.

Sweetbreads Balsam House

cold water	1 tbs vinegar
1 tsp salt	4 tbs butter
1 lb sweetbreads	4 slices bacon
1 large onion, diced	
1/2 cup red wine	2 carrots, diced
salt & pepper to taste	

Cover sweetbreads with cold water to which the vinegar and 1 tsp salt have been added. Soak for 2 hours. Next, blanche sweetbreads in 2 quarts boiling water for 10 minutes. Drain and plunge immediately into cold water. Strain and let cool. Remove nerve and skin and separate into 4 parts. Melt 4 tbs butter in very hot skillet, adding diced onion, carrot, and sweetbreads. Saute until brown (10 minutes maximum). Shake pan or stir constantly. Remove from heat. Line sides of two ramekins with two slices bacon each. Press carrots, onions, and sweetbreads into ramekins with bottom of wine bottle or wooden mallet. Bake at 350° for 15 minutes. When top is brown, add 1/4 cup wine to each ramekin and cook 5 minutes longer. Serve with rice and vegetables. Serves 2.

Friends Lake
Chestertown, NY 12817
Tel (518) 494-2828

Barnard-Good House

The Barnard-Good House recalls the days of the Victorian era when Cape May attracted national and international society to its beaches and boarding houses. There were no less than five American presidents who found it an inviting retreat from Washington, including Benjamin Harrison who established Cape May as his "summer" White House.

This charming inn stands in the heart of the historic city and was built in 1869. Complete in its Victorian architecture, the wraparound veranda is filled with old-fashioned, comfortable rockers, making it the perfect spot for getting to know other guests or to relax with a good book and enjoy the light sea breezes. Bicycles and beach tags are added amenities.

A gourmet breakfast is lovingly created and includes Freshly Squeezed Orange Juice with Apricot Nectar, Swiss Souffle with Yogurt Sauce, a Leek and Potato dish, Swedish Spice Cake, Homemade Breads, and Blueberry Grents.

Blueberry Grents

1 egg	1/3 cup whipping cream
2/3 cup flour	
2 tbs sugar	1 tsp baking powder
1/4 tsp salt	

Beat egg with 1/3 cup whipping cream in small bowl. Whisk in flour, sugar, baking powder, and salt. Combine with:

2 tbs fresh lemon juice	1/2 cup sugar
1/2 cup water	1/2 tsp allspice
1/2 tsp freshly grated nutmeg	

Bring to boil, adding:

2 pints fresh or frozen blueberries

Return to boil and reduce to a bare simmer. Drop in rounded tablespoons of butter, leaving 1/2" between each. Cover and simmer gently without peeking for 15-20 minutes. Uncover and test for doneness with toothpick.

238 Perry Street
Cape May, NJ 08204
Tel (609) 884-5381

BISHOPSGATE INN

Bishopsgate Inn was built by merchant and shipbuilder Horace Hayden in 1818 and, as should be expected, the inn is just what New England architecture is all about: Early American clapboarding covering a saltbox-type house. Each tastefully furnished floor has its own sitting room. The guest rooms have family antiques and period pieces, and four of the rooms have fireplaces. Naturally, no two rooms are alike.

Within easy walking distance to the Goodspeed Opera House, fine restaurants, antiques, craft and gift shops, the private grounds are reminders of the beautiful East Haddam countryside. "Bishopsgate Inn is a gem" is one of the many favorable comments from publications such as *The East Coast Bed and Breakfast Guide.*

Breakfast is served each morning in the spacious country kitchen. Fragrant coffee, freshly baked goods from the oven, and preserves from the pantry greet the morning. A favorite from Julie Bishop, the previous owner, was this recipe.

Cheese-Filled Apricot Bread
(Tangy apricots and cream cheese in a handsome loaf)

1 box dried apricots
3 tbs butter
3 eggs
1 cup sugar
2-1/2 cups flour

1/2 tsp salt
2 tsp vanilla
1 cup nuts
1 tsp soda
1 tsp baking powder

Filling:

1 egg
2 pkgs (3 oz) cream cheese
1/3 cup sugar

1 tbs flour

Cut apricots in small pieces. Place in large bowl and add baking soda, butter, and 1 cup boiling water. Mix well and allow to cool. Beat eggs and add sugar, then combine with apricots. Sift flour, salt, and baking powder and add to apricot mixture. Stir in vanilla and nuts.
For Filling: Soften cream cheese. Beat in sugar, flour and egg. Beat and smooth. Grease and flour a loaf, putting 3/4 bread mixture into pan, then spread cheese mixture on top. Cover with remaining bread mixture and bake at 350° for 60-65 minutes.

Goodspeed Landing
East Haddam, CT 06423
Tel (203) 873-1677

NORTHEAST

BLACK BASS HOTEL

Black Bass Hotel provided a fortified haven for river travelers against Indian attacks during the turbulant days of the 1740's, and today the Black Bass is still an ideal retreat. The hostelry has given warmth and hospitality for generations based upon the old provedb, "Make new friends, keep the old, these are silver, those are gold." During the Revolutionary War the hotel was loyal to the Crown and it was recorded that George Washington was refused accommodations.

The inn was saved from a nearby disastrous fire in 1832-33 when Major Anthony Fry broke into the cellar and carried to safety blasting powder that had been stored by the Canal Company. In 1949 Black Bass underwent its last restoration.

The ancient rooms are filled with 18th and 19th century furnishings, and some of the rooms face the Delaware River with private balconies. A Continental breakfast is placed each morning outside the guest's door.

Meals are served in either the Stone Room, Lantern Room or Jackson Room. Roast Duckling Normandie, Charleston Meeting Street Crabmeat, and other delightful fare await the guests.

Roasted Sea Scallops with Pistachio Nut & Cognac Butter

1-1/2 lbs sea scallops	6 oz unsalted butter
4 oz peeled pistashio nuts	2 tsp chopped parsley
1 fl oz cognac or to taste	2 tsp fine chopped shallots

Soften butter and add in pistachios, shallots, and parsley. Add cognac and salt to taste. Place whole scallops in casserole, split butter on top, and roast at 450° for 10 to 15 minutes. Serve with combination of brown or wild rice and fresh broccoli.

Route 32
Lumberville, Bucks County, PA 18933
Tel (215) 297-5770 or 5815

NORTHEAST

Blueberry Hill

Blueberry Hill's quiet environment and 1800s charm is a reflection of early traditional living. This friendly two-story inn is surrounded with views of mountains and valleys in the Green Mountain National Park. The open kitchen is a favorite gathering place, filled with aromas of imaginative food. Comfortable guest rooms are pleasantly decorated with antiques and warm, colorful quilts.

Directly across from the inn stands the Blueberry Hill Ski Touring Center. An expert staff devotes itself to skiers of all ages and abilities. Although skiing is the main winter activity, summer months offer an inn-to-inn hiking program, canoeing, sightseeing, and fishing.

Early morning coffee is served in the greenhouse with Blueberry Muffins and Scones.

Blueberry Scones

2 cups flour	1 tbs baking powder
1 tsp salt	3 tbs sugar
1/3 cup butter	2/3 cup milk
2/3 cup blueberries	1 egg yolk & 1 tbs water
	beaten together

Mix flour, baking powder, salt, and sugar. Cut in butter until mixture resembles coarse meal. Stir in milk, add blueberries. Shape dough into flat rounds 9'' diameter. With sharp knife cut into 8 wedges. Brush top with egg yolk and water. Bake at 400° 12-15 minutes until lightly browned.

Goshen, VT 05733
Tel (802) 247-6735

NORTHEAST

The Bradley Inn

ISAIAH 11 1-10

The Bradley Inn was built around the turn of the century at the end of Pemaquid Point with views of John's Bay. An authentic air of days long since past still lingers in this gracious old inn that is a short walk from the historic and picturesque Pemaquid Lighthouse. Visitors may take in Fort Henry, New Harbor, and interesting restorations. The white sandy beach and woods are beautiful for walking and exploring. A golf course is seven miles away.

The comfortable lounge, woodburning stove, sundeck, and large screened-in porch provide a very pleasant atmosphere. Each guest room is airy with homelike comforts.

A Continental breakfast is prepared each morning, and the old-fashioned dining room serves the public as well as guests. The menu includes Maine Lobster, Shrimp Scampi, Southern Chocolate Pie, and other temptations.

Bradley Inn Oven-Style Shrimp Scampi

1/2 lb butter, melted
1/4 cup cooking sherry
1/4 cup chopped parsley
1/8 cup lemon juice
4 minced garlic cloves
2 lb shrimp (smaller the better)

1 tsp Worcestershire
1/2 tsp Tabasco sauce
1/2 tsp salt
1/2 cup bread crumbs
1/2 tbs basil

Combine everything but shrimp and blend well. Mix in shrimp. Put into 5-6 individual baking dishes and bake at 350° for 15 minutes or until bubbly. Can be prepared in a large casserole and can be made ahead and refrigerated until ready for use.

Route 130, 361 Pemaquid Point
New Harbor, ME 04554
Tel (207) 677-2105

NORTHEAST

The Bramble Inn

The Bramble Inn is located in the heart of Cape Cod's historic district and is made up of three charming buildings, two of which are Greek Revival in style, constructed during the Civil War era. The Capt. Bangs Pepper House is a Federal style Colonial built in 1793. Each restored structure offers country charm and cozy accommodations in a friendly atmosphere.

Within easy walking distance of Cape Cod Bay, guests enjoy swimming, sailing, wind surfing, and fishing. Also, just a stroll away, antique shops and summer theatre add activities that help make a visit to Bramble Inn memorable.

Excellent meals are served in the inn's restaurant that enjoys acclaim in the Boston Globe and three stars from the Boston Herald. Featured in the Providence Journal and '' Bon Appétit'', the inn is chosen one of the Cape's top three restaurants noted for fine dining.

White Chocolate Coeur A La Creme

1 8 oz. package cream cheese, room temperature
1 1/2 cups whipping cream
3/4 cup powdered sugar, sifted
3 oz. white chocolate, melted and slightly cooled

1 12 oz. bag frozen unsweetened raspberries, thawed
1/3 cup sugar
1 8 oz. can unsweetened apricots, drained
Amaretto liqueur
Fresh mint leaves

Line six 1/2-cup coeur a' la creme molds with double thickness of dampened cheese cloth, extending enough beyond edges to enclose filling completely. Using electric mixer, beat cream cheese with 1/4 cup cream and powdered sugar in large bowl until fluffy. Add chocolate and beat until smooth, about 2 minutes. Whip 1 cup cream to stiff peaks in another bowl. Gently fold into cream cheese mixture. Spoon 1/2 cup cheese mixture into each prepared mold. Fold cheesecloth over tops. Place molds on rack set over pan. Refrigerate for at least 8 hours or overnight.

Drain raspberries, reserving juice. Puree berries with 1/3 cup sugar in processor. Press through fine sieve into medium bowl to remove seeds. Add just enough reserved juice to thin puree to sauce consistency. Cover and refrigerate. Puree apricots in processor. Add amaretto to taste. Transfer to small bowl. Cover and refrigerate. (Sauces can be prepared 3 hours ahead.) Whip remaining 1/4 cup cream to stiff peaks. Spoon into pastry bag fitted with star tip. Pull back cheesecloth and invert 1 mold onto right side of large plate. Carefully remove cheesecloth. Pour 3 tablespoons raspberry sauce on left side of plate. Spoon 1 tablespoon apricot sauce in center of raspberry sauce. Draw knife through center of apricot circle, forming heart pattern. Repeat with remaining molds and sauces. Pipe rosettes of cream onto each plate and garnish with mint leaves.

6 Servings

Route 6 A
Brewster, Cape Cod, MA 02631
Tel (508) 896-7644

NORTHEAST

THE BRASS-BED

The Brass Bed's Cape May location is what attracted 19th century visitors to the "Queen of Seaside Resorts" during the Victorian era. The two-story Carpenter Gothic Cottage with dormers, gables and wraparound porch was built in 1872 and lends itself fittingly to the Victorian architecture that line the streets. The bright, cheerful guest rooms are furnished with original antiques and the atmosphere is "just like a visit to Grandma's house." Open all year and close to everything, a leisurely stroll or bicycle ride takes the guest into America's "Golden Age".

A hearty Continental breakfast is served every morning to the delight of the guest.

The Brass Bed Breakfast Log

2 6-oz boxes croutons
(cheddar cheese, preferably)
cup sliced mushrooms
1 8-oz pkg cheddar cheese
1-1/2 doz eggs

1 lb bulk sausage
2 cups milk

Use large greased 9 x 13 pan. Put croutons on bottom, add cooked sausage, drained mushrooms, and cheddar cheese. Beat eggs and milk together, then pour over the rest of the ingredients. Refrigerate overnight before baking 40-50 minutes in 325 degree oven. Serves 16.

719 Columbia Avenue
Cape May, NJ 08204
Tel (609) 884-8075

NORTHEAST

The Breakwater is nestled among four acres of gardens, lawns and woods on Hancock Street in Bar Harbor, Maine.

Built in 1904 as a summer cottage for John Innes Kane, great-grandson of John Jacob Astor, the mellow half-timbered building with its gables and rock stone walls is a classic example of an English Tudor estate.

Listed on the National Register of Historic Places, the picturesque rooms bring back the spirit and feeling of a bygone era with breathtaking views of sailing ships and the spruce-capped islands of Frenchman Bay.

The rooms are luxurious. They are furnished with queen-sized canopied beds, fireplaces and outstanding ocean front views. Mr. Kane's chamber and Abigal's offer views of the courtyard and rose garden.

Morning temptations are graciously served in a sun-filled dining room.

Tomato Florentine Strata

8 slices white bread, crust removed
1-1/2 cups cheddar cheese
1-1/2 cups monterey jack cheese
1/3 cup sautéed onion
4 cups fresh spinach

2/3 cup diced, seeded tomatoes
1 tsp fresh basil
8 large eggs
3 cups milk
pepper to taste

Preheat oven to 350°. Spray a 9 × 13 pan with vegetable oil. Wash spinach and remove thick stems. Dry completely and coarsely chop, then lightly square until just wilted. Toss the tomatoes with the basil. Line the pan with bread slices. Spread cheeses evenly over bread. Layer with onion, spinach, and tomatoes. Beat eggs well. Add milk and pepper to eggs, blend well and pour over cheese and vegetable layers. Bake for 45 to 50 minutes or until knife comes out clean. (This dish can be covered and refrigerated overnight before baking.) Serves 6-8.

45 Hancock Street
Bar Harbor, ME 04609
Tel (207) 288-2313

The Cameron Estate Inn was originally built in 1805 as the centerpiece of one of the largest estates on the Susquehanna frontier. It was the home of Simon Cameron, Abraham Lincoln's first Secretary of War, four-time U.S. Senator and Ambassador to Russia.

The Cameron is Federal in style and has been restored to one of Pennsylvania's most elegant inns. A central stairway sweeps to the third floor where an enormous skylight is filled with plants. The wide hall, wood floors, oriental rugs, antiques, and period reproductions are gentle reminders of its former life. There are eighteen guest rooms furnished in a variety of styles ranging from baronial suites to cozy little rooms tucked beneath third floor dormers. Some of the rooms have working fireplaces, and each gives its guest its own special view of 15 wooded and landscaped acres.

French and American country cuisine are right at home in the candle-lit dining room with gleaming stemware and warming fire.

Chicken Saute Simon Cameron

Start with boneless chicken breast, flattening with wooden mallet. Lay a thinly-sliced piece of ham on top of chicken breast, rolled like a pinwheel; fasten with toothpick. Saute in white wine and garlic butter until golden brown. Serve over bed of wild rice and white asparagus. Top with cheese sauce.

Cheese Sauce

Heat 1 cup milk, add 1/4 cup white wine and a dash of paprika. Add 1 cup grated cheese to wine mixture. Stir until blended well. Season with salt and white pepper. Serve warm.

Box 305
Mount Joy, PA 17552
Tel (717) 653-1773

NORTHEAST

The Captain Lord Mansion

The Captain Lord Mansion shares a picturesque seacoast village with stately homes from the early 18th and 19th centuries. Among its outstanding features, the handsome building has a three-story elliptical staircase, blown glass windows, double Indian shutters, Trompe l'oel hand-painted doors and a hand pulled elevator. In addition to fourteen working fireplaces and original "pumpkin pine" floorboards, the National Landmark offers an unusual octagonal cupola and a seldom seen gold vault.

The inn has been graciously restored and renovated to reflect the warmth and charm of its elegant past. Each guest room is richly appointed with antiques, velvet settees, four posters, fine linens, lace and swags. One room still retains the original 1812 wallpaper. The Captain Lord Mansion is also the setting for a children's book entitled *Ghost Doll* by Bruce McMillan.

Activities include sandy beaches, fine shops, art galleries, and Kennebunkport is home to the Seashore Trolly Museum which houses over 100 trolleys from around the world. Guests may also enjoy cross-country skiing, hiking and deep sea fishing.

A complimentary breakfast is served family style in the kitchen. Soft Boiled Eggs, Coffee, Tea, Juice, and Fresh Baked Breads and Muffins piping hot from the oven await the early riser.

Blueberry-Bran Muffins

Mix together and let stand 2 minutes:

2-1/2 cups 40 Bran Flakes	1 egg
1-1/4 cups milk	5 tbs melted margarine

In separate bowl place:

1-3/4 cups flour	1/4 tsp salt
1/2 cup sugar	3 tsp baking powder
1/2 cup blueberries	

Layer blueberries on top of wet mixture. Pour dry mixture into wet and stir only until moist. Place into muffin tins and sprinkle with sugar. Bake 20 minutes in greased tins at 375 degrees.

Box 527
Kennebunkport, ME 04046
Tel (207) 967-3141

NORTHEAST

- 15 -

The Inn at Castle Hill was built in 1874 as the summer home of renowned naturalist and explorer Alexander Agassiz. He concluded that the location was the very spot on the Atlantic coast to study marine life. With envious views of Newport Harbor and the Ocean, the home's design is reminiscent of Agassiz's native Switzerland.

The character of the house has changed very little since the last century, and many of the original furnishings remain. Handcrafted wood paneling combined with the warmth of oriental rugs reflect the elegance of the Victorian era. The sitting room welcomes with a crackling fire in winter and cool sea breezes in summer. Notables such as Thornton Wilder have been included among Castle Hill's frequent visitors, and Presidents Eisenhower and Kennedy often summered in this city of fabulous mansions built by the "400" of Newport's Guilded Age.

Guest rooms are comfortably furnished and spacious. A brisk walk or leisurely stroll provides companionship along the rocky and secluded coastline.

The public is invited to dine at Castle Hill and enjoy the same hospitality and service that is pampered on guests. An extensive menu includes specialties of Boneless Duck Breast sauteed with black and green peppercorns flambeed with brandy and finished with cream, Stuffed Quail with goose liver pate and truffles, Poached Seafood with saffron, and Medallions of Beef, Veal and Pork.

Tarte Linzer
(Raspberry Nut Tart)

1 cup all-purpose flour
1/2 lb unsalted butter
1 cup rasperry preserves
1 cup chopped toasted
1/2 cup toasted chopped almonds
pinch salt, cinnamon, ground

1/2 cup granulated sugar
2 egg yolks
vanilla extract to taste
hazelnuts

cloves, baking powder

Toast all nuts slightly and let cool at room temperature. Whip egg yolks until fluffy, combining the sugar slowly. Mix butter until soft and smooth and add all sifted dry ingredients (flour, spices). Combine the nuts with the dough and then finish by adding the egg and sugar mixture to nutty dough. Line bottom of spring form pan with approximately 2/3 of dough. Place preserves in center of dough and spread evenly, leaving a 1/2-inch border around the edges. With remaining dough roll out pencil-size strips and form lattice or simple cross pattern on top. Bake at 350 degrees 1/2 hour or until top browns.

Ocean Drive
Newport, RI 02840
Tel (401) 849-3800

NORTHEAST

Century Inn

Century Inn was built in 1794 as a stagecoach stop on the Nemacolin Indian Trail, the historic road used by young George Washington and his militia during the French and Indian Wars. The inn has hosted many notables through the years, including General Lafayette on May 26, 1825 when he made his grand tour of this country, and Andrew Jackson stopped by on two different occasions: once for breakfast, and again on the way to his inauguration as president.

In 1945, Century Inn was purchased by Dr. and Mrs. Gordon Harrington who restored and furnished it with rare antiques. These include a display of Monongahela glass, a cherry highboy made in 1750, and a Whiskey Rebellion flag. The original kitchen contains a massive fireplace with a hand-forged crane and cooking utensils. A small room with hand-plastered walls painted with stencils cut from tracings by Moses Eaton, and a collection of dolls and toys from yesteryear can be enjoyed at this National Landmark. Guest rooms are comfortable and charming.

Excellent meals are served in five historic dining rooms.

Indian Corn Pudding

3 eggs, well beaten
2 tsp salt
8 tbs butter
3 15-1/2 oz cans whole kernel corn,
well-drained, reserving liquid

4 cups milk
4 tbs flour
8 tbs sugar

Place half the corn in blender with a bit of the liquid to puree. Preheat oven to 375 degrees, and in large bowl combine beaten eggs, the remaining ingredients, and the rest of the corn, blending well. Pour into buttered 9x12 casserole and bake 45 minutes. Halfway through baking time, top with buttered bread crumbs.

Scenery Hill, PA 15360
Tel (412) 945-6600 or 5180

NORTHEAST

The Chalfonte, located on the corner of Howard and Sewell streets in historic Cape May, helps to set off one of the nation's finest collections of Victorian architecture. This architectural beauty has been in continuous operation since it opened in 1876 and graciously run by the Satterfield family since 1906. A treasured remnant from the past, The Chalfonte is one of those rare places many guests call their second home because they come back year after year to meet old friends sitting on gingerbread porches.

The guest rooms are comfortable with marble-topped dressers, other Victoriana, and fresh sea breezes. The inn is listed on the National Register of Historic Places.

Meals are served family-style both to guests and the public. The menu is prepared by Chef Helen Dickerson and daughter Dot who is a fourth-generation cook at the hotel. It has been said that people come to Cape May for sun, sand, and Helen Dickerson's tasty food. Southern specialties are Fried Chicken, Country Ham, Roast Beef, Lamb, Spoonbread, and Corn Pudding.

Spoonbread

1 cup stone-ground yellow cornmeal
3 cans (13 ozs each) evaporated milk
2 tbs shortening   4 eggs, beaten
1-1/2 tsp salt   1 tbs baking powder

Bring meal, shortening, and 2 cans of milk to boil over medium heat, stirring constantly. Remove from heat. Combine eggs, remaining milk and salt; add to meal mixture. Quickly stir in baking powder. Pour mixture into two greased, 1-quart casseroles or one 2-quart casserole. Bake at 450° for about 30 minutes, until top is golden brown.

301 Howard and Sewell Streets
Cape May, NJ 08204
Tel (609) 884-8409

NORTHEAST

CHARLES HINCKLEY HOUSE
— circa 1809 —

The Charles Hinckley House is a fine example of federal colonial architecture. Built by ship-wright Charles Hinckley in 1809, the inn is located in the historic district of Barnstable Village, and is surrounded by profuse wildflower gardens. Restored to recapture its earlier years, The Charles Hinckley House's guests can expect to find special touches such as baskets of fresh fruit, bedside chocolates, English country breakfasts, fresh flowers, country quilts, and other attentions to detail that make a visit memorable.

Located on the unspoiled northside of Cape Cod, Country Living Magazine said, "The Charles Hinckley House brims with wild flowers outside and down-home hospitality inside," and the Los Angeles Times called it "the most photographed inn on Cape Cod."

Four-poster beds, working fireplaces, and private baths are in each of the guest rooms — fine old books, raised paneling, wide pine floors warmed by colorful rugs — all await the guest.

Fresh fruits and puff pastries are available each morning along with coffee and tea. Scrambled eggs with smoked salmon, poached eggs on crab cakes, or French pancakes with homemade raspberry butter and Vermont maple syrup are served in a well appointed, sunlit dining room.

Spicey Shrimp

2 lbs	16-20 count shrimp	½	cup crushed red pepper
2 tbs	cumin		in liquid
1 tbs	cayenne	1½	cups tequila
3 tbs	rosemary	½	cup olive oil
4-6	cloves chopped garlic		

Peel shrimp leaving tail on. Marinate in cumin, cayenne, rosemary, garlic, pepper, tequila, and olive oil at least 4-6 hours. Drain and grill, serving with Cranberry Cocktail Sauce, which is made by mixing 1 cup Ketchup, ½ cup cooked cranberries, and 4 tbs. horseradish.

Old Kings Highway
P.O. Box 723
Barnstable, MA 02630
Tel (508) 362-9924

The Churchill House Inn

The Churchill House Inn, ideally situated to explore the magic of Vermont, has offered hospitality to the traveler from the very beginning. The old farmhouse was built by the Churchill family in 1871, and served as a stopover for farmers taking their lumber and grain to the mills. That same spirit of friendly neighborliness remains today.

During the summer, outdoor activities abound with hiking, fishing, and stump-jumping. Wintertime lures skiers from around the country and, conditions permitting, an old-fashioned sleighride is enjoyed each Thursday. Cozy fires and antique furnishings bring back long-lost memories.

Spicy New England Pot Roast

4 to 5 lb beef (rump or round)
2 tbs vegetable oil or bacon grease
1 cup water
1 large onion, chopped
1/2 cup red wine
2 tbs horseradish
1/2 lb cranberries

1 cup sugar
2 cinnamon sticks, broken
1 1/2 cups beef broth
2 tbs flour

Place roast and oil in heavy Dutch oven. Brown well over medium heat. Pour off fat and combine with flour. Reserve. Combine cranberries, water, and sugar. Bring to boil and simmer 10 minutes. Combine with remaining ingredients and pour over roast. Simmer 3 to 4 hours. Strain liquid and serve. Delicious on a cold winter evening.

Route 73
East Brandon, VT 05733
Tel (802) 247-3300

NORTHEAST

The Claremont, established in 1884, is Mt. Desert Island's oldest operating summer hotel. The resort has cottages and two guest houses in addition to the main building. Some of the lodgings have fireplaces and ocean views.

Clay tennis courts, dock and moorings, badminton, bicycling, rowing, and a library are available. During August, The Claremont Croquet Classic is held, and all guests are both welcomed and encouraged to participate as part of the gallery. Fresh water swimming, summer theatre, and the Acadia National Park are also frequent activities of guests to this National Landmark.

Fine meals are served to guests and the public alike rivaled only by the striking views of Somes Sound and the mountains. (Gentlemen are asked to wear jackets and ties.)

Baked Stuffed Shrimp

In small saucepan melt 1/2 stick unsalted butter over low heat, stirring in 1/2 tsp hot Hungarian paprika, cooking the mixture while stirring for 5 minutes. Remove pan from heat and add 1/4 cup cracker crumbs, 3 tbs freshly grated Parmesan, 2 tbs crushed potato chips, and salt and pepper to taste. Rinse 12 very large shrimp, pat dry, and cut a deep slit down length of inside curve of each to within 1/8'' of tail without cutting through shell. Flatten shrimp slightly and stuff with 1/2 lb lump crab meat, picked over. Divide cracker crumb mixture among shrimp and divide shrimp among four individual gratin dishes. Spoon 2 tbs water around shrimp in each dish, drizzling 1 tbs melted butter over each serving, and baking in preheated moderate 350° oven for 20 minutes, or until stuffing has turned golden brown. Sprinkle with minced fresh parsley. Add lemon wedges. Serves 4 as first course.

Southwest Harbor, ME 04679
Tel (207) 244-5036

NORTHEAST

COLLIGAN'S
STOCKTON INN

Colligan's Stockton Inn was a stagecoach stop on the line between Philadelphia and New York. The small hotel with a wishing well is truly a step back in time with its weathered thick walls, narrow windows, random width flooring, and low ceilings. Guest rooms in the main inn and historic Carriage House are furnished with period antiques and have fireplaces. Two of the rooms have large balconies. Adjacent to the Carriage House is the Wagon House, a stone building erected in 1795.

The main dining room has four huge wood-burning fireplaces that fill the air with aromas and flickering lights as they have since 1710. Murals line the walls depicting local countryside scenes of the late 18th century. Weather permitting, guests dine in the outdoor gardens surrounded by waterfalls. The menu offers superb American and Continental cuisine.

A Continental breakfast is served each morning.

Turkey Waldorf Salad

1 1/4 lb cooked turkey, cut into chunks
1 apple, cored and diced, leaving skin on for color
1 stalk celery, diced or angle-sliced Chinese style
1/2 cup slivered toasted almonds
1/8 pkg dark raisins

Mix together with a dressing of mayonnaise and sour cream, consisting of one part sour cream to three parts mayonnaise. Season to taste. Diced, skinned, cooked chicken can be substituted for turkey. Serve cold in a nest of iceberg or Boston lettuce. Serves 4.

Route 29
Stockton, NJ 08559
Tel (609) 397-1250

NORTHEAST

Country Inn At Princeton was built in 1890 and enjoys a setting of rolling lawns, gardens, fieldstone walls and a pine grove. Authentic Victorian elegance is evident upon entering the reception area of this Queen Anne style mansion. The six spacious parlor suites are tastefully furnished and beautifully decorated.

Downhill and cross-country skiing, and the two-thousand acre Massachusetts State Audubon and Wildlife Preserve are right at hand.

In three well-appointed dining rooms, excellent meals are graciously served for discerning diners. An extensive, constantly changing menu is an experience, as the inn's consistant 4 and 5-Star ratings attest. "There was no doubt, dinner done, we had dined grandly", wrote the Providence Journal. Critics have also said, "Dedicated to serving...food with an elegance...", "Benchmark of fine dining", "...food very, very good!" Tournadoes of Beef with Sauce, Chateaubriand, Rich Cream of Celery Soup c.1890, Lemon and Lime Souffles, and Snails en Strudel are but a few of the dishes to be savored.

Baked Goat Cheese, Rochambeau

12 oz mild goat cheese
2 cloves garlic, minced
1 tsp oregano
salt and pepper
1 oz olive oil or salad oil
1 small can whole plum
tomatoes seeded and diced

1 small onion, diced
1 tsp basil
1 tsp tarragon
1 lemon
bread crumbs

Divide goat cheese into 4 equal rounds, roll lightly in oil to coat, then roll in fresh bread crumbs. Place on plastic and refrigerate. (this can be done a day ahead.) For a sauce, saute onion over low heat in half the oil until wilted, adding garlic and spices and cooking 1 minute. Add tomatoes with juice and simmer 35 minutes, or until sauce begins to thicken. Pre-heat oven to 350°, placing cheese on baking sheet and baking 5 to 7 minutes or until cheese softens, but still holds its shape. Place hot sauce on plates, putting hot cheese rounds on top. Garnish with lemon wedges and serve piping hot.

Mocha Mousse

8 oz heavy cream
1/8 tsp creme tartar
1/2 cup melted sweet chocolate

1/2 cup sugar
1/4 cup egg whites
1-1/2 tsp instant expresso coffee powder

Whip cream until soft and firm. In small sauce pan combine sugar and creme tartar. Add 1/4 cup water. Stir and cook slowly until sugar dissolves and water boils. Boil without stirring until syrup reaches 242°. Beat egg whites stiff. Fold in coffee and chocolate. Fold in the whipped cream. Serve in parfait glasses. (Whipped cream topping optional.)

30 Mountain Road
Princeton, MA 01541
Tel (617) 464-2030

Curtis House

Curtis House was known as the Orenaug Inn when it opened its doors to the traveler in 1794. Built by Anthony Stoddard and located in an area rich in both 17th and 18th century homes, the inn is just a ten minute walk to the Glebe House, birthplace of American Episcopacy.

Over the years changes and renovations have been made and records show that in 1900 a handsome third floor addition was made at the cost of $400.00. Many of the old details include beamed ceilings, wood floors, and fireplaces. One owner aptly said "Every Modern Comfort, Every Ancient Charm". There have been four Curtis owners, none related.

The guest rooms are warmly furnished with wallpaper, ruffled tiebacks, canopied beds, and area rugs on wood floors. The former Carriage House also provides lodging and is connected to the main grounds by a picturesque footbridge. The large sign at the entrance of the inn is the work of artist and writer Wallace Nutting.

Meals are served in dining rooms that seat up to 350. The menu, includes Rice Stuffed Duckling with Orange Sauce, Roast Leg of Lamb, Prime Rib, and seafood from Stuffed Trout to Broiled Baby Flounder.

Indian Pudding

4 cups milk	1/2 cup dark molasses
2 oz sugar	2 oz yellow corn meal
2/3 tsp cinnamon	1/3 tsp nutmeg
1/8 oz salt	2 oz butter

Heat 4/5 of the milk and add molasses, sugar, corn meal, spices, salt and butter. Cook 20 minutes or until mixture thickens. Pour into baking dish and add remaining cold milk. Do not stir. Put into slow 300 degree oven and bake 3 hours without stirring. Serve warm with cream, hard sauce, or ice cream.

Main Street
Woodbury, CT 06798
Tel (203) 263-2101

NORTHEAST

Dana Place Inn

Dana Place Inn is perhaps best known for its outstanding cuisine and collection of classic and creative dishes. Located at the foot of Mt. Washington on 300 acres dotted with apple orchards and mountain pools of the sparkling Ellis River, this rural retreat is surrounded by the White Mountain National Forest.

The Colonial farmhouse was built by Mr. and Mrs. Otwin Dana and has welcomed visitors since the 1890s except for one brief period when it was a private summer home.

Guest rooms and suites are comfortable and pleasantly decorated, reflecting the charm of the countryside. Year 'round activities abound, and even a hammock is provided for the less energetic.

Meals in the dining room include Smoked Nova Scotia Salmon, Escargots Bourguignonne, Veal Marsala, Fruit de Mer, Club Steak Cafe du Paris, Chicken Veronique, Roast Long Island Duckling a L'Orange, Pork Tenderloin Calvados, and Cranberry Torte.

Cranberry Torte

2 cups fresh cranberries
1/2 cup chopped nuts
1 stick butter
3/4 cup flour
2 eggs, beaten

1/2 cup sugar
1 cup sugar

Butter 9'' pie plate. Pour cranberries into plate. Mix 1/2 cup sugar and nuts and pour over berries. Melt butter, and when slightly cooled, add beaten eggs, 1 cup sugar, and flour. Pour over berry and nuts in pie plate and bake at 350⁰ for 45 minutes to 1 hour until golden brown.

Pinkham Notch Road
Jackson, NH 03846
Tel (603) 383-6822

NORTHEAST

HISTORIC 1776
Dobbin House Tavern

The Dobbin House Tavern is Gettysburg's oldest and most historic building. Constructed of native stone in 1776 by Reverend Alexander Dobbin and his wife Isabella, the inn sits nearby where President Lincoln delivered his immortal Gettysburg Address.

During the Civil War the inn served as a hospital for both the North and South. It was also a link in the Underground Railroad for runaway slaves and its secret crawl space has been featured in the *National Geographic*. Listed on the National Register of Historic Places, the inn remains much the same as it did over 200 years ago.

The hand-carved woodwork has been restored to its original beauty, and its five great rooms are decorated with antiques reflecting the era. Several fireplaces add to its charm and ambiance.

Meals are served in six dining rooms. A menu of colonial and continental cuisine includes New York strip, prime rib of beef, and fresh seafood.

An array of mouth watering desserts are part of the fare.

Fine Fowl with Shrimp

1 8-oz. Boneless, skinless chicken breast	Flour
2 pieces raw shrimp (peeled and deveined)	1-1/2 oz. butter
1 tsp old bay	Chablis
Pinch salt	1 tsp dry parsley flakes
Pinch black pepper	

Melt butter in a sauté pan on medium heat. Sprinkle both sides of chicken breast with small amount of flour. Place chicken along with shrimp into hot butter. Sprinkle seasonings evenly over chicken and shrimp. Cook till golden brown on one side. Turn chicken and brown other side. Add chablis and simmer until chicken breast is tender and cooked through. Remove from stove and place chicken on plate. Place shrimp on top and pour pan juices over. Garnish with parsley flakes.

89 Steinwehr Avenue
Gettysburg, PA 17325
Tel (717) 334-2100

NORTHEAST

The Edgartown Inn was built in 1798 as the home of Captain Thomas Worth, and Fort Worth, Texas was named in honor of his son who was a hero in the Mexican War.

During its long and distinguished career, the inn has played host to many notables. Nathaniel Hawthorne wrote *Twice Told Tales* while he was a guest, and at the height of his career, Daniel Webster was refused accommodations because of his dark skin (he was thought to be an Indian). He later returned and the innkeeper asked his children not to "sop the platter" in Mr. Webster's presence (not to dip bread in the gravy). To the children's delight, Mr. Webster himself "sopped the platter", putting everyone at ease. Other celebrities include Charles Sumner, a 19th century opponent of slavery, and John F. Kennedy when he was senator.

The structure has changed very little over the years and would be easily recognized by its first owner. Guest rooms and two adjacent buildings are furnished with antiques, serving as a reminder of the rich history of the seacoast's early whaling days.

The inn is not elaborate, nor does it make any effort to be, but is comfortable and has been serving discriminating guests for a great many years.

A full country breakfast is served in a warm paneled dining room. During summer months a charming patio garden is the scene for specialities of homemade Breads, Muffins, and Griddle Cakes.

Oatmeal Bread

In large bowl, combine:

2 cups old fashioned oats	**4 tsp salt**
1 cup molasses	**1 stick Oleo (1/4 lb)**
4 cups boiling water	**12-14 cups bleached**
3 pkgs yeast	**flour**

While this cools sufficiently so as not to kill the yeast, add yeast, mixing well. Mix in 12-14 cups unbleached flour and let rise 1 hour. Punch dough out and divide into three equal portions. Roll out, form into loaves in pans and let rise another hour. Bake 40 minutes at 350 degrees. Remove from oven and coat with Crisco. Pop out of pans onto cooling racks.

Edgartown, Martha's Vineyard Island, MA 02539
Tel (508) 627-4794

NORTHEAST

1811 HOUSE

1811 House is an early Colonial home amidst English flower and rock gardens that dates back to the 1770s. Except for one very brief period when it was the home of Mary Lincoln Isham, granddaughter of the Civil War's president, the handsome two-story structure has operated as an inn since 1811.

The building has been faithfully restored to reflect the early nineteenth century and is filled with English and American antiques. Guest rooms are furnished with oriental rugs, fine paintings, canopied beds, and some of the rooms have fireplaces.

A complimentary breakfast is served with varied dishes, such as Fresh Juice, Fruit, Bacon, Apples, Home Fries, Farm Fresh Eggs, and Tomatoes.

1811 House Sauteed Mushrooms

sliced mushrooms   **salt**
white pepper
heavy cream & butter

Saute mushrooms in butter, adding a little heavy cream. A dash of salt and a little white pepper should be thrown in before covering and simmering.

Manchester Village, VT 05254
Tel (802) 362-1811

NORTHEAST

Evermay-On-The-Delaware is a fine example of the many early country homes built in Pennsylvania, and it looks much the same today as it did in 1871. The history of the building dates back to the mid-18th century and is now elegantly restored in character of the grand family home that it was.

The library parlor has two fireplaces and a grand piano. Guest rooms are furnished with beautiful Victorian and period pieces. Some are quite spacious, while others are very cozy. Freshly cut flowers and fruit add the welcoming touch. The restored Carriage House also provides cozy accommodations.

Tea is served at 4 p.m. either in the parlor or, weather permitting, outdoors. Breakfast is served in the conservatory. An innovative menu brings the finest and freshest foods available from local markets, New York, and Philadelphia, making up five-course evening meals in the dining room.

Crab Bisque

2 shallots, minced
1/2 cup flour
1 tbs tomato paste
2 cups cream
salt, paprika, and white pepper to taste

1/2 cup butter
1 qt milk
1/4 cup sherry
1 can fresh crab meat

Lightly saute minced shallots in butter, adding flour to make roux, then adding milk and tomato paste. Add whipping cream, then sherry, and season with salt, white pepper, and paprika. Gently fold in crab that has been carefully picked over.

River Road
Erwinna, Bucks County, PA 18920
Tel (215) 294-9100

the Exeter Inn

The Exeter Inn, situated on the campus of Exeter Academy, was founded over 200 years ago by John Phillips who envisioned a school for boys, especially those with limited incomes. The inn was the gracious gift of Mrs. William Boyce Thompson and her daughter Mrs. Anthony J. Drexel Biddle, Jr., in 1932. Today, the Academy operates more than 60 impressive buildings exemplifying its early traditions of warm hospitality. There are 50 attractively decorated guest rooms furnished in a variety of styles. Close to everything, the region abounds in historic places and nearby sandy beaches.

Meals are served in the dining room that has tall, graceful windows, chandeliers, and crisp, white linens. The menu includes Fresh Shrimp Cocktail, New England Clam Chowder, assorted sandwiches, Baked French Onion Soup, and delicious desserts.

Ravioles De Homard
(Lobster-filled pasta with garlic and herb sauce)

Filling:

lobster meat from 4 small lobsters
2 cups fresh bread crumbs
pinch basil, rosemary, thyme
bunch chopped scallion greens

3 cloves finely chopped
  garlic
vegetable oil, salt, pepper

Pasta:

14 oz sifted flour
1 egg white
2 tbs vegetable oil

3 beaten eggs
5 tbs cold water
pinch salt

Filling:

Chop 2/3 of fresh lobster meat fine, mix in a small bowl with garlic, herbs, and scallion greens. Season with pinch salt and fresh ground pepper. Add fresh bread crumbs and mix thoroughly. Add vegetable oil a spoon at a time and keep mixing until filling holds together (about 4 tbs oil). Cover and refrigerate.

Pasta:

Put sifted flour in medium size bowl. Add beaten eggs, salt, and egg white. Mix loosely 15 seconds, add water and oil. Mix again into a ball (do not over-work dough). Sprinkle with flour and roll out half on floured board (thin) into rectangle. Put large pot with 5 gallons of water and 1/4 cup vegetable oil to boiling.

Assembly:

Roll out all of the filling into 1 oz balls. Place on flat tray. Lay the balls in a straight line down the center of rolled-out dough, about 2 inches apart. Fold one side of the dough over the filling. Press around each ball loosely with floured hands, then cut around each ravioli with ravioli cutter, making sure all sides are closed. Repeat until all dough and filling are used. Drop ravioles into boiling water for about 5 minutes. Drain and cool completely with cold water, being careful not to break up ravioles.

Sauce:

3 cloves chopped garlic	2 cloves chopped shallots
Pinch basil and thyme	4 tbs good white wine
1tbl spoon butter (unsalted)	3 cups heavy cream

Remaining lobster (diced medium) Salt and pepper to taste.

Reduce garlic, shallots, basil, and thyme in small sauce pan with wine about 3 minutes. Add unsalted butter. Reduce again 2 minutes. Add heavy cream and reduce until creamy. Add lobster meat and adjust seasoning.

To Serve:

Drop ravioles into hot water for 2 minutes or until hot. Strain well. Place on serving platter, 6 ravioles per person. Ladle hot sauce over them and sprinkle with freshly grated parmesan cheese. Serve with piping hot French or garlic bread.

90 Front Street
P.O. Box 508
Exeter, NH 03833
Tel (603) 772-5901

NORTHEAST

Fairfield Inn and Guest House is truly an historic inn eight miles west of Gettysburg on Route 116. The original plantation home of Squire William Miller, who settled in Fairfield in 1755 and laid out the town in 1801, the inn has been in continuous operation since 1823 serving as a stagecoach stop and a drover's tavern. Headquarters of Thaddeus Stevens when he constructed the famous Tapeworm Railroad and the Maria Furnace, Fairfield Inn hosted Confederate General Jeb Stuart on two occasions: once in 1862 when his men stole 700 horses from the valley, and again in 1863 when the town was occupied by the Confederate army during the Battle of Gettysburg. It is also believed that Patrick Henry was an early guest.

The Guest House was known as the Cunningham House for the Cunninghams who lived there for five generations. This building was used as a hospital for wounded officers during the Civil War. Today, six comfortable guest rooms are restored and furnished with antiques.

Meals are served at the inn.

Apple Cake

3 cups flour	2 tsp baking soda
1 tsp salt	3 eggs, beaten
1 cup oil	2 cups sugar
3 cups chopped apples	2 tsp vanilla
1 cup chopped walnuts or pecans	

Beat eggs and add oil. Beat in other ingredients. Bake for 1 hour at 325 degrees in 9 x 12 buttered and floured baking pan. Start cake in cold oven only. Serve with powdered sugar.

Main Street
Fairfield, PA 17320
Tel (717) 642-5410

NORTHEAST

Fitzwilliam Inn

Innkeepers the McMahon Family welcome you to the Fitzwilliam Inn to relax and enjoy country living in the beautiful Monadnock Region of New Hampshire. Since 1796, the Fitzwilliam Inn has provided food, grog and lodging to the weary traveler every day of the year. The stately Inn overlooks the Historic Town Common in the quaint New England town of Fitzwilliam. The view from the front porch provides an unmatched example of the understated architectural elegance as true to New England today as it was in the early 1800s. Twenty-five charming bedrooms; renowned fireside dining; breakfast, lunch & dinner; cozy pub with fireplace; free Sunday afternoon concerts during February & March; murder mystery dinners; outdoor swimming pool; ten kilometers of cross-country trails; antique shopping; Mt. Monadnock; Rhododendron State Park; Cathedral of the Pines. Just 65 miles from Boston. Authorized agent and stop for Vermont Transit Bus Line. 1996 Yankee Travel Guide Editor's Pick.

Fitzwilliam Inn Pumpkin Bread

4 eggs
3 cups sugar
1 cup oil
1 (16 oz.) can pumpkin filling
3/4 cup water
4 cups all-purpose flour

2 tsp baking soda
1 tsp baking powder
1-1/2 tsp salt
1 tsp ground cinnamon
1 tsp ground nutmeg

Beat eggs until fluffy then gradually beat in sugar. Blend in oil, pumpkin and water. Combine flour, baking soda, salt, baking powder, cinnamon and nutmeg. Blend into pumpkin mixture and beat well. Pour into two greased 9 x 5 inch loaf pans. Bake at 350° for 55 to 60 minutes, or until cake tester comes out clean. Cool on rack ten minutes; remove from pans and cool completely. Makes two loaves.

On the Common
Fitzwilliam, NH 03447
Tel (603) 585-9000
Fax (603) 585-3495

GARNET HILL

Garnet Hill Lodge, tucked away high in the Adirondacks, overlooks secluded Thirteenth Lake. The Log House, constructed in 1936, and The Big Shanty, built in the early 1900s, have quiet fireside areas for warmth and conversation. Guest rooms all share a particular charm.

Garnet Hill and the adjacent Siamese Ponds Wilderness Area are crossed with over 70 miles of marked and maintained hiking trails. Two tennis courts and white water rafting on the Hudson River make this an exciting vacation spot. During winter, Garnet Hill is a complete ski touring center with over 40 kilometers of scenic groomed and track trails for both the beginner and expert alike.

Meals are served in the restaurant to both guests and travelers. Breads and desserts are baked daily.

Yogurt & Cucumber Soup

1-1/2cups diced cucumber	1 tsp salt
1 large clove garlic	2/3 cup ground walnuts
1 tsp salt	2 cups plain yogurt
2 tbs olive oil	1-1/2cups water

Peel cucumber and slice lengthwise into ¼'' strips, then crosswise into thin slices. Place in bowl and sprinkle with 1 tsp salt and refrigerate 1 hour. Mince clove of garlic and mash in bowl with walnuts and 1 tsp salt. Blend in yogurt along with 1½ cups water to walnuts, adding cucumber and liquid which have been marinating 1 hour. Add olive oil and more salt if needed. Serve chilled.

North River, NY 12856
Tel (518) 251-2821

The Genesee Falls Inn

Genesee Falls Inn was built in 1870 by Joseph Ingram and it still maintains the atmosphere of a bygone era that saw John L. Sullivan fight exhibition matches in the former ballroom. The inn is located one-half mile from the south entrance of Letchworth State Park.

Over the years many changes and renovations have been made and, in 1964 five modern units were added. The guest rooms are decorated with period furniture and wallpaper. Some of the rooms have antiques. A guest book is filled with names from around the world who have enjoyed its fine dining and hospitality.

Breakfast and lunch are offered in the Coffee House. The evening meal is graciously served in the Victorian dining room.

Clams Genesee Falls Style

3 tbs butter
2 cans chopped clams
6 tbs fresh bread crumbs
dash lemon juice
dash Worcestershire sauce

1/2 cup minced onion
3 tbs mayonnaise
3 tbs dried parsley flakes
dash Tabasco sauce

Saute onions in butter. Add drained chopped clams, saving half the juice. Mix in remaining ingredients and add juice if needed. Bake at 350° for 20 minutes or until bubbly hot and golden on top. Can be frozen. Serve as appetizer or as main course.

Box 396, Main and Hamilton Streets
Portageville, NY 14536
Tel (716) 493-2484

NORTHEAST

Glen Iris Inn

GLen Iris Inn is located in an area that is one of the premier examples of gorge and water fall scenery in the eastern United States. The three-story clapboard building was the home of William Pryor Letchworth who granted Letchworth State Park's original 1000 acres to New York State in 1907.

On a ridge directly behind the inn is a restored Seneca Indian Council House and the grave of Mary Jemison, reminders of the area's turbulent history. Both a pioneer and museum are nearby. In addition to the main inn, Pinewood Lodge is close by and has light housekeeping units. The park is open from April until early November and is ideal for the outdoorsman.

Meals are graciously served in the dining room.

Cucumber Soup

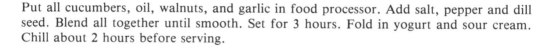

9 cups chopped, seeded cucumber	4 tbs dill seed
3/4 cup olive oil	3 tsp salt
5 cloves garlic	3 cups plain yogurt
2 tsp white pepper	1-1/2 cups finely chopped walnuts
6 cups sour cream	

Put all cucumbers, oil, walnuts, and garlic in food processor. Add salt, pepper and dill seed. Blend all together until smooth. Set for 3 hours. Fold in yogurt and sour cream. Chill about 2 hours before serving.

Letchworth State Park
Castille, NY 14427
Tel (716) 493-2622

NORTHEAST

The Golden Stage Inn

Golden Stage Inn, originally an old stage coach stop, served as a link in the charitable Underground Railroad and as the home of Cornelius Otis Skinner. (The locals still call it the Skinner Place). The charming inn has had only six owners during its long, colorful history of nearly 200 years. The peaceful four-acre estate of rolling lawns, gardens, spectacular pines and maples offer a place for guests to stroll or relax and enjoy views of Black River Valley and Okemo Mountains. The atmosphere is best reflected by a guest's comments: "We came back, and it's still our favorite place." The public rooms include a library and a large plant-filled living room with a fireplace. Ten guest rooms are comfortable and attractive.

Meals are served combining traditional New England fare with Continental cuisine. Specialties include delicate soups, Pink Chicken Saute, and Bavarian Apple Cheese Torte.

Stage Puffs

1 cup water	**1/4 lb butter**
1 cup flour	**4 beaten eggs**

Boil water and butter. At once add flour, mixing over low heat until mixture clings together. Slowly add eggs, blending well. Drop by large tablespoon onto cookie sheet, or use a pastry bag for more decorative puffs. Bake 30 minutes at 400 degrees.

Filling:

2 8-oz pkgs soft cream cheese	**1 cup confectioner's**
1/2 cup heavy cream	**sugar**
1/2 cup mini chocolate chips	**3 drops cinnamon oil**
1/2 orange rind grated	

In processor mix cream cheese, sugar, and cream until smooth, then mix in remainder of ingredients. Chill until firm. Fill each puff. Drizzle with chocolate fudge sauce or dust with powdered sugar. Can be frozen for up to 2 weeks.

Box 218
Proctorsville, VT 05153
Tel (802) 226-7744

Greenhurst Inn

Greenhurst Inn was a most welcomed haven for travelers between Boston and Montreal when it opened as an inn in the 1930's. It is now listed on the National Register of Historic Places.

Built by the Harrington family of Philadelphia in 1891, this Victorian mansion with its porches, gables and fireplaces is crowned with a large corner turret. With a library of 3,000 volumes and a parlor with the sounds of a victrola and piano guests have said, "memories are made of this."

The guest rooms are furnished with antiques, Martha Washington spreads, and mints on the pillows are the added touch. A complimentary breakfast is served each morning in a period dining room beside a crackling fire. Guests may choose from Fresh Fruit, Juices, Home Baked Muffins, Biscuits and array of Jams, Preserves, Coffee and Tea.

Smoked Eggs

6 eggs	2 tbs soy sauce
1 tsp honey	1 tps salt
1/2 cup water	1 tbs sherry
1 tsp liquid smoke	

Boil eggs 5 to 7 minutes. Cool and shell. Pierce each egg once with sharp knife and place in wide-mouthed quart jar. Bring soy sauce, water, salt and honey to a boil. Remove from flame, add sherry and pour over eggs. Cool and refrigerate over night. Next day, add liquid smoke and let eggs stand at least 2 hours. Cut eggs into quarters and serve. Makes 24 appetizers.

Bethel, VT 05032
Tel. (802) 234-9474

NORTHEAST

Greenville Arms

Greenville Arms is ideally located near the Hudson River and the northern Catskills on a seven-acre estate covered with green lawns, old oaks, maples and flower gardens. Built as the home of William Vanderbilt, this 1889 Victorian structure has comfortable porches to sit on, bays and a sky pointing corner turret. The spectacular beauty of the countryside has attracted people from around the world since the early 1800's, and today with its many trout streams, hiking trails and cultural events, visitors are lured to the area more than ever.

An inn since 1952, guest rooms are comfortably decorated with antiques. Old fashioned country cooking includes Ham, Turkey, Fresh Vegetables, Homemade Bread, Pies and Cakes.

Raspberry Cheese Pie

4 oz raspberry gelatin	1/4 cup sugar
1-1/4 cups boiling water	1 tbs fresh lemon juice
10 oz frozen raspberries	dash salt
4 oz softened cream cheese	1 cup heavy whipped cream
1/3 cup confectioners sugar	1 tsp vanilla
Baked 9 inch pie shell	

Red layers: Dissolve gelatin and granulated sugar in boiling water. Add frozen berries and lemon juice and stir until berries set. Chill until partially set.

White layers: Blend cheese, confectioners sugar, vanilla and salt. Fold in whipped cream. Spread half of white mixture on cooled, baked 9 inch pie shell. Cover with half of red mixture and repeat process. Chill until set.

Greenville, NY 12083
Tel. (518) 966-5219

NORTHEAST

Griswold Inn

Griswold Inn recalls the days of 1776 when it welcomed travelers to the old river town of Essex, and to this day there have been only five owners. Essex, an early commercial center, was also a battlefield in the War of 1812.

Inside, firearms dating from the 15th century, a potbellied stove, fireplaces, Currier & Ives steamboat prints and an historic collection of Jacobsen marine art are on display. Collectors from around the world visit the 'Gris' to view the Jacobsens. Favorable comments from Mobil Travel Guide and others attest to its extraordinary atmosphere. With 20 guest rooms, the inn caters to persons who cherish privacy. Some of the rooms have brass beds and port or starboard lists that are over a century old. A Continental breakfast is offered each morning.

The four charming dining rooms serve delicious New England cuisine where everything is genuine and fresh.

Griswold Inn Hunt Breakfast Creamed Ham and Mushrooms

1 lb. smoked Virginia ham in half-inch cubes
1-1/2 qts whole milk   8 ozs butter, melted
1 cup flour   1 tsp Outerbridge's Sherry
1/2 tsp Tabasco Sauce   Pepper Sauce
1 tsp Worcestershire Sauce   salt & white pepper to taste
2 cups fresh mushrooms, quartered

Melt butter in a pot and stir in flour while milk is brought to a crust (almost to boil) in another pan. Add hot milk to flour and butter mixture, whisking until smooth. Add Outerbridge's Sherry Pepper Sauce, Worcestershire Sauce, Tabasco, then salt and pepper to taste. Steam ham cubes and mushrooms until mushrooms are al dente and add them to hot cream sauce. Mix and serve over toasted English Muffins. Serves 6-8.

Essex, CT 06426
Tel (203) 767-1812

NORTHEAST

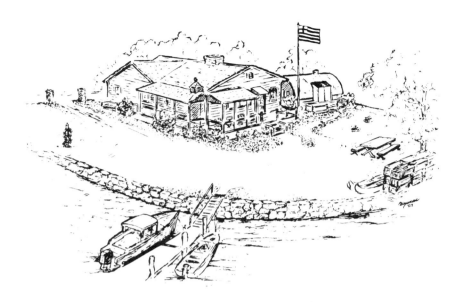

HHarbour Inne and Cottage is a rustic retreat located at the end of Edgemont Street, two blocks from the railroad. In this early shipbuilding and whaling port guests are within walking distance to shops, restaurants, and the Mystic Seaport Marine Museum. The museum houses more than 300 historic vessels, including the Charles W. Morgan, the only wooden whaling ship in existence from the early 19th century.

One of the original 13 states, Connecticut is rich in history at every turn. Guests should ask about Mystic and other nearby attractions. The rooms, recently redecorated, are comfortable with outside views of Mystic River and Fishers Island Sound. The cottage's interior is cedar and can accommodate up to six. Visitors to this friendly inn on the waterfront may enjoy fishing, canoeing, rowing and waterfront picnicking.

Charley's Lemonade

**juice from 2 lemons and 1 lime with 2 qts water
sugar to taste**

Serve with cracked ice.

RFD –1, Box 398
Edgemont Street
Mystic, CT 06355
Tel (203) 572-9253

NORTHEAST

Hawthorne Inn

The Hawthorne Inn, built around 1870 on the famed "Battle Road" of 1775, is nestled among beautiful old trees that once belonged to Ralph Waldo Emerson, the Alcott's, and Nathaniel Hawthorne. Two of the trees still stand by the pathway that were planted by Hawthorne and can be seen on the west side of the inn.

The common room is furnished with a selection of books, magazines, and a warm fire. Original works of art, both ancient and modern, antique Japanese Ukiyoye prints, and sculpture by innkeeper Gregory Burch are handsomely displayed throughout the building.

Guest rooms named Emerson, Alcott, Musketequid, Walden, and Concord are colorful and furnished with antiques, handmade quilts, and wood floors warmed with oriental and rag rugs. A bowl of fresh fruit and flowers welcome guests.

Directly across the road stands the Hawthorne House, the Wayside, and Alcott's Orchard House. This is also the home of the Concord Grape and closeby is the Old North Bridge where the "shot heard around the world was fired."

A Continental breakfast is served each morning in the common room. Baked Breads, Fresh Fruit, Juice, Tea and Coffee and, when in season, Raspberries are enjoyed.

Morning Cake Delight

1 lb butter	6 eggs
1/2 cup sour cream	1/2 cup milk
1-1/2 tsp almond extract	1 tbs baking powder
2 cups sugar	1 banana
4 cups flour	1 cup berries

Mix butter, eggs, sour cream, milk, almond extract, baking powder, sugar and banana extremely well until a smooth consistency is reached. Beat in flour until well coated but do not overbeat. Pour one-half of the mixture into pan, adding a layer of berries, and pour the rest of the mixture in over berries. Bake at 375° for 1-1/4 hours in a buttered and floured Bundt pan.

Hawthorne Inn Topping

1/2 cup fresh whipped cream	1/2 cup fruited yogurt
1/2 cup sour cream	

Fold yogurt and sour cream into whipped cream and serve over Morning Cake Delight.

462 Lexington Road
Concord, MA 01742
Tel (508) 369-5610

NORTHEAST

HICKORY BRIDGE FARM

Hickory Bridge Farm is located in the foothills of the Appalachian Mountains where beauty abounds during all seasons. The clapboard structure has the homey look it was meant to have amidst tall shade trees, old farm implements, and a rail fence. Besides the main inn, cottages that have Franklin stoves overlook a trout stream. Antiques in the guest rooms provide a country charm, while nearby activities include golfing, skiing, swimming, antique hunting, the Totem Pole Playhouse, and historic Gettysburg.

A Continental breakfast is offered each morning. Meals are served in a century-old barn with antique farm implements. Home-cooked dinners are served family style. Many of the fresh fruits and vegetables are grown right on the farm or neighboring farms.

Adams County Apple Dip

8 red apples
1/4 cup lemon juice
few drops red food coloring

1 cup strawberry jam
1 large pkg cream cheese
1 large container Cool Whip or
1 recipe of Dream Whip

Core and cut apples in wedges (16 to 1 apple). Drop into bowl with lemon juice. Blend cream cheese, jam, and food coloring well. Fold in whip cream lightly. To serve, place apple wedges around plate, put dip in bowl.

Hot Spiced Apple Cider

1 qt apple cider
10 whole cloves

3 sticks whole cinnamon

Place spices in small cloth or tea strainer, and then into apple cider. Warm apple cider, but not to boiling. Remove spices and serve.

Ortanna, PA 17353
Tel (717) 642-5261

NORTHEAST

The Holloway House

The Holloway House has catered to the traveler as far back as the early 1800s. Built as a tavern in 1808 by blacksmith Peter Holloway, good food is served to today's guests in the same restful surroundings that attracted the coach-worn passenger well over a century ago. An important event in the history of the inn goes back to 1812 when Rochester's first mayor, Jonathan Child, operated a store in part of the building. It was his father-in-law, Nathaniel Rochester, who established a city bearing his name at the Falls of the Genesee. Hand-hewn beams and square nails used in the construction add to the charm of the historic old house. Several interesting attractions are within walking distance.

The Dutch oven brought from the cellar where cooking was carried on in earlier days and the original fireplace add to the country-style dining room that serves good food.

No overnight lodgings are provided.

Southern Peanut Cream Pie

1 baked pie shell
1/2 cup smooth peanut butter
2/3 cup sugar
2 cups milk (scalded)
1/4 tsp vanilla
3 egg whites, 6 tbs sugar for meringue.

1 cup confectioner's sugar
1/4 cup cornstarch
1/4sp salt
3 egg yolks beaten
3 tbs butter

Combine confectioner's sugar and peanut butter, blend until it appears like biscuit mix. Spread half of mixture on baked pie shell. Now combine cornstarch, sugar and salt. Add scalded milk and mix well. Pour small amount over beaten egg yolks and mix well, then return all to milk mixture. Cook in top of double boiler until mixture thickens. Add butter and vanilla. Cool. Pour into pie shell and top with meringue and sprinkle remainder of peanut butter/sugar mix on top. Bake 325° until meringue browns.

East Bloomfield, NY 14443
Tel 1-716-657-7120

NORTHEAST

The Homestead Inn

The Homestead Inn sits on land that was a proprietorship grant issued to Colonel Benjamin Bellows by King George II. It was Colonel Bellows who built the inn in 1762, thirteen years before the American Revolution.

The inn is very rich in history. Having served as a major station on the Underground Railroad in pre-Civil War days, it has heard the whispers of escaped slaves and the war whoops of attacking Indians. Strong shutters built into the "Indian Room" window frames were designed as protection against the shooting arrows. They are still there.

More than two hundred years later, Homestead Inn still provides hospitality and lodging in the spirit of its early beginnings.

Meals are graciously served, offering the very best in country cooking.

Bread Pudding

12 slices stale bread	4 tbs butter
1 cup sugar	6 eggs, beaten
6 cups scalded milk	1/2 tsp salt
1/2 tsp cinnamon	1 cup moist raisins

Toast bread lightly and spread with butter while hot. Break into buttered baking pan 14x10x2. Stir the salt and all but 3 tsp of sugar into beaten eggs, adding milk and stirring. Pour over bread and let stand 10 minutes, then stir in raisins. Mix 3 tbs sugar with cinnamon and sprinkle over the top. Bake at 350° for approximately 45 minutes. Serves 12.

Walpole, NH 03608
Tel (603) 756-3320

THE
HOTEL
HERSHEY

Hotel Hershey is a grand example of Mediterranean architecture in a Pennsylvania setting of manicured lawns, formal gardens, and exotic sculpture. The beautiful all-seasons hotel has provided elegance, and warm hospitality since 1933. With 270 tastefully-appointed guest rooms, activities include three championship golf courses, tennis, lawn bowling, swimming, and horseback riding. Winter guests are lured by tobogganing and cross-country skiing.

Just minutes away, Chocolate Town, U.S.A. entertains millions of visitors each year. At this unusual and fascinating place there is a Swiss-designed monorail, and the street lamps are shaped like Hershey's Kisses.

Meals are served in a spectacular setting of the Circular Dining Room with views of shimmering ponds, sweet scented flowers, and stained glass. Specialties prepared by Executive Chef Heinz E. Hautle include Brandied Chicken Livers, Beef Wellington, Rice Pilaf, Roast Leg of Lamb, Chilled Strawberry Bisque, and Frozen Saboyan.

Smoked Porkloin with Braised Red Cabbage

1 med. head red cabbage	1-1/2 large onions
1 large apple	1 cup wine vinegar
2 cups apple juice	1/2 cup sugar
1 4-lb smoked porkloin	1 carrot
1 stalk celery	2 cups beef broth
1 tbs cornstarch	3 tbs water
salt	

Dice one onion and one peeled, cored apple. Saute in large pot. Add sliced cabbage, vinegar, apple juice , and sugar. Mix well. Cover with tight fitting lid. Cook over medium heat for about 45 minutes or until cabbage is tender. Place seasoned porkloin in hot oiled roasting pan. Brown all sides. Roast at 325° for 35 minutes. After 10 minutes, add 1/2 onion, carrot, and celery (all diced) to roasting pan along with beef broth. Let finish roasting. When finished, remove porkloin from broth and thicken with cornstarch (mixed with water). Maintain heat on sauce by placing pan on stove. When thickened, season to taste, then strain. Serve porkloin with the cabbage and sauce.

Hershey, PA 17033
Tel (717) 533-2171

NORTHEAST

HOWARD HOUSE

Howard House Motor Lodge, an Alpine-style structure, is about a mile from the waterfront of fascinating Booth Bay Harbor. With high beamed ceilings and natural wood walls, the accommodations have a decidedly country-like air. The guest rooms are spacious and furnished in the warmth of Early American. Each room has a deck for sunning and relaxing.

Guests may enjoy sightseeing, dining out, boating, and fishing at Booth Bay.

A complimentary homemade Continental breakfast is served each morning. Treats are Best Ever Coffee Cake and Blueberry Muffins.

Best Ever Coffee Cake

3 cups flour
2 eggs
1 cup shortening

3 tsp baking powder
1 cup sugar
1 cup milk

Topping:

1 cup light brown sugar
3/4 cup melted butter
1-1/2 cups chopped walnuts

3 tbs flour
1-1/2 cups chopped dates

Make batter by creaming sugar, eggs, shortening, and milk very well with whisk. Pour half the batter into 9x13 pan. Mix together topping and sprinkle half onto batter. Layer again with batter and top with remaining date mixture. Bake 50 minutes at 350°. Serve very warm.

Route 27
Booth Bay Harbor, ME 04538
Tel (207) 633-3933

NORTHEAST

Jared Coffin House

Jared Coffin House is an outstanding example of 19th century craftsmanship. Located in the heart of Nantucket's Historic District, the stately three-story English brick building has a Welsh slate roof and dates back to 1845. Elegantly restored, the inn recaptures the days when Nantucket was the reigning queen of the world's whaling ports.

Made up of five charming old homes - one of which dates to the 1700's - the inn's rooms are furnished with period antiques, art work, and island-woven fabrics that reflect the wide travels of the Nantucket sailors.

Hailed as an intimate hotel for those who appreciate fine accommodations and service, the Jared Coffin House brings back a way of life that has passed forever from the American scene. Stores on Main Street and Steamboat Wharf are just a minute's stroll away.

A Continental breakfast is served each morning, and the quiet and elegant atmosphere of the main dining room hosts an innovative menu. Classical American cuisine including Baked Noel, Poached Salmon Fillet with Oysters, and Pumpkin Cheesecake are part of the fine fare.

Jared's Cranberry Nut Bread

3 cups flour	2 cups sugar
2 tsp baking powder	1-1/2 tsp salt
2 tsp baking soda	2 tsp vanilla
2 tsp cinnamon	1 lb cranberries
1-1/3 cups vegetable oil	4 eggs
l lb chopped walnuts	

Combine all ingredients except eggs, which need to be added one at a time. Bake in a greased, floured bread pan for 40 minutes at 325°.

Nantucket Island, MA 02554
Tel (617) 228-2400

NORTHEAST

THE JOHN HANCOCK INN

The John Hancock Inn has welcomed travelers to the beautiful hills of New Hampshire and the lovely village of Hancock for almost two centuries. Near other historic buildings, the inn was a stagecoach stop during its early years.

Sitting before a blazing hearth in the Carriage Room, guests enjoy the atmosphere with tables of old bellows and seats from early buggies. The Mural Room has a pastoral scene painted around 1825 by itinerant artist, Rufus Porter. Ten guest rooms are comfortably furnished with canopied and four poster beds, braided and hooked rugs, rockers, and wingbacks . . . gentle reminders of days gone by.

The area is rich in activities that include mountain climbing, golf, Alpine and cross-country skiing, concerts, and summer theatre.

Meals are served in three dining rooms. The main dining room is decorated with recreated stencil designs by Moses Eaton. The menu offers hearty New England fare of Prime Rib, Seafood, and Poultry selections. Specialties include Hancock Dressing and Daniel's Pumpkin Bread. At Thanksgiving, each family receives a loaf as they leave.

Daniel's Pumpkin Bread

Mix together:

1-1/2 cups granulated sugar	**1 cup oil**
1-1/2 cups firmly packed brown sugar	

Whip in:

3 eggs	**2 cups pumpkin**

Separately, sift together:

3 cups flour	**1-1/2 tsp ground cloves**
1-1/2 tsp cinnamon	**1/2 tsp allspice**
1-1/2 tsp nutmeg	**1/2 tsp baking powder**
1 tsp baking soda	**1/2 tsp salt**

Add dry ingredients to creamed mixture. Pour into lightly greased loaf pans. Bake at 350 degrees for 1 to 1-1/4 hours. Raisins, nuts, or chopped dates may be added. Yields 5 loaves.

Main Street
Hancock, NH 03449
Tel (603) 525-3318

NORTHEAST

Welcoming guests for 170 years, the Kedron Valley Inn is the eighth oldest continually running inn or tavern in Vermont. Its 26 rooms are spread amongst three buildings, two of which are brick and clapboard structures from the 1820s. An authentic Vermont Log Home building houses the remainder. Over half the guest rooms have wood-burning fireplaces, and all rooms have private baths and TVs. A 60-piece heirloom antique quilt collection is on display throughout the guest and common rooms.

The 100 seat dining room is a focal point of the experience at Kedron Valley Inn. Contemporary American Cuisine is served, using the freshest local products and seafood straight from Boston and Florida.

Kedron Valley Salmon

Serves 4

18 oz. fillet of Norwegian Salmon, cut into four 4 oz fillets, then slice each fillet in half lengthwise, so that one piece can be put on top of the other with the mousse in between. Save 2 oz. of salmon for the mousse.

Mousse

2 oz salmon saved from 18 oz. fillet	**1/4 tsp white pepper**
3 oz. shrimp - raw, peeled and deveined	**1/2 pint heavy cream**
3 oz. fresh sea scallops	**1 egg white**
1 tsp chive, fresh or dried	**4 - 5x5 frozen puff pastry squares**
1 tsp tarragon	**1 egg and 1 tbs milk lightly beaten together**
1 tsp parsley	

If using food processor or blender, place bowl in freezer 1/2 hour prior to start. Preheat oven to 425°. Place all seafood in bowl. Pulse once or twice to mix. Slowly add heavy cream and egg white while blending (1 minute). Remove and place in clean dry bowl. Add all herbs and pepper to the mixture and fold gently with rubber spatula. Place bottom salmon in the middle of puff pastry. Place 3 or 4 tbs of mousse on bottom half of salmon and cover with top half. Bring four corners of pastry together on top and squeeze to secure. Lightly butter baking pan and invert salmon on pan. Brush with egg wash lightly. Cook in preheated oven for 7 minutes or until golden brown. Remove and let sit for 2 minutes. Serve with assorted fresh vegetables. Chardonnay would be a good accompaniment.

Route 106
South Woodstock, VT 05071
Tel (802) 457-1473

Lincklaen House

Lincklaen House has been a local landmark since 1835 when it was built and named for John Lincklaen, founder of the town. For many years the Georgian brick structure was a luxurious stopover for colonial travelers. Notables who have enjoyed its elegant hospitality include President and Mrs. Grover Cleveland and John D. Rockefeller.

Inside, the character of the hotel has been well preserved, though updated for the comfort of its guests. The spacious public rooms have high ceilings, handsome carved mouldings, painted wood panels and impressive Williamsburg chandeliers. Three huge fireplaces for warmth create an atmosphere of days past. Guest rooms are comfortable in the Early American theme and many of the rooms have antiques and stenciled ceiling borders.

Meals are served in two dining rooms. The main dining room's table setting of white linens and gleaming silver are in contrast to the garden atmosphere of the Terrace Room's yellow brick walls and bright water colors. The menu includes seafood bisque as the house soup, scallops in sundried tomato pesto sauce, baked salmon with dill beurre blanc sauce, 16 oz. porterhouse steak with burgundy barbeque sauce, and creative specials.

Sundried Tomato Pesto Sauce

1/2 cup whole garlic
2 cups (loose pack) fresh basil
4 cups sundried tomatoes
   (soaked or in oil)
1 cup walnuts

1 tbs black pepper
1 tsp salt
2 cups olive oil
1 cup grated romano

In food processor blend all but oil and cheese. With machine on, add oil in steady stream. Add cheese and pulse 2-3 times. Add 1-2 tbs paste to 1 cup cream, heat and toss with pasta and veggies.

79 Albany Street
Cazenovia, NY 13035
Tel (315) 655-3461

NORTHEAST

LOGAN INN, NEW HOPE

Logan Inn has been in continuous operation since 1727. Because of its location on the river and "Old York Road", the inn was the scene of the final planning of the American attack on Trenton, which originated with the crossing of the Delaware on Christmas Day, 1776.

Built by John Wells, founder of the town and operator of the ferry, the inn played host to many important men during the Revolution documenting five visits by General George Washington. Logan Inn has also served as official Broadway headquarters for many famous celebrities.

The public rooms are filled with antiques, fine paintings and a sizeable collection of old ticking clocks. Guests rooms are furnished with antique brass and tall Lincoln type wooden beds, marble topped dressers and armoires. Many of the interesting lamps have been made from antique vases and figurines.

The elegant glass-roofed conservatory dining room presents such specialties as Shrimp Logan, Swedish Lamb Bernadotte, Filet Mignon, Loin of Veal Esterhazy, Supreme of Chicken Tarragon, Sole Veronique, and Apple Cake with Hot Buttered Rum Sauce.

Chicken Logan au Peche

1 tbs brown sugar	2 tbs sweet butter
salt	white pepper
flour for dusting	1 beaten egg
3/4 cup dry white bread crumbs	vegetable oil for deep fryer
4 large half breasts of chicken,	1 ripe peach peeled, pitted, and sliced
boned and skinned	1/4 tsp grated fresh ginger root
	(or 1/2 tsp minced candied root)

Flatten chicken breasts between sheets of wax paper as thin as possible without tearing. Salt and pepper to taste. Melt butter in small saucepan. Add sugar and ginger root, stirring until sugar is dissolved. Add peach slices and simmer for 1 minute. Cool. (A tbs Major Grey's Chutney, chopped, may be added at this time.) Place peach slices on each flattened breast. Fold envelope style (long bottom side of breast up and over peach, fold sides in next, fold top flap over all). Chill for at least 1 hour. Dust with flour, dip in beaten egg, roll in bread crumbs. Chill. Heat oil to 350⁰ and fry for about 10 minutes. Drain and serve.

New Hope, PA 18938
Tel (215) 862-2300

NORTHEAST

THE LONDONDERRY INN

The Londonderry Inn, nestled in a grove of trees just minutes from Stratton, Bromley, and the Magic Mountains, was built in 1826 as a home overlooking the West River and quiet village of South Londonderry. The region has been a favored resort for decades and a pamphlet written about South Londonderry in 1881 records: "The tourist and pleasure seeker will find no spot more inviting."

Today, more than a hundred years later, little has changed and the inn extends an equally warm welcome. Operated as the Melendy Dairy Farm over 150 years ago, its early beginnings are still a part of the charm. The twenty-five comfortable guest rooms are restful and just steps away from endless outdoor activities.

Meals are served in the dining room that is housed in the former woodshed enhanced by Audubon prints and soft candlelight. An innovative menu changes nightly and features traditional American fare, Continental specialties, and creative surprises.

Curried Lamb & Apricots

1/8 cup sherry
1/4 cup apricot preserves
1/4 cup raisins
1/4 cup coarsely chopped walnuts
1/4 tsp ginger powder
(1/8 tsp if fresh ginger)
1 apple cored and cubed into
half-inch pieces
1 lb cubed lamb
(leg or tenderloin)

1/4 tsp curry powder
1 cup dried apricots
1/4 cup butter

Heat butter in saute pan, but do not burn. Add lamb pieces, stirring to brown evenly. When browned add curry and ginger. Stir to evenly distribute spices, then add all remaining ingredients. Lamb should be cooked on rare side, unless preferred otherwise. Serve immediately on rice pilaf or your own favorite rice dish.

Route 100
South Londonderry, VT 05155
Tel (802) 824-5226

NORTHEAST

Longfellow's Wayside Inn

Longfellow's Wayside Inn, the scene for early American patriots who conspired revolution against the British that ultimately led to the birth of our country, is America's oldest operating inn and has provided hospitality to nine generations.

Built in 1702 as the two-room home of Daniel How and later established as the How Hotel and Tavern, the early (1647) laws of Massachusetts Bay Colony required an innkeeper to provide for a man, his horse, and his cattle. By 1796 it was known as the Red Horse and had become a popular gathering place for people from all walks of life. After Henry Wadsworth Longfellow visited in 1862 and published "Tales" a year later, the National Landmark was called Longfellow's Wayside Inn.

Open for tours, the main portion of the inn has been restored by the Ford Foundation, and its guest rooms are home to period furnishings. Adjacent to the inn stands The Redstone School of "Mary and Her Little Lamb" fame, The Wayside Gristmill, and the Martha-Mary Chapel...all a part of the Ford Foundation.

The bill of fare served in the dining room reflects the inn's rich colonial heritage with dishes of Roast Goose with Apple Stuffing and Tangerine Sauce, Chicken Pie, Yankee Pot Roast, Baked Scallops, Creamed Finnan Haddie (smoked haddock), Baked Indian Pudding, and Pear and Apple Pies.

Sauteed Rainbow Trout Almondine

4 8 oz trout, boned and gutted	1 stick melted butter
flour to dredge	2 cup sliced, blanched almonds

Melt butter and place clarified portion in saute pan. Place pan on stove and heat. Dredge trout in flour and place in saute pan and cook for approximately 5 minutes on each side, being careful not to burn. Take fish out and place on serving tray. Saute almonds for about 1 minute, then pour almonds over fish and serve. Garnish with parsley and lemon wedges.

Rhubarb Pie

5 cups diced rhubarb stalk	1/3 cup flour
1 tbs cornstarch	1-1/2 cups sugar
5 fresh strawberries	pastry crust for 9" pie

Mix all ingredients in bowl and place in unbaked pie crust. Egg wash rim and place top crust over filling. Crimp edges and cut steam vents in crust. Egg wash and bake in 350° oven until golden brown.

Sudbury, MA 01776
Tel (508) 443-8846

NORTHEAST

LOVETT'S

Lovett's is now 200 years old and is listed as a National Landmark. The clapboard structure is located in the White Mountains of New Hampshire, and has been run by the Lovett family for two generations. Characteristic of many early homes, the inn is a rambling connection of comfortable rooms in a variety of sizes and styles. All are light and airy.

In addition to the main inn, several contemporary cottages are tucked among evergreens. Some are warmed by fireplaces, have private terraces, and all enjoy walls of windows that look out on Franconia Range.

Just fifteen minutes to three major ski areas, Lovett's is the very place for the outdoorsman. Mountain trails lead everywhere, and trout streams, brooks, ponds, and stone walls are added charms to this AAA all-season inn.

The dining room's meals are prepared from garden-fresh vegetables.

Black Bean Soup, Lovett's Style

2 cups dried black beans
1 carrot scraped and chopped
1-1/2 tsp dry mustard

1 large onion, chopped
1 ham bone
2 celery stalks and leaves, cut fine

Pick over and soak beans overnight. Drain, saving the soaking liquor. Add enough water to make three quarts in all. Put all ingredients in a pot. Bring to a boil, then simmer for about three hours until beans are soft. Remove ham. Season with salt and freshly ground pepper. Serve chilled with dash of dark rum and a thin lemon slice. (Can be pureed in blender or food processor.)

Franconia, NH 03580
Tel (603)823-7761

NORTHEAST

The Lyme Inn

Lyme Inn was built in an old settlement chartered in 1761 and this fine example of New England architecture dates back to 1809. During the mid-1800's, Lyme was the largest sheep-producing village in the region.

The inn is filled with antiques, comfort, and informality on all four floors. Ten fireplaces, Currier and Ives samples, stenciled wallpaper, and a screened-in porch distinguish Lyme Inn as a place to sit and relax...not just to stop by. An extensive library ranging from science fiction to the classics is right at hand. Guest rooms are, of course, very different and furnished with antiques, poster beds, colorful handmade quilts, and hooked rugs on wide floorboards.

Activities include canoeing the Connecticut River in summer and skiing in the winter. Nearby, concerts, plays, festivals, and art exhibits take place the year 'round. The well-known Appalachian Trail passes right through Lyme.

A Continental breakfast is served each morning, and meals prepared to perfection are served in an unhurried country setting. Fresh seafood being the specialty, the changing menu also offers traditional New England fare of Veal, Lamb, Beef, and Pork.

Brandy Alexander Pie

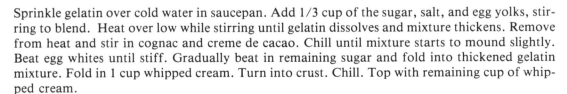

1 envelope unflavored gelatin
2/3 cup sugar
2 eggs, separated
2 cups heavy cream, whipped
9'' chocolate crumb crust

1/2 cup cold water
1/8 tsp salt
1/4 cup cognac
1/4 cup creme de cacao

Sprinkle gelatin over cold water in saucepan. Add 1/3 cup of the sugar, salt, and egg yolks, stirring to blend. Heat over low while stirring until gelatin dissolves and mixture thickens. Remove from heat and stir in cognac and creme de cacao. Chill until mixture starts to mound slightly. Beat egg whites until stiff. Gradually beat in remaining sugar and fold into thickened gelatin mixture. Fold in 1 cup whipped cream. Turn into crust. Chill. Top with remaining cup of whipped cream.

Chocolate Crumb Crust

Mix 6 tbs melted butter and 1 1/2 cups finely crushed chocolate wafer crumbs well before patting firmly into 9'' pan, covering bottom and sides. Either chill thoroughly before filling or bake at 300° for 15 minutes.

Lyme, NH 03768
Tel (603) 795-2222 or 4404

NORTHEAST

THE MAINSTAY

The Mainstay is bordered by a green picket fence and bright colorful flowers in one of the nation's oldest summer resorts. Located on the corner of Columbia and Stockton Streets, no expense was spared when this exclusive men's club was built in 1872.

The gingerbread embellishments, sweeping veranda, and stately windows flanked by tall green shutters, are fitting complements to its 14-foot ceilings and ornate plaster mouldings. The very finest walnut furnishings were used, and many of the original pieces remain. Twelve foot mirrors, brass chandeliers, marble-topped sideboards, and beautiful loveseats are reminders of those opulent days. Guest rooms have antique beds with lofty headboards and equally high wardrobes.

Afternoon tea is served on the veranda or in the drawing room. Breakfast is given in the dining room or, weather permitting, out on the porches. The hospitality includes Juice, Fruit, Cereal, Cakes, and Breads.

Hummingbird Cake

3 cups flour	1 tsp soda
1 1/2 tsp vanilla	1 tsp cinnamon
2 cups sugar	3 eggs
1 tsp salt	2 cups diced bananas
1 1/2 cups cooking oil	1 cup chopped pecans
1 8-oz can crushed pineapple, undrained	

Preheat oven to 325 degrees. Grease tube pan. Sift dry ingredients and add pineapple, oil, vanilla, eggs, bananas, and pecans, mixing by hand until just blended. Bake 1 hour. Serves 10-12.

635 Columbia Avenue
Cape May, NJ 08204
Tel (609)884-8690

NORTHEAST

Built in 1802

Founded as an artists colony, Camden later become the getaway for the high society of Boston, New York and Philadelphia. Its shady tree-lined streets are filled with century-old homes, small churches and interesting shops.

The Maine Stay is located in the heart of Camden, two blocks from the village common and harbor dotted with fishing and sail boats. The white clapboard home is listed on the National Register and dates back to 1802.

Oriental rugs, cozy parlors with fireplaces, and eight guest rooms tastefully decorated with antiques await the traveler. A focal point is the country kitchen with its pine floors, beamed ceiling, and handsome Queen Atlantic coal burning stove dating from the 1800s.

Many activities include hiking, white water rafting, fishing, bird-watching and windjamming.

Open year round. Full complimentary breakfast and afternoon refreshments are offered.

Sausage Strata

1 lb sausage	5 large eggs
1/3 cup ea. green & sweet red pepper (chopped)	2 cups Half and Half
	1/2 tsp Worcestershire sauce
1 tsp Grey Poupon Country mustard	1/8 tsp black pepper
8 slices white bread (crust removed)	1/4 tsp ground nutmeg
2 cups grated swiss cheese	1/8 tsp salt

Sauté sausage until browned. Add diced peppers and cook for just a few minutes — don't get them soggy. Drain off fat. Add mustard. Arrange bread in bottom of greased 13 x 9 baking pan. Top with sausage mixture and cheese. In a large bowl, lightly beat eggs. Add milk, Worcestershire sauce, pepper, nutmeg and salt. Pour over layers in baking pan. Cover tightly and refrigerate overnight. Preheat oven to 350°. Bake strata, uncovered, for 40-45 minutes or until center seems set.

22 High Street
Camden, Maine 04843
Tel (207) 236-9636

Middletown Springs Inn

Middletown Springs Inn was built in 1879 and was in the same family for 66 years. Listed on the National Register of Historic Places, the inn is located in the heart of the historic town of Middletown Springs, Vermont - once a fashionable spa.

The impressive Italianate structure was converted to an inn in 1971, and most of its architectural features still remain.

Downstairs, the entrance hall with its handsome curved staircase and five public rooms welcome visitors with period elegance complemented with antiques. There are seven upstairs guest rooms tastefully furnished, in addition to an 1840s carriage house with comfortable accommodations.

A continental breakfast is offered, and dinner by request. Only the finest cuisine is featured.

Chicken Middletown

3	skinned boneless chicken breasts	1	chopped green pepper
1	large onion	1	chopped red pepper
1	small can crushed tomatoes	¼	pound mushrooms
1	cup Ragu sauce		curry powder
1	cup white wine		salt
1	clove garlic		pepper

Chop chicken breasts in half. Spread a layer of crushed tomatoes in bottom of baking dish, place chicken on top. Place chopped onion, crushed garlic, green and red pepper combined with Ragu sauce and remainder of crushed tomato on and around chicken. Add cracked pepper, small amount of curry powder, and salt to taste. Cover contents with white wine and bake at 400 degrees for one hour. Twenty minutes before completion add chopped mushrooms. Serve with rice and mixed green salad.

On the Green
P.O. Box 1068
Middletown Springs, VT 05757-1068
Tel (802) 235-2198

Middlebury Inn

Middlebury Inn has presided over happenings in Addison County with hospitality and friendly service since it was established in 1827. The building is very stately and Federal in design. Besides the main inn, the Porter House and attached Hubbard House provide lodging. The public rooms are spacious with wide hallways, high ceilings, cozy little libraries, and sitting rooms. Each area has its own charm. Guest rooms are individually decorated with colorful wallpaper, antique beds of maple and cherry, and some have hand-cut lamp shades.

Activities in this lively college town abound in every season, including downhill and cross-country skiing, ice skating, antiqueing, and maple sugaring. There is also a walking tour of museums.

Plentiful New England fare is offered in a variety of dining choices, depending upon the season. During the warmer weather, the wide sweeping porch is a natural for lunch or dinner with views of the "goings on" on the green. An innovative menu provides many superb specialties.

Chef Tom Phelps's Chilled Strawberry Soup

1 pt. fresh strawberries	1 cup sour cream
2 cups coffee cream	
3 tbs brandy	sugar to taste

Chop strawberries in blender. Add sour cream, sugar, brandy; blend until smooth, then mix in coffee cream. Chill and serve. (Tom's Chilled Fruit Recipe was requested by Gourmet magazine.)

Box 631
Middlebury, VT 05753-0631
Tel (802) 388-4961

NORTHEAST

Mill House Inn

The Millhouse Inn is a rebuilt sawmill where returning guests are known to ask for their favorite room. Its architectural design has an Alpine look that blends in very well with its Berkshires setting. The rough-hewn walls and beams add a distinctive charm of friendliness and informality. The common room is a favorite gathering spot to meet old and make new friends before a crackling fire on chilly evenings. Guest rooms and suites are tastefully furnished with antiques where, along with modern conveniences, the overnight guests can still warm up to a blazing hearth.

Activities include hiking, golf, downhill and cross-country skiing, and, close by, the Hancock Shaker Village, Clark Art Institute, flea markets, and the Williamstown Theatre can be visited.

Afternoon tea is served, and each morning a full breakfast is available either in the Europa Room or on the garden deck, weather permitting.

Stone Ground Wheat Cakes

2 tbs corn oil
1 egg
1/2 cup unbleached white flour
1 cup stone ground wheat (graham)

2 cups milk
2 tbs sugar
1/2 tsp salt
3-1/2 tsp baking powder (Rumford)

Mix dry ingredients in large bowl. Mix wet ingredients in small bowl. Pour wet mixture into dry and stir until blended. Makes 3 to 4 servings of 3 pancakes each. Top with favorite syrup.

Route 43
Stephenville, NY 12168
Tel (518) 733-5606

NORTHEAST

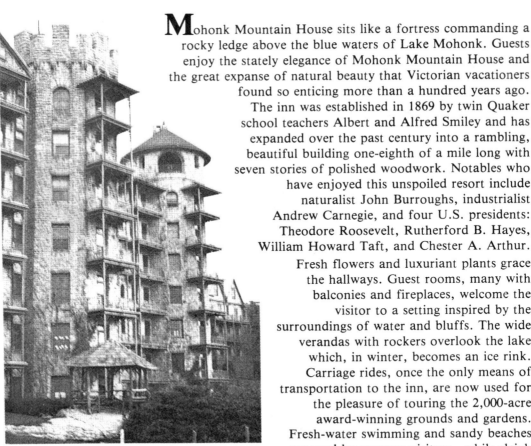

Mohonk
Mountain
House

Mohonk Mountain House sits like a fortress commanding a rocky ledge above the blue waters of Lake Mohonk. Guests enjoy the stately elegance of Mohonk Mountain House and the great expanse of natural beauty that Victorian vacationers found so enticing more than a hundred years ago.

The inn was established in 1869 by twin Quaker school teachers Albert and Alfred Smiley and has expanded over the past century into a rambling, beautiful building one-eighth of a mile long with seven stories of polished woodwork. Notables who have enjoyed this unspoiled resort include naturalist John Burroughs, industrialist Andrew Carnegie, and four U.S. presidents: Theodore Roosevelt, Rutherford B. Hayes, William Howard Taft, and Chester A. Arthur.

Fresh flowers and luxuriant plants grace the hallways. Guest rooms, many with balconies and fireplaces, welcome the visitor to a setting inspired by the surroundings of water and bluffs. The wide verandas with rockers overlook the lake which, in winter, becomes an ice rink. Carriage rides, once the only means of transportation to the inn, are now used for the pleasure of touring the 2,000-acre award-winning grounds and gardens. Fresh-water swimming and sandy beaches are used by summer visitors, while sleigh rides through the snow await winter guests. A hundred gazebos perched along rocky precipices make ideal retreats. Elegant meals are served in the beautifully old-fashioned, polished wood dining room that seats 500 and whose ceiling soars overhead.

Mohonk Cabinet Pudding

Leftover Danish pastries baked fresh every morning by the hotel's baking staff are used in Cabinet Pudding.

In a 1 1/2 qt glass baking dish, place 2 1/2 to 3 cups stale Danish, cut into 1/4 inch cubes. Add 2 tbs raisins. To prepare custard, beat with wire whisk:

3 eggs   **pinch salt**
5 tbs sugar

Gradually beat in 2 cups milk and 1 tsp vanilla. Pour custard over Danish-raisin mixture and sprinkle with cinnamon. Set baking dish in larger pan and fill with water to halfway up sides of baking dish. Bake at 375° until knife inserted comes out clean, approximately 1 hour. Serve warm or at room temperature. Serves 4-6.

Lake Mohonk/New Paltz, NY 12561
Tel (914) 255-1000

Moose Mountain Lodge

Moose Mountain Lodge offers miles of hiking and ski trails right from the front door step. An authentic woodland lodge, built in 1938 of native logs and stones, Moose Mountain Lodge overlooks the Connecticut River Valley with views of the Green Mountains. In addition to trails, bicycle trips through New Hampshire and Vermont can be arranged along with ever-popular canoeing from inn to inn on the Connecticut River.

A complimentary breakfast is offered, and hearty meals are served in the dining room. The interesting menu reflects the philosophy of the innkeepers: Food should be healthy, delicious, and plentiful.

Moose Mountain Blueberry Gems

2 cups flour
1/2 tsp salt
1 tbs fresh lemon juice
1/4 cup melted butter

1/2 cup sugar
1 tbs baking powder
3/4 cup orange juice
1 egg

Combine dry and wet ingredients and add 1 cup fresh or frozen blueberries. Bake in heated cast iron pans 20 minutes at 400 degrees.

Etna, NH 03750
Tel (603) 643-3529

MORRILL PLACE

Morrill Place, with its rooftop widow's walk, characterizes the many dignified homes built in the days when Newburyport was a prosperous commercial and shipping center. Imports from Europe and China made it the seventh largest port in the nation. Built in 1806 by sea Captain William Hoyt and owned by succeeding mariners, this elegant Federal-style mansion's fine architectural details include cornices, mantels, balustrades, and a graceful hanging staircase. Daniel Webster was a frequent visitor when his law partner bought the house in 1836. For nearly a century it was the property of the Morrill family.

Since 1979, the historic home has been serving as a gracious inn with overnight, year 'round lodging. Ten guest rooms, summer and winter porches, a formal front parlor, and library all reflect a charming legacy of the past.

Afternoon tea is served at 4 p.m. A Continental breakfast brightens each morning with offerings such as Squash muffins, Juice, Coffee or Tea, and Cereal.

Maple Squash

3 cups squash puree   1/4 cup maple syrup
2 tbs butter   dash nutmeg and ginger

Heat squash puree on low heat with syrup and butter, adding nutmeg and ginger for a nice touch.

Squash Puree

Slice 2-3 medium squash lengthwise and scoop out pulp and seeds. Oil, cut sides as well as baking sheet and lay squash cut side down. Bake in preheated 375 degree oven for 45-55 minutes. When knife can be inserted easily into squash, it is done. Remove from oven and let cool slightly. When you can handle squash, scoop out insides and either puree in food processor, mix with electric mixer, or mash. If necessary, add a little water (should be consistency of whipped potatoes). Or cut squash into chunks and boil 25-35 minutes until tender, following method to obtain final product.

209 High Street
Newburyport, MA 01950
Tel (508) 462-2808

NORTHEAST

Mountain View Inn has remained a treasured hideaway of loyal guests for over forty years. The eleven guest rooms are warm and informal in this Victorian inn where nearby activities include golf, tennis, water sports, hiking, and cross-country and downhill skiing. Looking for antiques, beautiful country drives, music, and theatre lend themselves to the enjoyable surroundings.

Meals are graciously served in the dining room where an innovative menu of international dishes complemented by a fine assortment of homemade breads and pastries await the diner.

Rotolo

Rotolo is pasta roll filled with ham and cheeses and served on a bed of marinara.

Pasta:

2 cups flour	1 tbs olive oil
4 eggs	1/2 tbs salt

Mix all ingredients in a bowl until it is like pie dough. Let set for 20 minutes. On a floured table roll until 1/8 inch thick and is 15'' x 15''.

Filling:

1/2 pt of Ricotta cheese	4 oz. cream cheese
1/2 cup parmesan cheese	1 egg

Mix the filling and spread over the pasta. Slice scallions thin and sprinkle over the filling. Slice about 1 pound of ham thinly and lay over the filling evenly. Roll the pasta like a jelly roll. Wrap in cheesecloth and tie at both ends. Poach in chicken stock for 25 minutes. Unwrap and slice, serve over marinara.

Marinara:

2 ozs olive oil	2 onions, chopped fine
3 cloves garlic	1 cup red wine
1 tbs thyme	1 tbs oregano
1 tbs basil	6 cups tomatoes, crushed

Heat oil in pot, add onions and cook until wilted. Add garlic and spices and stir. Add the red wine, bring to a boil and reduce to one-half. Add tomatoes and cook about 1 hour. Serve.

Route 272
Norfolk, CT 06058
Tel (203) 542-5595

NORTHEAST

The Nauset House Inn

The Nauset House is just a short stroll from the Cape Cod seashore, and with its dormer windows and clapboard siding, it has the look of warmth and comfort. Family owned and operated, guests feel as if they are visiting good friends.

There are fourteen guest rooms, bright and cheerful with fresh flowers and handmade quilts on the beds. Some of the rooms have sitting areas, while others have balconies. All are restful havens from art galleries, antique and craft shops, and excellent restaurants.

The Victorian conservatory, built in 1908, was moved from Greenwich, Connecticut piece by piece, and overlooks an arbor filled with plants, colorful flowers, and antique lacey furniture.

The one meal served at The Nauset House Inn is a very hearty country breakfast.

Flat Top Orange Date Muffins

1 orange rind, chopped
1/2 cup orange juice
1 large egg, slightly beaten

1 orange quartered, no pith
1 stick soft, unsalted butter
1/2 cup chopped, pitted dates

Mix ingredients and set aside. In large bowl, sift together:

1 1/2 cups all-purpose flour
3/4 cup sugar
1 tsp double-acting baking powder

dash salt
1 tsp baking soda

Add orange mixture to dry ingredients and stir until just combined (batter should be lumpy). Spoon into greased muffin tins 2/3 full and bake 15-20 minutes in 400° oven. Makes 16.

Beach Road
East Orleans, MA 02643
Tel (508) 255-2195

NORTHEAST

The Okemo Inn was one of the district's first traditional New England-style homes, built in 1810. With the Okemo Mountains in the background, this clapboard structure served as a summer boarding house during the early 1900s and, later, again as a private home. Major renovations began in 1962 and the doors were opened once more to travelers. The twelve guest rooms are comfortable and decorated with antiques - some of the furnishings going back to the early settlement days. The original hand-hewn beams, wide pine flooring, and eight fireplaces provide the expected setting.

Cross-country ski trails lead from the front door, and maple sugaring is an attraction in the spring.

Family-style meals of Roast Beef with Oven Roast Potatoes, Homemade Breads, Tender Carrot Tips, Soups, and Crisp Salads are served.

Easy 'n Elegant Brunch Casserole

6 hardboiled eggs, sliced
1 lb hot bulk sausage
1-1/2 cups grated cheddar

salt & pepper
1-1/2 cups sour cream
1/2 cup dry bread crumbs

Place sliced hardboiled eggs in buttered casserole dish and season to taste. Cook sausage, drain, crumble, and sprinkle over sliced eggs. Pour sour cream over sausage. Combine bread crumbs and grated cheese and sprinkle over casserole. Place in 300° oven to heat thoroughly, 20-30 minutes and then brown the top briefly under broiler. To serve, cut into six equal sections. Garnish each plate with crisp lettuce leaves and tomato halves.

Route 103, Box 4-A
Ludlow, VT 05149
Tel (802) 228-8834

NORTHEAST

Old Drovers Inn

Old Drovers Inn opened in 1750 by John and Ebenezer Preston and was known as the Clear Water Tavern. In those days the inn catered to cattle drovers, a group of men who bought herds of cattle and swine from New England farmers and drove them to the New York City markets. These New England traders hired others to do their work while they traveled from inn to inn making arrangements and enjoying the hospitality.

Today the cattle drovers are gone, but the inn remains and continues to offer fine food and lodging to the traveler. Guest rooms on the upper floors are luxuriously furnished with antiques. Across the road stands the Coach House Shop with an unusual collection of early Americana.

Excellent meals are served in the Federal Room with polished mahogany tables and glistening Georgian silver. Specialties made famous since 1937 by Olin Chester Potter include Old Drovers Cheddar Cheese Soup, Shrimp Rarebit, Partridge with Stuffing, Genuine Indian Curries and locally grown Pheasants, roasted in Burgundy and carved at the table.

Old Drovers Inn Key Lime Pie
As presented on Channel 7's Eyewitness News, Bob Lape, Gourmet Reporter.

5 egg yolks	4 oz. fresh squeezed lime juice
19 ozs sweetened condensed milk	grated rind from 1 lime
(Magnolia brand)	1 8-inch graham cracker crust

Beat egg yolk with wire whisk, and blend in condensed milk, add lime juice and grated lime. Pour into crust and refrigerate for two hours.

Dover Plains, NY 12522
Tel (914) 832-9311

NORTHEAST

OLD FORT INN

Old Fort Inn is an 1800s rebuilt barn that resides in harmony with an area where the flavor of early clipper ships still lingers. The beautiful streets, winding river, and lovely sea captains's homes are reminders of those early days.

The living room walls of weathered pine, huge ceiling beams and a massive brick fireplace complement its antique furnishings of many pine and oak pieces. Guest rooms are located in a turn of the century carriage house made of brick and stone. Each room is colorful and decorated in country charm. Close to the beach, swimming, tennis and shuffleboard are on the grounds, and golfing is just minutes away. An antique shop features country furniture, primitives and china.

A Continental breakfast of Home Baked Breads, Juices, and Coffee is prepared at this Mobil Guide 3-Star Inn.

Sheila's Cranberry Almond Bread

1 cup butter
1-1/2 cups sugar
3 eggs
1-1/2 cups sour cream
1 tbs almond flavoring
1 can whole cranberry sauce

1-1/2 tsp baking powder
1-1/2 tsp soda
2-1/2 cups flour
1/2 tsp salt
1/2 cup chopped nuts

Combine baking powder, soda, flour and salt. Cream butter and sugar, adding the eggs. Add dry ingredients alternately with sour cream: add almond flavor. Alternate layers of batter and cranberries in loaf pans. Sprinkle with nuts, bake at 350° for one hour.

Old Fort Avenue
Box 759
Kennebunkport, ME 04046
Tel (207) 967-5353

NORTHEAST

Old Lyme Inn

Old Lyme Inn is a classic example of New England's colonial residences and dates back to the 1850s. It has a main street location in the historic district. Rescued from the ravages of time and restored to its former self, guests are greeted by the original ornate iron fence, tree-shaded lawn, and banistered front porch. the antique furnishings, hand-painted murals, and curly-maple staircase leading to five upstairs guest rooms are gentle reminders of the family home that it once was. Each room is decorated with handsome Victorian and Empire pieces. Witch Hazel and mints on the pillows are the added touch.

Directly across the street stands the Lyme Art Association and Academy.

The dining rooms are appointed with white table linens, polished silver, fine stemware, and antiques complemented by royal blue chairs and rug. Twice given 3-Stars by the New York Times, the inn prepares an innovative menu. Duck with Lincolnberry Sauce is found among the fine offerings.

Scallops Steamed with Spinach and Red Peppers

4 oz Bay scallops	3 tbs butter (reserving one to
1 tbs pimientos, finely chopped	finish sauce)
4 oz fresh spinach	2 tsp chopped shallots
2 tbs white wine	1 tsp chopped parsley
2 rings red pepper	salt & pepper to taste

Sweat shallots in 2 tbs butter just till tender. Add rest of ingredients, cover, and steam until scallops are cooked, stirring occasionally. (Scallops do not take long to cook.) Remove from heat, stir in remaining butter and save.

Lyme Street
Old Lyme, CT 06371
Tel (203) 434-2600
1-800-434-5352

NORTHEAST

THE OLD RED INN & COTTAGES

The Whites' Old Red Inn dates back two hundred years in the village of North Conway, New Hampshire. Within easy walking distance of restaurants, interesting shops, and the summer theatre, a short drive puts the visitor at Echo Lake State Park and Saco River for tennis, golf, swimming and fishing. Of course, skiing and ice skating are the popular wintertime sports.

Newly renovated guests rooms are furnished in English country style. In addition to the main inn, cottages frame the driveway on the property. Some have screened-in porches, kitchenettes and two bedrooms. All overlook award-winning flower and herb gardens. Delightful herb lunches are served on the lawns during summer months. Specialties include Tomato Herb Bread, British Cream of Carrot Soup, and Herb Tart.

British Cream of Carrot Soup

4 slices bacon, chopped
2 lbs carrots, pared and chopped
1 cup chopped celery
2 qts chicken broth
1/2 cup whipped cream
thin carrot strips
2 tsp parsley
1 bay leaf

1/4 cup butter or margarine
1/2 cup flour
1-1/2 cups milk
Salt & pepper to taste
1 turnip
1 tsp thyme
1 med onion, thinly sliced

Fry bacon in soup pot until limp. Add butter. Add chopped carrots, onion, celery, and turnip. Saute until onion is transparent, about 5 minutes. Stir in flour, cooking and stirring 2 minutes. Stir in chicken broth, heat to boiling, stirring constantly. Reduce heat, adding herbs. Simmer covered over medium heat 15 minutes. Place carrot mixture, three cups at a time, in blender and puree. Pour back into soup pot. Stir in milk, heat to boiling, constantly stirring, and reduce heat. Cook uncovered over medium heat 5 minutes, stirring frequently. Season with salt and pepper. Pour into serving bowls. Swirl thick whipped cream on top and garnish with carrot strips.

Box 467
North Conway, NH 03860
Tel (603) 356-2642

Old Riverton Inn

Old Riverton Inn was built by Jesse Ives in 1796 as a stagecoach stop on the Hartford-Albany turnpike. Enlarged and completely renovated in 1940, the inn overlooks the west branch of Farmington River with ten guest rooms decorated in a variety of furnishings that include canopied beds, four-posters, ruffled tie-backs, colorful wallpaper, wood floors and warming fireplaces. The country store has the original wooden beams and wide floor boards that bring back long ago memories.

Meals are served in two dining rooms. The Colonial Room and the Grindstone Terrace with floors made of grindstones which, according to old records, were quarried in Nova Scotia. The menu includes many specialities. A complimentary breakfast is served.

Veal Maison

Take thinly sliced veal, floured and sauteed in clarified butter. Season with salt and white pepper. Add freshly sliced mushrooms. Next, add brandy and flambe. Finely, add heavy cream. Reduce until thick and garnish with freshly chopped parsley. DO NOT LET CREAM OVERCOOK or it will separate.

Box 6
Riverton, CT 06065
Tel (203) 379-8678

NORTHEAST

PHILBROOK FARM INN

Philbrook Farm Inn's visitors are sure to find simplicity and warm hospitality that started in 1861 when Harvey and Susannah welcomed their very first guests. It was built in 1834 as a farm house and enlarged over the years to its present size.

The inn has been operated by the same family for five generations and is listed on the National Register of Historic Places. Spectacular scenery of the White Mountains and Androscroggin Valley abounds with wildflowers, trees, birds and interesting rock formations, making it the perfect location for artists and writers.

Guest rooms in a variety of sizes and styles show off family treasures, and summertime cottages are tucked about to continue the privacy.

Meals are served family style "from scratch" in the dining room with aromas of good New England Pot Roast, Lamb, Vegetables from the inn's garden, Dark Bread and tempting desserts.

Frozen Lemon Pie

1 graham cracker crust
juice and rind of 1 lemon
3 egg whites, stiff
1 cup cream

3 egg yolks well beaten
1/2 cup sugar
1 tsp sugar

To egg yolks add 1/2 cup sugar along with juice and rind of lemon. Beat 3 egg whites stiff with 1 tsp sugar and fold into egg yolk mixture. Beat 1 cup cream stiff and fold into all ingredients. Place in graham cracker crust and freeze. Makes one delicious 9-inch pie.

North Road
Shelburne, NH 03581
Tel (603) 466-3831

NORTHEAST

Publick House

Publick House was the setting for Colonel Ebenezar Crafts when he recruited Sturbidge's Revolutionary militia, drilled them at his own expense, and joined with General Lafayette to help Washington's army at Cambridge. Lafayette later honored the Colonel with a visit.

Founded by the Colonel in 1771, this National Landmark continues to greet visitors with a warm welcome. Guest · rooms are colorful and cozy, overlooking hills and valleys. Four lodgings have been added under apple trees, old elms, and maples. Sleigh rides, chestnut roasts, and Boar's Head Revels at Christmastime make this a very memorable place to visit in all seasons. Old Sturbridge Village, the largest outdoor living museum in the Northeast, is close by.

Fine Yankee cooking is served in the Publick House dining room or Crabapple's Restaurant. Scotch Egg with Onion Relish, English Lamb Chops, Fresh Vegetables, Garden Salad, and Strawberry Layer Cake have been enjoyed by guests for years. The Lobster Pie and Breakfast Muffins date back to 1771.

Yankee Cornsticks

2-3/4 cups all-purpose flour
2 tbs baking powder
3/4 cup granulated sugar
1 cup cream style corn
1-1/2 cups milk

1 cup corn meal
2 tsp salt
2 eggs
1/4 cup vegetable oil

Stir together flour, sugar, baking powder, and salt; stir in yellow cornmeal. Blend together well beaten eggs, cream style corn, milk, and vegetable oil; add to dry ingredients. Stir just until moistened. Preheat corn sticks pans in oven, then grease generously. Fill prepared corn stick pans 2/3 full with batter and bake at 425 degrees until done, about 20 minutes. Makes about 24 cornsticks.

Box 187
Sturbridge, MA 01566
Tel (508) 347-3313

NORTHEAST

THE QUEEN VICTORIA

The Queen Victoria, named in honor of the British Monarch who loved the sea, easily captures the flavor of the Golden Age with its porches, bays and hand-crafted touches.

The public rooms are decorated with authentic Victorian furnishings of walnut, wicker, oak, and pine. The parlor has the Wells collection of arts and crafts "mission" furniture, and on display for the guests are volumes about art, architecture, decorative arts, history, and fiction collected by the innkeeper when she was executive director of the Victorian Society in America.

Hospitality, comfort and service define this inn that has been a "Cover Girl" in several books and magazines, Sherwin Williams chose the Queen Victoria to illustrate its line of Victorian paints and McCall's recommended it for "getting away from it all". It is rated AAA and 3-Star by Travel Mobil Guide.

The guest rooms are beautifully appointed with antique high headboards, colorful quilts, and fresh flowers.

Activities include exploring Cape May, strolling along the beach, bird watching, or beachcombing for "Cape May Diamonds."

A Continental breakfast is graciously served in the dining room. Imported Coffees and Teas, Fresh Fruit, Eggs, and Homebaked Breads are to be savored.

Blueberry Muffins

1-1/3 cups milk
3-1/2 cups flour
2 cups blueberries
1/2 cup melted butter
2/3 cup sugar

2 tsp lemon rind
4 tsp baking powder
4 eggs

Beat eggs. Add melted, cooled butter and milk and mix well. Combine dry ingredients, then add beaten liquid ingredients in a few swift strokes. Add blueberries and lemon peel before the dry ingredients are completely moist. Fill paper-lined muffin tins 2/3 full. Sprinkle tips of muffins with cinnamon sugar and bake at 400° for 20-25 minutes.

102 Ocean Street
Cape May, NJ 08204
Tel (609) 884-8702

NORTHEAST

RABBIT HILL INN

Rabbit Hill Inn has contributed to the hospitality of New England since 1795 and is located in one of Vermont's most photographed villages. Within view of New Hampshire's White Mountains, the inn is a delightful find for the weary traveler. The Briar Patch opened as a tavern and general store by Samuel Colby, and the adjacent main inn, which dates to 1825, was the home of Jonathan Cummings.

During the early days this bustling center catered to the traveling needs of teamsters on their way to and from Montreal and the coast of New England. It is said that as many as a hundred teams a day rolled by.

Guest rooms and dining rooms provide a true New England decor of painted woodwork, old fashioned wallpaper, fireplaces, and good food. Just a hop away from the Connecticut River, visitors may enjoy fishing, sailing, golfing, antiquing, and mountain climbing.

Meals are served in two cheerful Colonial dining rooms.

Carrot Mousse

3/4 lb carrots	2 tbs butter
1/3 cup chicken stock	1 tbs maple syrup
1 tsp chopped tarragon	salt & pepper
2 eggs	1/2 cup heavy cream

Peel and cut carrots into 1'' pieces. Saute briefly in butter and add chicken stock, syrup, and pinch of salt and pepper. Cover and simmer slowly 40 minutes until very soft. Puree in food processor or through food mill without any of cooking juices (the liquid will have nearly evaporated). Add cream, eggs, and tarragon and beat lightly. Fill individual souffle dishes with mixture, place in baking dish of water, and bake at 300° 30-40 minutes, or until set and no longer sticky to the touch. Unmold, and serve as vegetable.

Pucker Street
Lower Waterford, VT 05848
Tel (802) 748-5168

NORTHEAST

THE RED LION INN

The Red Lion Inn appeared in one of Norman Rockwell's well-known Christmas scenes. Built originally in 1773 by Silas Pepoon as a tavern and stagecoach stop, today's Red Lion was reconstructed in 1897 after a fire destroyed the older inn. Five U.S. presidents, including Cleveland, McKinley, Theodore Roosevelt, Coolidge, and Franklin Roosevelt, along with Nathaniel Hawthorne, William Cullen Bryant, and Henry Wadsworth Longfellow have enjoyed The Red Lion's hospitality down through the years.

Gradually enlarged and filled with 18th century furnishings, Staffordshire china, and pewter, guests feel a very warm welcome as they enter the main parlor. Rooms are spacious with outside views of Stockbridge and the rolling Berkshires. Just down the street is the Old Corner House, historical museum and home of Norman Rockwell's paintings.

Meals are served in the elegant dining room or in the more intimate Widow Bingham Tavern. Traditional New England fare and Continental specialties are served.

Indian Pudding

4 cups milk
4 tbs butter
1/2 cup cornmeal
1/2 cup molasses
1/4 cup sugar
1 cup chopped apples

1/2 cup raisins
4 1/2 tsp cinnamon
1-1/2 tsp ginger
1/2 tsp salt
1 egg

SINCE 1773

Combine 2-1/2 cups milk with butter and scald. Combine 1/2 cup milk and cornmeal, add to scalded milk and butter. Cook 20 minutes, stirring slowly so mixture does not burn. Add molasses, sugar, apples, and raisins. Stir in cinnamon, ginger, salt, and egg. Cook 5 more minutes. Pour into well-greased shallow pan. Pour remaining cup of milk over this. Bake at 325° for 1 1/2 hours or until pudding is set. Serve warm with ice cream or whipped cream. Serves 8-10.

Stockbridge, MA 01262
Tel (413) 298-5545

NORTHEAST

The Redcoat's Return

The Redcoat's Return sits at an elevation of 2200 feet in the scenic Catskills overlooking fields, forests, and Schoharie Creek.

The four-story hotel, built in 1910 by Willie Dale and his new wife, Sadie, became the much-loved retreat for hundreds during the flourishing age of the summer boardinghouse. Mock weddings for children, Maypole dances, and Willie's hayrides became annual events along with feasts that included "second helpings galore and all the fresh milk you can drink." Today, the tradition of fine food and hospitality of that bygone era still lingers.

The rooms are colorful and cozy, furnished with period antiques and paintings. Leading from the doorstep are hiking trails into the mountains that hold magnificent views of the Hudson Valley.

A Continental breakfast is offered. Dinner is served in a library dining room every evening except Thursday.

Dilled Cheese Cubes

1 loaf unsliced French bread	1/2 cup butter
2 tsp dried dill weed	1 tsp Worcestershire sauce
1 tbs grated onion	2 eggs, lightly beaten
4 cups (1 lb) grated cheddar cheese	

Remove crust from bread and cut into 1'' cubes. Set aside. In medium saucepan stir butter and cheese over low heat until melted. Stir in dillweed and onion. Beat in eggs and remove from heat. Dip each cube of bread with fork into hot cheese mixture. Turn to coat all sides, shaking off excess. Arrange on an ungreased baking sheet and refrigerate 1-2 days. Preheat oven to 350°. Bake refrigerated cubes just 10 minutes. Serve hot. (Quick-frozen cubes should be baked 15 minutes.)

Platte Cove
Elka Park, NY 12427
Tel (518) 589-6379

NORTHEAST

The Inn At Sawmill Farm blends perfectly with the natural beauty of the Vermont landscape. A rebuilt barn in the village of West Dover, the hand-hewn posts, beams, and weathered boards are all reminders of the inn's former life. Guest rooms are attractive and individually decorated, some having sitting areas and fireplaces. All the rooms are immaculate with fine linens.

Open the year 'round, winter guests enjoy ice skating, downhill and cross-country skiing, and snow shoe hikes into quiet woods. The heat of the summer brings tennis and swimming.

The dining room's menu includes both American and Continental cuisine.

1980 Travel and Leisure describes Sawmill Farm as *"one of the twelve most perfect hideaways in the world."*

Medallions of Pork

pork loin	**unbleached flour**
salt	**brandy**
reserved fat	**heavy cream**
coarsley ground or crushed walnuts	

Ask butcher to debone pork loin, saving tenderloin for future use and bones for stock. Cut loin section into 3/4" - 1" slices. In bottom of 1-qt widemouth canning jar, sprinkle 1/2 tsp salt. Layer pork slices into jar, being sure to leave air spaces. Place jar(s) on rack in a canner with cold water up to bottom of lids. Bring to boil and, keeping water at same level throughout cooking period, cook at slow boil for 3-1/2 hours. Remove from canner and let stand until cool. Refrigerate until ready for use. To remove meat from jar, place jar in warm water to melt gelatinous stock resulting from canning. Carefully take slices out, reserving any fat that has risen to top. For each serving, brown 2 medallions in 1 tsp fat on both sides. Remove and keep warm. Stir 1/2 tsp flour into skillet, stir, and cook several minutes and blend in 1 tbs brandy. Bring to boil, stirring constantly, and add 1/4 cup cream. Bring again to boil, stirring, and blend in 1/4 cup walnuts. Heat and pour over medallions. Serve immediately.

Box 367 Mt. Snow Valley
West Dover, VT 05356
Tel (802) 464-8131

NORTHEAST

Sea Chambers Motor Lodge is situated at the very edge of the sea and provides a peaceful retreat after visiting summer playhouses, excellent restaurants, antique shops and art galleries. The magnificent Maine coast shoreline stretches for miles and the picturesque "Marginal Way" is within easy walking distance. Guest rooms are comfortable with large windows and balconies that capture views of the ever changing wonders of the sea.

Adjacent to the lodge is the Sea Bell, built around 1800. It was once a tea room and lodging spot for old sea captains and has remained in the same family for one hundred and forty five years. Today's guests recall the atmosphere of the old cape as they enjoy a Continental breakfast, served in the manner befitting the charm and hospitality of old New England. Offerings include Homebaked Muffins, Coffee Cakes and Sweetbreads.

Sea Chambers Lemon Tea Bread

3/4 cup margarine	2 tsp baking powder
2 cups sugar	1 cup milk
4 eggs	1/2 tsp salt
3 cups sifted flour	grated rind of 2 lemons

Cream margarine and sugar, adding grated lemon rinds and beaten eggs. Add flour sifted with baking powder and salt alternately with milk. Bake in greased loaf pans for 1 hour at 325-350°. Glaze while still in loaf pans with mixture of the juice of 2 lemons and 1/2 cup sugar.

37 Shore Road
Ogunquit, ME 03907
Tel (207) 646-9311

NORTHEAST

The 1740 House, built by the Nesslers, is a charming inn with at least one very interesting distinction: It's exactly as one would hope a country inn to be. Tastefully furnished and decorated, hospitality, seclusion, and privacy are hallmarks of this Mobil Guide 3-Star inn. Singled out by **Esquire** as one of the five outstanding East Coast inns, **Glamour** picked it as one of the ten best inns in the country.

Outside terraces overlooking the canal are there for quiet moments, and close to the Delaware River and historic Bucks County, both beauty and Revolutionary War history are around every turn.

A complimentary buffet is served each morning.

"Tia Maria Cake"

3/4 cup sugar	1 cup ground walnuts
1/2 cup ground Ritz crackers	2 cups heavy cream
4 tbs Tia Maria	2 squares shaved semisweet chocolate
6 eggs, separated, plus one whole egg	

Preheat oven to 350°. Lightly grease two 9'' layer cake pans and line with wax paper. In medium-size bowl, beat the whole egg and egg yolks with sugar until lemon-colored and foamy; add ground walnuts and cracker crumbs. In large bowl, beat egg whites until they peak. Gradually fold egg yolk mixture into egg white mixture. Pour equal amounts of mixture into both pans. Bake 20 minutes. Cool on racks. Whip the cream and Tia Maria together for icing. Sprinkle top and sides with chocolate shavings.

River Road
Lumberville, PA 18933
Tel (215) 297-5661

NORTHEAST

The town of Kennett Square was occupied in 1771 by British Gen. Howe who brought fellow troops to engage in the battle of Brandywine against Gen. Washington. The Scarlett is located at the foot of Hessian Hill where the soldiers were quartered and dates back to 1910. Beautifully constructed of local granite, the inn provides a comfortable atmosphere in a historic setting.

Guests enter through a double leaded-glass door flanked by exquisite woodwork. It is said that the original lady of the house chose each piece of chestnut and cherry wood so there would be no blemishes. There are two charming parlors with fireplaces and four guest rooms.

The Chantrell room has a soft country feel with its four poster bed, princess dresser and stenciled walls. It has a private sitting area. The Bayard Taylor Room, named for Kennett Square's most famous author, is light and airy decorated with Queen Anne furniture. All the rooms are elegant with scented soaps, fluffy robes and ceiling fans.

Activities abound — Longwood Gardens, Brandywine River Museum, Chads Ford Winery, Hiking and Antiquing.

A complimentary breakfast is served.

Fresh Muselix

1 cup old fashioned Quaker Oats - uncooked	1/2 cup chopped walnuts
1 cup heavy cream or lt. cream, reg. milk, 1% milk	1 banana cubed
	1/2 cup cubed cantaloupe
2 tbs confectioner's sugar	1/2 cup cubed honeydew
1/2 cup diced dried apricots	1/2 cup blueberries
1/2 cup diced dried figs	1/2 cup cubed apple
1/2 cup Dromedary chopped dates w/sugar	1/2 cup cubed pear
	1/2 cup raisins

Mix oatmeal, cream (milk), sugar. Cover and leave in refrigerator overnight. In the morning it will be a glob. Add milk (enough to make pourable but not too loose). Add fruits and nuts, mix, garnish (I use either slice of kiwi or star fruit) and serve. I always serve in antique compotes. Any blends of fruits and nuts can be used as long as there are a lot of contrasts in textures.

503 W. State Street
Kenneth Square, PA 19348
Tel (610) 444-9592

NORTHEAST

SHARTLESVILLE HOTEL

Shartlesville Hotel was founded in 1915 and is located on Old Route 22. This very American picturesque two-story hotel with its pitched tin roof and sweeping front porch lined with benches provides a gentle nostalgia and longing for a step back in time.

Although additions have been made, the original log structure built 200 years ago is still part of the building. Over the years the hotel has served as a stagecoach stop, post office and general store. Situated in the back, barns still stand that once stored feed and sheltered horses for stagecoaches. The fifteen guest rooms are all occupied.

This truly unique hotel began serving a never-to-be-forgotten meal of 7 sweets and 7 sours Pennsylvania Dutch family style exclusively in 1915. An "all you can eat" menu in three dining rooms includes Chicken, Ham, Sausage, Chicken Croquettes, Sweet Potatoes, Corn and more than 30 other good dishes.

Pearl Tapioca Pudding

1 cup tapioca	2 cups warm water
2 qts milk	6 eggs
1 cup sugar	1 tsp vanilla
pinch salt	

Soak tapioca overnight in warm water and drain. Heat milk in double boiler. Mix eggs, sugar, and tapioca. Add to hot milk and cook until thick. Add salt and vanilla.

Shartlesville, PA 19554
Tel (215) 488-1918

NORTHEAST

Shelter Harbor Inn

Shelter Harbor Inn consists of two guest houses (one a beautifully converted barn) besides the original farmhouse that dates to the early 1800s. The stately, yet unpretentious clapboard structure sits at the entrance of Shelter Harbor.

Each guest room is comfortably furnished, and some have fireplaces and private sun decks. All the rooms in the main house have access to a third floor deck with views of Block Island Sound. A reception room, library and fireplace, cheerful sunroom, and several dining rooms occupy the first floor of the old farmhouse. Open the year 'round, this restful inn has two paddle tennis courts conveniently located on the grounds and a hot tub on the third floor.

Traditional New England fare using the freshest seafood from the Sound tempt the guest.

Hazelnut Chicken with Orange Thyme Cream

Hazelnut Crumb Mixture:

> **1/3 cup hazelnut pieces**
>
> **1/4 tsp thyme leaves**
> **1 egg, lightly beaten with 1 tbs water**
> **flour to dredge**

> **1/3 cup fresh bread crumbs**
>
> **salt & pepper**

Orange Thyme Cream:

> **1 tbs Frangelico**
> **1 cup heavy cream**
> **1 orange, sectioned, with juice**
> **2 whole chicken breasts, skinned**
> **and lightly pounded**

> **1/8 tsp thyme leaves**
> **salt and pepper**

Cut each breast into halves. Bread chicken by first dredging in flour, then dip into egg wash and coat with hazelnut crumb mixture. Shake off excess. Chill until ready to use. Melt butter in heavy pan. Over moderate heat cook chicken until golden brown on both sides. Add orange juice, thyme, Frangelico, and heavy cream. Simmer gently, basting often until chicken is just cooked and sauce has thickened slightly. Add orange sections and season to taste with salt and pepper. Remove chicken from pan and pour sauce over. Serve immediately. Wild rice is an excellent complement. Serves 2-4.

Route 1
Westerly, RI 02891
Tel (401) 322-8883

NORTHEAST

The Sherwood Inn

Sherwood Inn has welcomed visitors to Skaneatles since 1807 and with so much to see and do in the area, it's no wonder the Finger Lakes is called Central New York's year 'round vacationland. It was built by Isaac Sherwood as a stage coach tavern and was a favorite stop for the Knickerbocker Tours in the 1820s. During that time the inn was the center for all town meetings and social events. Enlarged over the years, the clapboard structure recalls its colorful past with traditions of fine cuisine and lodging that pleased the coach and rail patrons of long ago.

The main lobby is warmed by a fire, and the comfortable front porch provides scenic views of Clift and Shotwell Parks in summer. Refurbished in 1978, guest rooms are furnished with period antiques. Some of the rooms have exquisite lake views.

The menu presents a combination of both Continental and American dishes, including Prime Rib, Fresh Boston Seafood, Brace of Lamb, Cape Scallops, Homemade Pies and Cheesecake.

Burnt Creme

12 egg yolks
1 tbs vanilla extract

1/2 pt heavy cream
21 oz sweetened condensed milk

Over medium heat scald milk and heavy cream. Temper the yolks with the hot mixture, then add yolks. Remove from heat, add vanilla, and pour into ramekins, being certain to fill to rim. Bake in water bath at 350 degrees for 20-25 minutes or until just browned. Cool. Cover custards with 1 tbs granulated sugar, then carmelize sugar with the broiler or an iron. Brown sugar can be substituted. Serves 12-14.

26 West Genesee Street
Skaneatles, NY 13152
Tel (315) 685-3405

SNOW DEN INN

Snow - Den - Inn is close to Mt. Snow, Carinthia, and Haystack - all famous for their downhill ski trails and offers endless activities for the winter visitor. Ideal during the summer, beautiful Deerfield Valley is the perfect spot for horseback riding, fishing, boating, and swimming. Fine restaurants, antique shops, summer playhouses, and the Marlboro Music Festival are in the area. Originally built as a farmhouse in 1885 by the Davis family, the clapboard structure opened its doors as an inn in 1952 and was totally renovated in 1976. Eight comfortable rooms await the guest, and five of the rooms have fireplaces.

Breakfast is served each morning, and during winter season an evening meal is prepared.

Coconut Pound Cake

1 lb butter	2 cups sugar
6 eggs	2 cups flour
7 oz coconut	1 tsp vanilla

Cream butter and sugar. Add 1 cup flour and mix well. Add eggs, one at a time, blending well. Add remaining cup of flour with coconut, then add vanilla. Bake 60-75 minutes in 9'' tube pan at 350.

Glaze

1 cup sugar	1/2 cup water
1 tsp coconut or almond flavoring	

Simmer glaze 10 minutes and apply to upside-down cake while still hot.

Route 100
Dover, VT 05356
Tel (802) 464-9355

NORTHEAST

Springside Inn

Springside Inn, established in 1851 as a boys' school by Dutch Reformed Minister Samuel Robbins Brown, probably served as a station on the Underground Railroad during the Civil War. The three-story clapboard structure opened as a summer resort in 1919 and started its career as a year 'round inn during the 1940s. It is now operated by the second generation of the Miller family.

The comfortable bedrooms are charming with period pieces and tie-back curtains.

A complimentary breakfast basket is offered each morning, while meals are served in the public Surrey Room. The massive beams, turn-of-the-century hanging lamps, and warming fire create an Old World charm. An extensive menu is prepared from family recipes that include Lobster Newburg, Roast Long Island Duckling, Chicken, and Baked Virginia Ham.

Chocolate Sauce

2 tbs butter
1 cup milk

2/3 cup sugar
1-1/2 squares unsweetened chocolate

Combine all ingredients in a double boiler and cook over medium heat. Dribble over rich ice cream. 4 servings.

Route 38
Auburn, NY 13021
Tel (315) 252-7247

NORTHEAST

The Squire Tarbox Inn

The Squire Tarbox Inn carefully preserves the best of the 18th and 19th centuries. Built in 1825 by Squire Samuel Tarbox, the core of the colonial-style inn dates back to 1763.

Just like the progression of years, The Squire Tarbox has progressively added on to the original building, which is quite common in old New England homes, yet the charm of antiquity has not suffered; it blends beautifully with the comforts of today. Guest rooms are comfortable and cozy.

An added character of the inn is the pure-bred dairy herd for natural cheesemaking. The sand dunes at Reid State Park, and a visit to one of the world's finest antique music box collections at the Musical Wonder House along with expected adventures of coastal Maine are all within a pleasant drive. Deep sea fishing, charters, and sailing at Boothbay add to the mariner's enjoyable visit.

A Continental breakfast is offered each morning, and meals served at a leisurely pace in the dining room are prepared in the evenings. Peach Cantaloupe Soup, Warm Peasant Bread, Marinated Tomato Salad, and Fresh Vegetables are found on the menu.

The Squire's Molasses Breakfast Pie

2 cups flour
1/2 tsp salt
1 cup molasses
1 tsp baking soda

1/2 cup Crisco
1 cup packed brown sugar
1 cup warm water

Combine flour, crisco, and salt as a mixture to make crumbs. Add brown sugar and molasses to the flour mixture and dissolve 1 cup warm water with tsp baking soda working in fast to other ingredients so as not to lose leavening properties before pie reaches oven. Pour into two unbaked pie shells and bake 35-40 minutes in 375 degree oven.

Rt 2, Box 2160
Wiscasset, ME 04578
Tel (207)882-7693

NORTHEAST

The Inn At Starlight Lake

The Inn at Starlight Lake is an old fashioned inn that has welcomed visitors to the Appalachian Mountains since 1902. The main house and adjacent cottages are comfortably furnished and overlook the lake for which it is named. An excellent library of recorded music is provided, and old movies from the McMahans's collection are shown weekly. The resort is open year 'round with activities for every season, including nearby canoe trips on the Delaware River.

Meals are served in the lakeside dining room. The menu features a variety of hearty Continental favorites such as Jagerschnitzel and Saurbraten along with traditional American fare.

Chocolate Walnut Pie

Line two 10'' pie pans with a good pie crust. Melt together 1 lb butter with 4 unsweetened chocolates. Mix together 4 cups sugar, 8 eggs, 8 tsp evaporated milk, and 1 tsp vanilla. Line bottom of pan with walnuts and pour in mixture of butter, chocolates, sugar, eggs, milk, and vanilla over nuts. Bake at 375 degrees for 55-60 minutes.

Starlight, PA 18461
Tel (717) 798-2519

NORTHEAST

The Sterling Inn

The Sterling Inn recaptures the relaxed graciousness and comfort one expects to find in an old-fashioned country inn. Distinguished by its good taste and warm hospitality, the setting of spacious lawns, tall shade trees, flower gardens, and walks beside the Wallenpaupack Creek have been fitting complements to this family resort since 1933.

The lounge has a huge fireplace of native stone, lots of easy chairs, wallpaper, and a small library. Besides the main inn, a variety of comfortable lodgings are on the grounds. Open all year, guests enjoy ice skating on the lake, cross-country skiing, sledding, hiking, tennis and swimming.

Meals are served in the Hearthstone Room. The menu consists of traditional American cooking of homebaked breads and an array of delightful pastries.

Sterling Inn Coffee Cake

1 cup butter	1/2 tsp vanilla
2 cups sugar	2 cups flour
2 eggs	1 tsp baking powder
1 cup sour cream	1/2 tsp salt

Mix butter and sugar. Add eggs, sour cream, and vanilla. Add dry ingredients. Pour half batter in greased and floured 9 x 13 pan. Sprinkle with cinnamon and sugar. Pour rest of batter in pan and sprinkle with cinnamon and sugar again and chopped nuts. Bake at 350 degrees approximately 1 hour.

South Sterling, PA 18460
Tel (717) 676-3311 or 3338

NORTHEAST

The Three Village Inn

Three Village Inn, according to Indian deeds dated 1665, resides in a community that actually began 300 years ago. The old shipping and fishing village rests in the hills of the North Shore and has its own harbor adjacent to Long Island Sound. In character with its charming surroundings, the Republican architectural-style inn was built in 1785 by Jonas Smith. Although thoroughly updated, the early 1800s atmosphere still remains. Open the year 'round, golf, fishing, and walking the sandy beach await the visitor.

Guest rooms are comfortable with colonial furnishings, exposed beams, ruffled tiebacks, colorful wallpaper, and views of the harbor and marina.

Beef, Pork, Fresh Seafood, and Colonial Grain Bread make up a part of the menu in the dining room.

Three Village Inn Apple Crisp

10 cups sliced apples	1 1/2 tsp cinnamon
2 tsp granulated sugar	

For topping:

1-1/2 cups brown sugar	6 tbs butter
6 tbs margarine	1/2 tsp cinnamon
1/4 tsp salt	
1 cup plus 2 tbs all-purpose flour	

Place apple slices, cinnamon, and sugar in bowl and mix thoroughly. Spread in lightly buttered 9x13x2 baking dish. In medium bowl combine brown sugar, flour, butter, margarine, cinnamon, and salt. Blend with pastry cutter. Do not allow mixture to get too moist. Spread crumbs evenly over apple mixture and pat down. Bake at 350° for 45 minutes or until apples are thoroughly cooked. If topping brown too fast, place sheet of brown paper on top. Serve slightly warm with whipped cream. Makes about 10 servings.

150 Main Street
Stoney Brook, Long Island, NY 11790
Tel (516) 751-0555

NORTHEAST

THE VILLAGE INN

The Village Inn is just four miles from Weston and Londonderry with marked ski trails leading into the National Forest right from the front door. An ideal spot for all season sports, this 1880s clapboard farmhouse is unmistakably "Vermont Continuous Architecture." Today, three generations of the Snyder family operate the inn, maintaining the original warmth and simplicity it was meant to have. The rustic Rafter Room lounge is warmed by low beamed ceilings, plank floors, and a blazing fire. Each guest room is spacious and comfortable.

Hearty meals are served in the old-fashioned dining room with candlelight and an open fire, and the menu includes traditional New England cooking at its best.

Cranberry Baked Chicken

1 can whole berry cranberries
1 cup creamy French dressing
1/3 cup dry leek soup mix

boneless breasts of chicken
1 tbs cornstarch (optional)

Prepare sauce and let set 3 hours. Lay chicken breasts in baking dish. Spread sauce over chicken and bake 20-30 minutes at 400°. Goes great with linguinni. Serves 12.

Landgrove, VT 05148
Tel (802) 824-6673

NORTHEAST

The INN *on Lake Waramaug*

The Inn on Lake Waramaug overlooks the lake amid spacious lawns and towering sugar maples in a country setting that lends itself well to the old colonial structure. It was built around 1795 as a home and enlarged in 1880 by Uncle Ben Norris "to keep up with the times." Luckily, he did not replace the hand-blown windows. This area was a flourishing summer resort in the 1890s and the inn accommodated its visitors.

In 1951 Dick and Bobbie Combs (grandson of an early owner) purchased the inn and restored it to the original style. Five guest rooms in the main building are furnished with pine and cherry antiques, heirloom collections of pewter, copper, brass, old maps, vintage tea services, and cupboards of lace fans. Guest houses on the property are tastefully appointed, and some have fireplaces and queen-sized beds. Just as in the beginning, warm hospitality is a main ingredient here.

Meals are served in the dining room whose fireplace is made of old bricks used as ship's ballast in the early 1700s. Lake views vie with Filet Mignon, Stuffed Shrimp, Fresh Fish, Veal, and Lobster for your attention. A specialty is Pepper Pot Soup, supposedly first served to Gen. George Washington's troops at Valley Forge.

Philadelphia Pepper Pot Soup

1/2 lb veal
1/2 med onion, chopped
1/2 med green pepper, chopped
1/2 tsp garlic, finely minced
3 qts chicken broth
4 oz prepared biscuit -5959

2 ribs celery
2 oz pimientos
4 oz butter
1/2 pt light cream
3-1/2 oz flour

Spices:

1 tbs thyme
4 bay leaves, crushed
1 tsp poultry seasoning
pinch ground clove
1 tsp Worcestershire sauce
1/2 tsp white pepper

1 tbs marjoram leaf
1/2 tbs oregano
pinch nutmeg
1 tbs dry mustard
1/2 tsp salt

Cook veal in chicken broth until tender. Remove veal, then cut into 1" x 1" x 1/4" pieces. Remove broth. Choose a 4-qt or larger heavy guage soup pot and combine butter, chopped onion, celery, green peppers, and garlic plus all spices. Saute until vegetables are tender. Add flour. Cook 3 minutes, not allowing flour to brown. Add reserved broth in 3 parts into sauteed mixture. Bring to light boil. If mixture seems too heavy, add a little water or more chicken broth, if available. Add dumplings made from biscuit mix. Continue to boil until dumplings rise to top. Reduce fire to a simmer and add veal, cream, and pimientos. Simmer 5 minutes more, and adjust seasoning as required.

New Preston, CT 06777
Tel (203) 868-0563 or (212) 724-8775

NORTHEAST

The Waterford Inne

The Waterford Inne's drive was once part of a busy stagecoach road, but now peace and quiet pervades the old colonial home with its pitched tin roof, shutters, and rockers.

The Oxford Hills region is truly an all-season resort where outdoor activities are endless. For the history buff, visitors enjoy discovering the rich heritage of the area while visiting its many museums and historic sites. Guest rooms are furnished with period pieces, fireplaces to ward off the chill, and fine outside views. An antique shop is on the property.

Breakfast and dinner are served each day. Baking from scratch and garden-fresh vegetables are specialties of the inn.

Beef Stroganoff

1 tbs flour
1/2 tsp salt
3 tbs flour
1 tbs tomato paste
1 1/4 cups beef stock
1 cup sliced mushrooms
1 cup sour cream
1/2 cup chopped onions
2 tbs sherry

2 tbs butter

1 lb beef sirloin
2 tbs butter

Combine 1 tbs flour and the salt. Thinly slice the meat (1/4" or less) and cut into pieces 1-2" long. Dredge meat in flour, heat skillet, and add 2 tbs butter. Brown meat quickly on both sides, and add mushrooms and onions, cooking 3-4 minutes or until onion is barely tender. Remove meat and mushrooms. Add 2 tbs butter to pan drippings. When melted, blend in 3 tbs flour. Add tomato paste. Slowly pour in cold meat stock, stirring until thickened. Return meat and mushrooms to skillet. Stir in sour cream and sherry, heating briefly. Serve over noodles.

Box 49
East Waterford, ME 04233
Tel (207) 583-4037

NORTHEAST

The Weathervane Inn recalls its early years with a beehive oven and original fireplace, things seldom seen in todays homes, but a necessity in olden times. Typical of many early homes of the area additions have been made through the years, and in 1835 a Greek Revival high-ceilinged section was completed. Other interesting details include wide floor boards and mouldings, all visible records of the long ago craftsmen.

Guest rooms are comfortable and pleasantly decorated. Adjacent to the Weathervane stands the Egremont Country Club with golf and tennis. Meals are served in the many windowed dining room with full country breakfast and candlelight dinners. The menu includes hearty New England fare.

Celery Seed Dressing a la Weathervane

1/2 cup sugar
l tbsp celery seed
1 tsp salt
1 tsp dry mustard

1/3 cup vinegar
1 cup salad oil
1 small onion, quartered

Put all ingredients, except oil in blender a few seconds at medium speed. Gradually add oil and blend until it mixes in completely. Store in glass jar in refrigerator. Keeps well.

Route 23
South Egremont, MA 01258
Tel (413) 528-9580

NORTHEAST

The
Wedgwood
Inn

The Wedgwood Inn, built in 1870 as the home of M. A. Slaughter, stands on the original foundation of the building that General Lord Stirling stayed in during the Revolutionary War. The Victorian Structure with its gabled hip roof, fancy wood brackets, and an inviting wrap-around porch has been open to visitors since 1950, and is now eligible for the National Registry. The hardwood floors, lofty windows, and antique furnishings are reminders of earlier days. The Wedgwood was voted 1989, "Inn of the Year" by inn guidebook readers. It is now part of a collection of historic 19th century homes that include the Aaron Burr House and the Umpleby House.

Guest rooms are individually decorated with canopied beds, oriental rugs, and colorful quilts. Original art, fresh flowers, and Wedgwood pottery complete the setting. Mints are left on the pillow.

A Continental breakfast is served each morning on the cheerful sun porch or in the gazebo with Fresh Kiwi and Pineapple Fruit Cup, Fresh Strawberries and Yogurt, Blueberry Preserves and Butter, Cheese Grits, Almond-flavored Croissants, Orange Juice, Coffee and Tea.

Irish Soda Bread

Sift together:

3 cups flour	**2 tsp baking powder**
1/2 tsp baking soda	**1 tsp salt**
1/4 cup sugar	

Stir with fork:

1 cup raisins	**1 tbs caraway seeds**

Pour in 1-1/2 cups buttermilk and knead. Place in greased and floured round pan. Bake 1 hour at 350°.

111 W. Bridge Street
New Hope, PA 18938
Tel (215) 862-2570

NORTHEAST

- 96 -

WEST MOUNTAIN INN

West Mountain Inn occupies a hill outside Arlington and provides good food, lodging, and old-fashioned hospitality. Professionals from the arts and crafts as well as other visitors find the large clapboard inn an ideal place to relax. With 150 acres of wooded trails, ponds, and pastures, activities such as canoeing, photography, swimming, and fishing the trout-filled Battenkill abound.

Twelve guest rooms named for famous persons are furnished in a variety of charming styles. Some have porches and patios. The Grandma Moses room has a fireplace, and the Norman Rockwell has a tree-top view of mountains and meadows.

Meals are served by the warmth of a country hearth. A full breakfast is available each morning.

Aunt Min's Swedish Rye

1 tbs oil or butter
1/3 cup brown sugar
1/4 cup dark molasses
8 cups white flour
1 pkg yeast with 1/4 cup warm water

1 tbs salt
4 cups warm water
2-1/2 cups rye flour
1 tbs fennel or anise seeds

Combine yeast and water. Add 4 cups water. Add all ingredients except flours and mix. Add the rye flour, then add 2 cups white flour and beat. Add remaining flour gradually and knead 10 minutes. Let rise at 85° for 1-1/2 to 2 hours. Punch down and form into three loaves. Place in greased bread pans. Let rise 1 hour and bake at 350° 1 hour.

Arlington, VT 05250
Tel (802) 375-6516

NORTHEAST

West River Lodge

West River Lodge lies just under the hill in a valley of trout pools and covered bridges. Near the West River and shaded by tall trees, the white clapboard farmhouse is furnished with antiques enhancing its country, yesteryear charm. The inn's stables house the area's oldest riding school established in the 1930's, and some of the finest backroad bridle trails in the state begin at the front door.

Hiking, cycling, canoeing, and nearby historic sites along with summer theatre are activities the guest can enjoy. Sleigh rides on the farm and cross-country skiing are winter activities, while the warming spring brings maple sugaring and bird and wildflower trips with trained naturalists. Autumn's lively colors invite discoveries around every bend. The summer '73 edition of "Vermont Life" described the people, the seasons, the horses, and the moments as printing indelible marks in the memories of West River Lodge's visitors.

Meals are prepared with local Vermont produce from New England and British recipes.

Welsh Cakes

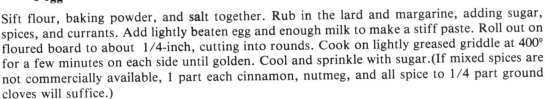

8 oz flour	1/2 tsp baking powder
2 oz margarine	2 oz lard
3 oz sugar	2 oz currants
1/2 tsp mixed spices	pinch salt
1 egg	little milk (1 tbs or so)

Sift flour, baking powder, and salt together. Rub in the lard and margarine, adding sugar, spices, and currants. Add lightly beaten egg and enough milk to make a stiff paste. Roll out on floured board to about 1/4-inch, cutting into rounds. Cook on lightly greased griddle at 400° for a few minutes on each side until golden. Cool and sprinkle with sugar.(If mixed spices are not commercially available, 1 part each cinnamon, nutmeg, and all spice to 1/4 part ground cloves will suffice.)

Rd 1, Box 693
Newfane, VT 05345
Tel (802) 365-7745

NORTHEAST

Westmoor Inn

Westmoor Inn, overlooking the moors of historic Nantucket, is a friendly and intimate inn that easily captures the old flavor and charm of the island. The island, which lies thirty miles at sea, was the whaling capitol of the new world during the early 1800s and its cobblestoned streets are lined with grand old homes that once belonged to sea captains and merchants from those early days.

The inn is located less than a mile from town and the secluded Cliff Beach is just a five-minute walk away. Guests may also enjoy bicycling, tennis, riding, reading, and strolls on the peaceful moors and beaches. As one guest said, "You can almost hear the stars."

The large living room with a fireplace makes an ideal place for get-togethers with other guests. Rooms are large and airy, furnished with period pieces in keeping with earlier times. Afternoon tea is served.

Breakfast is served each morning on the glassed-in terrace and a box lunch is provided for the beach or bike trips.

Advance reservations for ferrying autos to the island are recommended well ahead of your arrival.

Cucumber Soup

1 medium onion, chopped
3 large cucumbers peeled,
1-1/2 qts chicken stock

1/2 cup butter
seeded, and chopped

In food processor chop cucumbers and onions. Saute in butter, adding hot chicken stock, salt and pepper. Simmer and garnish with chopped chives.

Cliff Road
Nantucket, MA 02554
Tel (508) 228-0877

NORTHEAST

The Inn at Weston

The Inn at Weston has welcomed visitors to the state of Vermont and surrounding area since 1974. Painted an unimposing green and shaded by tall trees, this rambling clapboard structure still retains much the same look as it had when it was built as a farm house in 1848.

The rooms flow from one to the next and are furnished with colorful wallpaper, exposed beams, pine plank floors, and wood stoves. It's an easy walk to country stores, churches, concerts, summer theatre, museums, and the village green.

Excellent and creative meals are served on the porch or in the rustic dining room. Winner of the 1983 Silver Spoon Fine Dining Award, the menu includes Loin of Pork with Chutney, Stir Fried Ginger Beef, Chilled Poached Salmon with Cucumber Sauce, and Roast Cornish Hen.

Chicken Nonie

3 lbs chicken, quartered	1 cup crushed pineapple
1/4 cup tamari or soy sauce	1/2 cup apple or other chutney

Flour lightly chicken pieces. Saute until golden in butter with a little oil. Drain on paper towels. Put chicken into casserole large enough to accommodate all chicken in one layer. Top with crushed pineapple, tamari sauce, and chutney. Bake at 325° 30-40 minutes, covering if drying out. Four boneless breasts cut into strips, skinned, and pounded may be used in place of quartered chicken.

Route 100
Weston, VT 05161
Tel (802) 824-5804

NORTHEAST

The Winter's Inn

Winter's Inn enjoys a hilltop setting in the western Maine mountains. The mansion was built by the Stanley twins, (famous for inventing the Stanley Steamer automobile), and wealthy A.G.Winters for Winter's bride from New York. Fine architectural features include a palladium glass window and side lights on the front door, pillars, verandas, fireplaces, and a handsome staircase leading from an elegant parlor furnished with antiques to upstairs chambers. The inn was restored by architect Michael Thom and listed on the National Register of Historic Places in 1976.

An extensive menu of fine French cuisine is served in the romantic fire light of the dining room.

Veal Normandy

butter
1 tbs cinnamon sugar
1/2 cup cream

1 apple, peeled and sliced
1/2 cup apple brandy
10 ozs Veal scallops, pounded and lightly
floured, salted, peppered, and garlicked

Saute veal until it loses pinkness and remove to warm platter. Add brandy to hot pan, scraping any residue into brandy, adding sliced apple and cinnamon, stirring. Add cream and allow to bubble to reduce (apples should be soft, not mushy). Pour over veal, serving at once topped with parsley and accompanied by favorite rice and vegetable. Serves 2.

Box 44
Kingfield, ME 04947
Tel (207) 265-5421

NORTHEAST

The Yankee Pedlar Inn occupies five separate buildings. Built in 1875 as a private home, this charming structure has gradually expanded through the years to house the Pedlar with 28 overnight guest rooms and suites, cooperate apartments, short-term office spaces, eight banquet facilities, an up-scale, creative American restaurant with exposed kitchen and a casual pub with a light fare menu and live entertainment.

The public spaces as well as all of the private rooms are furnished with antiques from several periods. Within the overnight rooms, our guests enjoy the vision and comfort of canopy beds, stained glass windows, cable television, air conditioning and private baths.

For more information, rates, and menu offerings, please access our Web Site at www.yankeepedlarinn.com.

Sweet Potato & Pumpkin Bisque

Yield 1 gallon

garlic, minced 1 tsp
chicken stock 1 qt.
celery, med. dice 3 oz.
onion, fine dice 3 oz
leeks fine dice 3 oz
sweet potato med. dice 2 lb
pumpkin med dice 1 lb
cinnamon stick 1/2

nutmeg 1/4 tsp
maple syrup 2 oz.
salt 1 tsp
evaporated skim milk 12 oz
Garnish
whipped cream 1/2 cup
currants, dried 2 tbs
almonds toasted 2 tbs

Sweat the garlic in 2 tbs of stock. Add the celery, onion and leeks and sauté them until the onions are translucent. Add the potatoes and pumpkin and remaining chicken stock. Bring the liquid to a boil, reduce the heat and simmer the soup until the potatoes are tender. Puree the soup in a processor or blender until smooth, then return to the soup pot. Add the remaining ingredients. Return the soup to a boil. Thin the soup with stock or water if necessary. Remove and discard the cinnamon stick. Serve the soup in heated bowls. Garnish with whipped cream, currants and almonds, or a dollop of sour cream.

1866 Northampton Street
Holyoke, MA 01040
Tel (413) 532-9494

NORTHEAST

The Bailey House

The Bailey House was built in 1895 and stands on land that was a wedding gift to Effingham W. Bailey and his new bride. Designed by architect George W. Barber of Knoxville, Tennessee, Bailey House is an outstanding example of the Queen Anne style. The wraparound porches, turrets, gables, bays, and fish scale decorations testify to the fine craftsmanship that is believed to have been done by boatwrights, since Mr. Bailey was an agent for a steamship company.

The reception hall is very impressive with its mantel inscribed "Hearth Hall, Welcome All", in addition to several large stained glass windows. It took three years to build this fine old home at the then outrageous cost of $10,000.

Located in the historic district within walking distance to restaurants, shops, and the City Marina, this National Registered home is filled with antiques. Six fireplaces, carved furniture, brass beds, pump organs, footed bath tubs, and marble-topped dressers allow guests the feel of elegance in those gentler Victorian days past.

A Continental breakfast is served each morning in the main dining room.

Datenut Bread

1 cup chopped dates, over which sprinkle: 2 tsp soda (rounded slightly) adding: 2 cups boiling water. When cool, cream 2 cups sugar and 6 tbs butter, to which add: 2 eggs well beaten. Add date mixture and: 2 tsp vanilla, to which add: 4 cups sifted flour, 1 tsp salt, 2 tsp baking powder. Beat well and add 1 cup chopped nuts.

Grease well 6 No. 303 size cans. Fill half full with batter and bake one hour and 20 minutes at 300°. Loosen edge with knife and take out while hot.

28 S. Seventh Street
P.O. Box 805
Fernandina Beach, FL 32034
Tel (904) 261-5390

SOUTHEAST

BALSAM MOUNTAIN INN

Balsam Mountain Inn is one of those seldom-found holdovers from earlier, quieter times, and is listed on the National Register of Historic Places. The very epitome of an old-fashioned country hotel sitting on twenty-six wooded acres with a Balsam Mountain Range as a back drop, the large white structure has provided food and lodging since 1906.

The spacious front porch is filled with rockers and delightful views of the countryside, while the lobby's polished wood floors, wicker furniture, and tall windows provide the perfect "home away from home." The guest rooms are comfortably furnished and some have large front corner windows.

Homecooked meals are served in an unhurried atmosphere of the dining room. A favorite breakfast dish is Hot Cakes served with Sausage and Syrup. Guests agree they are the best they have ever eaten.

Hot Cakes

5 cups plain flour	3 tbs baking powder
1 tsp salt	3 eggs
1-1/2 cups Wesson Oil	1 cup sugar
1 tsp vanilla	1 can evaporated milk
1 can water	

Mix well with electric mixer. Cook on hot griddle and serve with good sausage and warm syrup.

Box 40
Balsam, NC 28707
Tel (704) 456-9498

SOUTHEAST

The Banyan

The Banyan, nestled in lush tropical gardens off Main Street in Old Town Key West, is made up of six elegantly restored Victorian homes, each on the National Register.

The Delaney House with its double front porches, shutters, and gingerbread was completed around 1898 as the home of William Delaney, a collector for the U.S. Customs. Guest rooms and suites are decorated in calming colors and furnished with voluptuous sofas, chairs, rattan, and paddle fans...just what one expects in a tropical setting.

From the historic homes, guests may take the Conch Train around the island, leisurely strolls to restaurants, shops, and museums, or to the famous sunset celebrations.

Luaus are special at The Banyan and add flavor to this tropical island. Ham, Pineapple, and Shrimp Kabobs are to be expected. Mamita's Key Lime Pie is WORLD CLASS and is shared by 81-year-old native Mrs. Felicia Bode.

Mamita's Key Lime Pie

3 eggs, separated
2 tbs confectioner's sugar
1/3 cup freshly-squeezed Key Lime Juice
pinch salt

1 can condensed milk
pinch creme of tartar

Mix milk and egg yolks and Key Lime Juice. Pour into prepared Graham cracker pie crust and set aside until firm, about 20 minutes. Beat egg whites with pinch of salt until soft peaks form. Gradually add sugar and creme of tartar and continue to beat until whites are stiff and shiny. Spoon this meringue onto filling and bake at 350° for 10 minutes or until meringue begins to brown.

323 Whitehead Street
Key West, FL 33040
Tel (305) 296-7786

SOUTHEAST

Beaumont Inn

Beaumont Inn, built in 1845 as a school for young ladies, is an outstanding example of Greek Revivalism. The two-story front porch of the red brick mansion is supported by six Ionic columns and many of the windows contain the original hand-rolled panes. Besides the main inn, operated by the same family for four generations, three impressive buildings stand on a 30 acre estate. Beaumont Inn is listed on the National Register of Historic Places.

Inside, double Victorian parlors are furnished with gilded mirrors, chandeliers, fireplaces, and wingbacks with rich velvets. Adding to the elegance are floral rugs, wallpaper decorated with a ceiling border of red poppies, and a Steinway Grand for sing-a-longs...all typifying the quiet gentleness and grace of a more leisurable time.

Directly through the hallway, dual stairways sweep to second-and third-floor guest rooms filled with antiques and family heirlooms. A poem written by Annie Bell Goddard entitled "The Pearl" is found in every room.

Fort Harrod, in downtown Harrodsburg, is one of the very first permanent fortifications in Kentucky, while just minutes away are Civil War battlefields, antebellum mansions, beautiful and incomparable Bluegrass horse farms, and a restored Shaker Village.

The dining room renowned for excellent service and traditional Kentucky fare serves with the tinkling of a bell. Specialties include two-year-old Kentucky Cured Ham, Old Fashioned Yellow-Legged Fried Chicken, and General Robert E. Lee Orange-Lemon Cake.

Beaumont Inn's Corn Pudding

4 eggs
1 qt milk
4 tbs butter, melted
2 cups white whole kernel corn, or fresh
white corn cut off the cob

8 level tbs flour
4 rounded tsp sugar
1 tsp salt

Stir into the corn the flour, salt, sugar, and butter. Beat up eggs well; put them into milk, then stir into corn and put into pan. Bake in oven at 450° 40-45 minutes.

638 Beaumont Drive
Harrodsburg, KY 40330
Tel (606) 734-3381

SOUTHEAST

The BOAR'S HEAD INN

The Boar's Head Inn's wide range of facilities and racquet sports have placed it among the top 50 tennis resorts in America. This luxury estate is located in the foothills of the Blue Ridge Mountains.

The public rooms are handsomely appointed with antiques from England, where an impressive collection of prints by wildlife artist John Ruthven are displayed. A hundred-seventy-five large, comfortable guest rooms and suites are furnished with custom pieces, warm chestnut paneling, and working fireplaces overlooking gardens, valleys, and lakes.

American and European cuisine is served in three dining rooms. Specialties include Virginia Country Ham with Liver Pate and Melon, Prime Rib, and Roast Duckling. served by waitresses in crisp white aprons and waiters in knickers and doublets.

Southern Pecan Pie

3 eggs, slightly beaten	3/4 cup dark corn syrup
3/4 cup light corn syrup	2 tbs melted butter
1/8 tsp salt	1 tsp vanilla
1 tbs flour	1 cup pecans
1 tsp sugar	1 unbaked 9'' pastry shell

Mix flour, sugar, salt, and butter until creamy and blend in light and dark syrups, eggs, and vanilla. Spread pecans over bottom of pie shell and pour in the mixture. Bake at 325° 1 hour or until firm.

Box 5185
Charlottesville, VA 22905
Tel (804) 296-2181

SOUTHEAST

Boone Tavern Hotel

Boone Tavern Hotel has played an important part in the economic and cultural life of Berea since it opened its doors in 1909. The architecture is Georgian brick and the atmosphere is pure Kentucky. Boone Tavern, owned and operated by the college, helps to carry on the unique tradition of the school's work-study program.

Inside, the drama continues with a student staff of smiling faces welcoming guests. The comfortable lobby is spacious and filled with colonial furniture and a portrait of the area's best known frontiersman, Daniel Boone, hangs on the wall. The guest rooms are furnished with antique reproductions handcrafted by a college staff and students. Housed within the hotel is a gift shop displaying colorful quilts and crafts made by students and talented local people.

Guests to this small college town may tour the many shops with their local color, college industries, weavers, and potters. A short drive puts the visitor either in the middle of the beautiful Bluegrass region of Kentucky with its manicured horse farms and white fences, antebellum homes, and Civil War battlefields, or into the folds of the Cumberland Mountains where Appalachian life makes its own special approach into the world.

Three gracious meals a day are served in the hotel's quiet dining room. Tasty regional dishes and gracious student service have earned Boone Tavern a much wider reputation than its small town setting would suggest. Chicken Flakes with Steamed Dumplings, Roast Kentucky Turkey with Southern Dressing, Roast Leg of Veal Oregano with Cinnamon Apple Jelly, and ever-present delicous Southern Spoonbread make up part of the temptations. A specialty graciously contributed by Chef Richard T. Hougen and found in his cookbook, *Look No Further,* is Cream of Pimiento Soup.

Cream of Pimiento Soup

2 tbs butter	5 tbs flour
1/2 tsp salt	3 cups milk
1 medium chopped fine onion	few flecks pepper
1/2 cup pimientos	
4 cups chicken stock (fresh stock or stock	
made by dissolving 5 tsp chicken crystals in 4	
cups boiling water)	
(Note: If chicken crystals are used, cut down	
on salt.)	

Melt the butter, add flour and seasonings, blending well. Add milk, meat stock, and pimientos (which have been put through a sieve). Cook in the top of a double boiler for 30 minutes until the mixture has thickened somewhat, remembering to stir frequently to keep mixture smooth. Taste for seasonings. Serve with a sprinkling of chopped parsley on top. Serves 8 to 10.

Berea, KY 40404
Tel (606) 986-9357

SOUTHEAST

The Inn at Buckeystown

The Inn at Buckeystown is situated on a 2-1/2 acre manicured site of a pre-Civil War cemetery in the historic district. The Victorian mansion was built in 1897 and has served as a gracious inn since 1981. The five public rooms have richly papered walls, polished wood floors, magnificent chandeliers, and three working fireplaces. Contributing to the hospitality is a wide selection of books, magazines, and games.

Five guest rooms sweep to the second floor and are furnished with period pieces that share space with hand-crocheted afghans, fresh flowers, and Victorian memorabilia. A collection of clown paintings is hung throughout the inn. All in all, the Inn at Buckeystown opens gracious doors into the past.

Excellent meals are served on tables appointed with old Victorian china, silver, and glassware. Specialities are Boston Clam Chowder, Salmon in Red Pepper Sauce, elaborate salads and homemade desserts.

West Virginia Blackwalnut Apple Cake

4 cups coarsely chopped apples
2 cups sugar
2 eggs
1/2 cup vegetable oil
2 tsp vanilla

2 cups sifted all-purpose flour
2 tsp baking soda
2 tsp cinnamon
1 tsp salt
1 cup chopped black walnuts

Preheat oven to 350°. Grease and flour a 9x13x2-inch baking pan. In a mixing bowl, combine apples and sugar and let stand for approximately 1 hour. In a separate bowl, beat eggs slightly then add oil and vanilla - set aside. In a large mixing bowl, combine sifted flour, baking soda, cinnamon and salt; stir into egg mixture alternately with apple-sugar mixture. Stir in walnuts. Pour into pan and bake for 1 hour (or until cake tests done). Let stand in pan until quite cool; turn out on rack to complete cooling. Frost with lemon butter frosting and decorate with black walnut halves, if desired. Cut into squares to serve. Makes 12-15 servings.

Lemon Butter Frosting

4 tbs softened butter
3 cups confectioner's sugar
2 tbs lemon juice

2 tbs cold water
1 pinch of salt

In mixing bowl, cream butter and add sugar gradually, creaming thoroughly. Beat in lemon juice and enough cold water to make a spreading consistency. Beat in salt. Makes approximately 3 cups of frosting.

3521 Buckeystown Pike
Buckeystown, MD 21717
Tel (800) 272-1190

BUTTONWOOD INN

This small and cozy country inn is a delight for people who enjoy simplicity and the rustic beauty of Mother Nature. Dogwood and rhododendron present a spectacular display every spring, and fall's foliage is brilliant. Nestled among tall pines, the inn is delightfully furnished in country home style with antiques, handmade family quilts, collectibles, and country crafts.

Each morning begins with a full breakfast, and dishes range from country to gourmet. Culinary treats may include puffy scrambled eggs, souffles, apple sausage rings, baked peaches and sausage, or stuffed French toast. Liz says she is addicted to cookbooks: "They are my trashy novels! I get more enjoyment out of recipes than I do reading a paperback."

Buttonwood Inn is located just a short distance from the Smoky Mountain and Blue Ridge Parkways. The area offers an abundance of activities including gem mining, white water rafting, horseback riding, and hiking, as well as excellent crafts shopping and restaurants.

Strawberry-buttered Omelet

3 large eggs (separate)	2 tbs sour cream
3-1/2 tbs sugar	2 large strawberries
1 tbs rum	2 sprigs mint for garnish
pinch salt	2 tbs strawberry butter

Heat oven to 325°. Separate eggs, beat yolks until frothy with 1 tbs sugar and the rum. Add remaining sugar and beat until stiff but not dry. Fold whites into yolks. Pour mixture into well-buttered omelet pan or skillet (9"). Place pan on middle rack in oven. Bake 20 minutes. Remove from oven, place strawberry butter on one side and fold over other side. Turn onto warm plate and serve at once with some cream. Garnish with strawberries and mint.
Strawberry Butter: Soften 1/2 cup unsalted butter, whip, and blend in 1/2 cup strawberry jam with 1 tsp lemon juice. Place in covered container and refrigerate. May be frozen. Use on toast, waffles, breads, or hot biscuits.

50 Admiral Drive
Franklin, NC 28734
Tel (704) 369-8985

SOUTHEAST

Chalet Suzanne, an unlikely architectural style that rambles in all directions on at least 14 different levels, has been under the ownership of the Henshaw family since 1931. The enchanting inn overlooks Lake Suzanne on a seventy-acre estate amid balconies, towers, and patios. Every corner glows with stained glass, old lamps from faraway places, and antiques. A collection of tiles from ancient Persia, ironwork from Spain, copper pitchers from Egypt, and colorful costumes from Switzerland lend to the unusualness of this inn. The guest rooms are warm, inviting and charmingly different.

Excellent dinners are served by candlelight in five quaint rooms on many levels with water views. No two tables are alike, nor are the chairs, silver, or table settings. Delicious meals include Baked Grapefruit with Cinnamon, Hot Homemade Potato Rolls, Tropical Fruit Relishes, Crepes Suzette, and Mint Ice. The inn has been given a 4-Star rating by Mobil Guide, and many prestigious publications have written about its merits. *Travel/ Holiday Magazine Fine Dining Award* selected it as "one of the outstanding restaurants of the world."

Cauliflower Rinaldi

1 large head cauliflower, steamed whole and drained
3 anchovy filets or 1 tsp anchovy paste
1 cup reconstituted Chalet Suzanne Chicken Consomme Condensed

5 tbs butter, separated	1 small onion, minced
1 tbs Wine vinegar	1/2 tsp chopped parsley
1/3 cup grated Parmesan cheese	1/2 tsp basil

Saute onion in 2 tbs butter. Add anchovies or paste, chicken consomme, vinegar, parsley, and basil, and simmer for 2 minutes, adding 3 tbs butter. Set drained cauliflower head in round cake pan. Pour sauce over top of cauliflower and sprinkle with Parmesan cheese. Place under broiler, basting twice during broiling time, and cooking until well browned. Most easily served by cutting into wedges. Serves 8-10.

U.S. 27
North Lake Wales, FL 33859
Tel (813) 676-6011

HILDA CROCKETT'S
CHESAPEAKE HOUSE

Hilda Crockett's Chesapeake House is a weathered New England-style clapboard structure sitting on Tangier Island in Chesapeake Bay. Discovered in 1608 by Captain John Smith, whose life was saved by Pocahontas, this great waterway has served our nation ever since.

The adventure begins when guests board a mail boat that leaves the quiet dock in Chrisfield, Maryland each day at 12:30 (except Sundays) and slips across the Sound to Tangier Island. On the following morning, a return trip is scheduled for 8 o'clock when visitors may see a sky full of ducks, geese, or sea gulls.

The inn is open from April to November. Family style dinners are served. Big seafood dinners are, naturally, a specialty.

Hilda Crockett's Corn Pudding

1 can white cream style corn	1 can Pet milk
1 cup sugar	3 tbs corn starch
2 eggs	

Use a 1-1/2-qt casserole and put sugar and corn starch in first. Mix, then add eggs. Next, add corn and milk and dot with butter, baking at 350° for about 1 hour.

Hilda Crockett's Pound Cake

3 sticks butter (not margarine)	
3 cups sugar	6 eggs
2 tbs lemon flavor	1 tbs vanilla flavor
3 cups flour	1 tsp baking powder
1 cup milk	

Mix in large bowl, butter, sugar, eggs, and flavorings until very light and fluffy, then add flour mixed with baking powder. Add alternately with milk and bake for approximately 1 hour (or until straw comes out clean when inserted) at 350°. DO NOT OVERBAKE

Tangier Island, VA 23440
Tel (804) 891-2331

SOUTHEAST

The Clewiston Inn

Clewiston Inn is operated by the United States Sugar Corporation and is located in one of the last small towns in South Florida. Noted for its colonial atmosphere and Southern hospitality, the inn is close to Lake Okeechobee, the nation's second-largest fresh water lake nationally known for its sponsored bass fishing contests.

The spacious lobby is warm and inviting with rich wood paneling, ceiling beams, comfortable sofas, and a fireplace...typical of the informal surroundings. Guest rooms are restful and pleasantly decorated.

Nearby activities include tennis, golf, strolls through the garden, and, of course, fishing and sunning.

Meals are served in the Colonial dining room with its Southern buffets.

The Clewiston Inn Pepper Steak

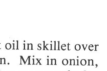

1 lb top round steak
1 clove garlic
2 cups sliced green pepper
1/4 tsp pepper
2 cups beef stock or bouillon

1/4 cup oil
1/2 cup sliced onion
1 tsp salt
3 tsp curry powder
2 tbs flour

Cut steak diagonally across grain in thin strips. Cut into strips 2" long. Heat oil in skillet over medium heat. Add garlic and remove after 3 minutes. Add meat and brown. Mix in onion, green pepper, salt, pepper, and curry powder. Cook over medium heat, stirring constantly for 3 minutes until just tender. Blend flour with stock. Stir into mixture. Bring to boil, stirring until liquid thickens. Serve over fluffy rice. Serves 4.

Box 1297
Clewiston, FL 33440
Tel (813) 983-8151

SOUTHEAST

The Cloister

The Cloister, a 5-Star, 5-Diamond resort off the sunny Georgia coast on tropical Sea Island, is surrounded by historic sites, antebellum plantations, hard-packed beaches, and 10,000 acres of marshland. In 1927 Howard Coffin built The Cloister and the Golf Club. The Golf Club was the three story cotton barn of Retreat Plantation. Today visitors are greeted with blooming flower gardens and a Spanish architectural style that is made-up of several guest houses which face the ocean in addition to the River House. The guest rooms are luxuriously decorated in a variety of styles.

Activities abound with championship golf, skeet, tennis, biking, fishing and horseback riding on the beach. Friday night plantation suppers lighted by torch and bonfire are always a delight.

Three meals served daily include an extensive menu of Chicken Breast Galliano, Braised Pork Flamande, and Lamb with Mint Sauce.

Mint Sauce for Lamb

2 lbs fresh mint   1 lb apple cider vinegar
1 lb sugar

Clean mint, discard stems and discolored leaves. Grind up mint using small blade. Mix in part of the sugar and vinegar and freeze. To finish sauce, defrost and add equal amounts of sugar and apple cider vinegar. Mix well. Chill.

Sea Island, GA 31561
Tel (912) 638-3611

Colonial Inn

Colonial Inn, one of the ten oldest inns in the United States, has been in continuous operation since it was built. The earliest part of the ancient hostelry dates to around 1759.

It was at Hillsborough that British General Cornwallis taunted colonial patriots by raising the Royal Standard five years after the Declaration of Independence. Staying at the inn, Cornwallis was but one of many notable guests, including American Vice President Aaron Burr.

The tradition of hospitality that defines the inn has been preserved, and none of the previous innkeepers have been more gracious hosts than the mother and daughter who welcome guests today.

Adjacent to the inn stands an antique store, and more than 100 buildings in Hillsborough date from the 18th and early 19th centuries.

Southern cooked meals are served in a cozy dining room. Pan Fried Chicken, Cornwallis Yams, as well as Homemade Breads and desserts are enjoyed by diners.

Cornwallis Yams

6 medium sweet potatoes
1/2 tsp cinnamon
1/4 lb butter
marshmallows
1/2 cup crushed pineapple
1 1/2 cups milk

1/2 tsp salt
1/2 tsp nutmeg
3 eggs
1/2 cup grated coconut
1 cup white sugar

Boil sweet potatoes; peel and mash with potato masher. Season with salt, cinnamon, nutmeg, and butter. Add eggs (beaten), coconut, pineapple, and milk. Place in greased casserole and top with marshmallows. Bake at 350° until lightly browned. Serves 10.

153 West King Street
Hillsborough, NC 27278
Tel (919) 732-2461

SOUTHEAST

THE
CORNER CUPBOARD
INN

The Corner Cupboard Inn, small and informal, is tucked away on a peaceful sand-covered side road 1-1/2 blocks from the Rehoboth Beach.

In addition to the main house, four guest rooms overlook a bricked courtyard. The living room, with its crackling fire is an invitation of hospitality and is a good spot to relax. With all the comforts of home, guests rooms are furnished with antiques and old prints. From mid-September to Memorial Day weekend a Continental breakfast is served and during the summer months offerings include both breakfast and dinner.

Meals are served in the large screened-in side porch. Although the food isn't fancy - a typical winter breakfast consists of eggs, sausage, home fries, toast, and strawberry preserves -guests are graciously served with fine appointments that include sterling silver and Wedgwood china. Full of understated elegance, its real attraction is its cheerfulness. Also prepared are Soft Shell Crabs, Roast Duckling, Broiled Fish of the Day, Sirloin, Lobster, Fresh Vegetables, and an array of very tempting desserts.

Scallops with Garlic and Tomatoes

1 lb bay or sea scallops
2 tbs butter or margarine
1 tomato, coarsely diced
1 tbs Worcestershire Sauce
1/4 tsp garlic powder

1/4 cup all-purpose flour
2 tbs olive oil
1 tbs chopped parsley
1 tbs lemon juice
lemon wedges

Cut sea scallops into halves or quarters and lightly dust with flour. Cook in butter and oil in medium-size skillet until lightly browned. Add tomato, parsley, Worcestershire sauce, lemon juice, and garlic powder. Continue cooking until tomatoes are heated and scallops are cooked. Serve with lemon. Serves 3 to 4.

The Corner Cupboard Inn
50 Park Avenue
Rehoboth Beach, DE 19971
Tel (302) 227-8553

SOUTHEAST

The Country Inn

The Country Inn is a handsome brick structure that has entertained numberless visitors to Berkley Springs, West Virginia since 1932. The architecture is colonial and the atmosphere is warm and inviting. The inn is very comfortable with its pillars, porches, and lawns.

The lobby is spacious and the guest rooms are bright and relaxing. Adjacent to the nation's oldest health spa dating back to 1748, the inn joins the village green of this small town.

From nearby Prospect Peak, scenes of the Potomac and Great Cacapon Valleys and three states - West Virginia, Pennsylvania, and Maryland can be seen. This view has been classified as the fifth finest in the United States. For those who enjoy golf, an 18-hole course is located 12 minutes from the front doorstep.

Delicious Southern cooked meals are served in a well-appointed colonial dining room.

Apple and Banana Fritters

Begin with four bright red apples (slightly tart) and four firm bananas. Core the apples, leaving the peel on and slice into 1/2"-thick rings, covering with lemon water to prevent browning. Peel bananas and cut into four equal parts. Next, prepare a thick consistency of good pancake batter. In a deep sauce pot heat liquid shortening for frying. Dip sliced apple and banana pieces individually into batter and place separately into hot grease. Cook until covering is slightly browned and remove with slotted spoon to paper towel. Sprinkle with confectioners sugar and serve immediately with heated syrup and link sausage.

Berkeley Springs, WV 25411
Tel (304) 258-2210

SOUTHEAST

Doe Run Inn is a weathered, fieldstone structure that has provided good food and lodging since 1927. The inn was an old mill that began about 1800, and stands on property that was deeded to Squire Boone (Daniel's brother) in 1786. It has walls thirty inches thick and was named for the deer that gathered in great herds around the stream. In addition to its history, the National Landmark can lay claim to the fact that Abraham Lincoln's father worked there as a stonemason.

The hand-hewn ceiling beams, sagging floors, antiques, and primitives immediately take the guest back in time. The rooms are furnished in a variety of styles with high headboards, marble topped dressers, old chests, colorful quilts, and wood floors. A delightful gift shop is downstairs with beautiful handmade crafts from the area.

Meals are served in three dining rooms. During the summer the screened-in porch above the running brook is a favorite spot. The menu includes Fried Chicken, Steaks, Seafood, and Kentucky Country Cured Ham.

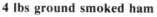

Country Ham Balls

4 lbs ground smoked ham
2 cups bread crumbs
4 eggs

2 lbs pork sausage
2 cups milk

Mix all together. Let stand two hours, then roll in marble-sized balls, baking about 35 minutes at 350°. Mix and bring to boil for about 5 minutes:

Sweet and Sour Sauce

1 cup vinegar
1 tbs prepared mustard

1/2 cup water
1 cup brown sugar

Bake Ham Balls in 2 cups of sauce, and serve with remainder of sauce.

Brandenburg, KY 40108
Tel (502) 422-2042

SOUTHEAST

∘DUDLEY'S∘
RESTAURANT

Dudley Square can trace its history back to the days when its halls and stairways were filled with the comings and goings of laughing children. An elementary school from 1851 to the early 1930s, this 1881 building is named in honor of Benjamin Winslow Dudley, a medical doctor at the Transylvania Medical School.

Enlarged over the years and completely renovated in 1979, this handsome old structure stands in the charming historic district of downtown Lexington, Kentucky, and houses a collection of interesting shops and Dudley's restaurant. Although no overnight lodgings are available a trip to Dudley Square puts visitors within walking distance of Victorian Square, Festival Market, Civic Center and moonlight horse-drawn carriage rides through old Lexington. (By reservation.)

Meals are served in the main dining room (third grade classroom) with high ceilings, paddle fans and crisp linens or, outside (weather permitting) in the warm red brick courtyard, filled with cozy little tables and chairs shaded by smart umbrellas. Offerings include Chicken Monterey, Fettucine Alfredo, Tournedos Maxwell, Soups, Salads, and delicious Muffins, all set off by a delightful array of desserts.

Country Ham Quiche

In a 9 inch unbaked pie shell, put 3 ounces cooked country ham, and 3 ounces grated cheese (swiss and gruyere mix). Mix 3 eggs and 2 cups half and half, pour over ham and cheese mixture. Bake at 325° for about 30 minutes, until golden brown. Cool before slicing. Yield 1 quiche.

386 South Mill Street
Lexington, KY 40508
Tel (606) 252-1010

SOUTHEAST

DuPONT LODGE

Dupont Lodge is named in honor of T.Coleman Dupont who donated land more than half a century ago to the Commonwealth of Kentucky for a park at Cumberland Falls. Enjoying a bird's-eye view of the river below, this handsome rock and log structure, with awnings and restful surroundings, has been a welcomed retreat for generations of returning visitors.

The warmth of the sandstone walls and the thunder of Cumberland River as it plunges 60 feet recalls memories in a setting of timeless beauty. On moonlit nights, guests may walk down to the precipice of the falls along wooded trails to view a "moonbow" created by the full moon's light reflecting against the rising mist. The only other place in the world to have a moonbow is Victoria Falls in Africa.

The large, comfortable lobby has exposed beams, gleaming wood floors, braided area rugs, and a massive stone fireplace. And just off the lobby is the Robert A. Blair Museum of native artifacts. Mr. Blair fought tirelessly to protect the environment of the falls for the enjoyment of future generations.

Guest rooms are attractively furnished and pleasantly decorated. Outdoor activities include hiking the many mountain trails, swimming, rafting, and horseback riding.

Meals are served in a dining room on the lower floor whose ceiling is supported by huge polished logs and beams. Floor-to-ceiling windows give outstanding views of the river below. The menu includes Lake Catfish and Hushpuppies, Southern Fried Chicken, Kentucky Cured Ham with Red Eye Gravy, and Cobblers.

Chef James Ruby Messamore's Yellow Squash Casserole

3-4 med. crookneck squash
salt & pepper to taste
1-1/2 cups shredded cheddar cheese
1-1/2 cups crumbled bread crumbs

1 medium size onion
2 tbs butter
1 cup whole milk

Slice squash and put in small boiler to cook at high temperature. Dice onion and add to squash along with butter, salt, and pepper. Boil on top of stove until squash is cooked to desired tenderness. Drain off 1/3 to 1/2 water and add 1 cup shredded cheddar cheese, 1 cup whole milk, and 1 cup bread crumbs. Mix by hand until mixture is creamy. Put in desired pan greased with spray. Take remaining cheese and bread crumbs and sprinkle over casserole, adding a little butter over the top. Place in oven at 300-325° approximately 30 minutes or until brown. Serves 4-6

Cumberland Falls State Park
Tel. (606) 528-4121
Corbin, KY

SOUTHEAST

ELMWOOD INN

Elmwood Inn stands gracefully in a grove of trees and faces the Chaplin River. The antebellum mansion has served as a private home, a prestigious academy, and, during the Civil War, a hospital for wounded soldiers who fought in the Battle of Perryville, called the "Gettysburg of the West." Many activities are centered in the rolling Bluegrass countryside, and Perryville itself is full of Civil War reminders, even though other and older landmarks are to be found.

Today, the inn is a centerpiece for Kentucky hospitality. Restored to the family home that it once was, the inn has opened its doors to visitors by including an English Tea Room and two overnight guest rooms.

A full gourmet breakfast is offered and a traditional English afternoon Tea is served daily in the Tea Room.

Tea Room Scones are a favorite at this inn.

Wedding Reception Punch

1 large can frozen lemonade	1 large bottle ginger ale
1 large can frozen fruit punch	2 pints pineapple sherbet
lemon slices and strawberries	

Dilute lemonade and fruit punch according to directions on cans. Pour the two into large punch bowl and stir in softened sherbet. Decorate with lemon slices and strawberries floating in punch. Just before serving, add ginger ale. Serves 25.

Perryville, KY
Tel (606) 332-2271

SOUTHEAST

Fryemont Inn

Fryemont Inn, covered with bark from huge poplar trees, is furnished with virgin cherry and walnut pieces made by local craftsmen. It was built of the finest chestnut, oak, and maple to be found by lumber baron Captain Amos Frye in 1923. The ornamental hardware on the doors was forged by blacksmith John Carson and the massive fireplace in the spacious lobby was fashioned by Cherokee stonemasons who knew how to build a chimney that would "draw a cat out of the room." Fryemount Inn is listed on the National Register of Historic Places.

Guest rooms are comfortable with some antiques and sitting areas. The porch is filled with rocking chairs and views of the city and mountains beyond.

Meals are served in the many-windowed dining room with another huge stone fireplace and outstanding views. An extensive menu offers a variety of entrees including Fresh Mountain Trout, Turkey with Pecan Dressing, and Southern Fried Chicken. Fresh vegetables are served family style along with tempting desserts.

Buttermilk Pie

1 unbaked pie shell	4 eggs
1-1/2 cups sugar	1/2 cup buttermilk
1 tsp butter flavor	1 tsp vanilla
1/4 cup butter, melted and cooled	

Beat eggs and sugar until fluffy. Add buttermilk and butter, mixing well. Stir in flavorings. Pour in shell. Bake on lower shelf at 375 degrees 45 minutes or until center is almost set but still soft. Cool thoroughly before slicing.

Box 459
Bryson City, NC 28713
Tel (704) 488-2159

SOUTHEAST

General Lewis Inn

General Lewis Inn resides in historic Lewisburg, rich in both Revolutionary and Civil War lore. The streets are lined with trees and interesting old architecture in warm red brick or frame. Many of these gracious homes have large porches, reminders of leisurely days past.

The original part of the inn dates back sometime around 1834 and was completed in 1929 by Randolph K. Hock and his wife, Mary. The parlor-lobby has hand-hewn beams, a fireplace, and an old-fashioned mantel clock in addition to other memorabilia. The front desk, built of walnut and pine about 1760, registered Thomas Jefferson and Patrick Henry when it stood in the Sweet Chalybeate Springs Hotel. Out front sits an old stage coach that traveled by the inn. Guest rooms are comfortably furnished with antiques and all have the original mantels.

The original part of the inn houses the dining room with its large hand-hewn beams and old cupboards filled with early glass, pottery, china, and curios. Fried Chicken, West Virginia Country Ham, Grilled Pork Chops, Candied Sweet Potatoes with Peanuts, Breast of Chicken Randolph, and Hot Corn Sticks await the guest.

Candied Sweet Potatoes with Peanuts

4 medium size sweet potatoes, peeled and sliced
1/2 cup firmly packed light brown sugar
1/4 cup butter or margarine   1 cup boiling water
1/2 tsp salt   2 tbs chopped peanuts
1 tsp French's, America's Favorite Yellow Mustard

Arrange potatoes in shallow 2-qt baking dish. Combine water, sugar, butter, mustard, and salt; pour over potatoes. Bake, covered with foil, at 325° for 45 minutes. Remove foil. Spoon syrup over potatoes and sprinkle with chopped peanuts. Bake 20 minutes longer, basting several times, until potatoes are tender and slightly glazed and peanuts are lightly browned. Serves 4-5.

Lewisburg, WV 24901
Tel (304) 645-2600

SOUTHEAST

Graves' Mountain Lodge

Graves' Mountain Lodge is a family-owned rustic resort in Virginia's Blue Ridge Mountains that prides itself on Southern hospitality and good home-cooked food. Guests enjoy the natural beauty of the great outdoors while horseback riding, fishing, hunting, or hiking trails that challenge them through the Shenandoah National Park to White Oak Canyon and Old Rag Mountain.

The lodge is centrally located to the log cabins, cozy cottages, and motels furnished in colonial comfort pleasantly tucked away in secluded woods. A paradise for the outdoorsman, local streams are full of native and stocked trout. The 8,000-acre Rapidan Wildlife Area is open to the public.

Close by are Civil War battlefields, Monticello, and the Hebron Lutheran Church which is the oldest church in America still in continuous use.

Meals are served family buffet style in the sunlit dining room by an open hearth. Specialties include Fried Chicken, Roast Beef, Rainbow Trout, Ribeye Steak, Country Ham, and Home Grown Vegetables.

Fruit Cream Pie

8-10 ozs blueberries, peaches, or
   strawberries
8 oz cream cheese
1 cup whipped topping

9" baked pie shell
1 cup confectioners sugar
pecans, chopped

Heat oven to 400°. Cover bottom of pie shell with pecans and bake until brown. Cool. Blend cream cheese and confectioners sugar. Fold in whipped topping and fruit. Pour into cooled pie shell and chill. Top with additional whipped topping before serving.

Syria, VA 22743
Tel (540) 923-4231

SOUTHEAST

The Inn at Gristmill Square

The Inn at Gristmill Square is a cluster of five charming buildings including a country store, an art gallery, and the Waterwheel Restaurant. Additional rooms and suites occupy a restored Federal-style structure. Each room is tastefully furnished and decorated quite differently. Some have antiques and old prints, while others enjoy a more contemporary atmosphere.

Besides a pool and three tennis courts, the historic Warm Springs pools are withing walking distance. Golf, fishing, horseback riding, and carriage rides are nearby. During the winter, skiing at The Homestead and Silver Creek are added pleasures. Rated 4-Star by Mobil Travel Guide, the original mill was built on the site in 1771.

Meals are served in the rustic surroundings of the Waterwheel Restaurant. Continental cuisine and American favorites are served, including fresh local trout.

Duck at Gristmill Square

1 4-1/2 to 5 lb duck	8 oz sliced fresh mushrooms
2 oz butter	2 oz flour
2 cups milk	1 tbs Worcestershire Sauce
salt & pepper to taste	2 tbs fresh chopped parsley
cognac to taste	1 box Greek filo pastry
1 lb melted butter	

Roast duck at 375 degrees for 1-1/2 - 2 hours. Cool and pull meat from bones. Reserve to the side. Add flour to melted butter to make a roux. Add milk to make heavy white sauce. Season with salt and pepper and Worcestershire Sauce. Saute mushrooms and lightly brown in butter. Deglaze with cognac. Blend duck, white sauce, mushrooms, and the adjust seasonings. Brush filo with butter. Layer 3 times. Cut in half lengthwise and add 3/4 cup of mixture and fold as you would a flag. Brush with butter and bake at 350° for 15-20 minutes until lightly browned.

P.O. Box 359
Warm Springs, VA 24484
Tel (703) 839-2231

SOUTHEAST

THE HASLAM - FORT HOUSE

The Haslam-Fort House dates back to 1872 when it was built by John Haslam, producer of minstrels after the Civil War. Italianate in style, the handsome building stands in the delightful historic district of Savannah, Georgia, renowned for its wide streets, flowers, ancient trees draped in Spanish moss, and lovely old homes. Savannah is also rich in Revolutionary and Civil War history.

Upon arrival guests are invited to the upstairs parlor for a tour of the restored townhouse. The host is eager to help the visitor in every way to thoroughly enjoy Savannah, and will arrange reservations for dinner, theatre, and other points of interest. An avid doll and toy collector, guests should ask to see his collection.

A garden suite is entered from the west side of the house. The spacious living room with high ceilings and a warming fireplace is cheerfully decorated with colorful wallpaper, antiques, and wingbacks. The two bedrooms are airy and pleasantly furnished.

A Continental breakfast is provided on a self-serve basis. Offerings include Coffee, Tea, Orange Juice, English Muffins, Bagels, and Cinnamon Buns.

Hot Broccoli Dip

1 6-oz tube garlic cheese
1 can cream of mushroom soup

1 10-oz pkg frozen chopped broccoli

Combine all ingredients (thawed broccoli) in top of double boiler or heavy pan. Cook over low heat for 20 minutes. Serve in chafing dish or fondue pot with triscuits or other crackers. Can be frozen and re-heated.

417 East Charlton Street
Savannah, GA 31401
Tel (912) 233-6380

SOUTHEAST

PHOTO BY DEAN M. HENSON

Herndon J. Evans Lodge

Herndon J. Evans Lodge sits high on a ridge not far from Cumberland Gap National Park. Many brave settlers with names like Daniel Boone, Dr. Thomas Walker, Skaggs, and Harrod forged into the unknown wilderness in the late 1700s to open up Kentucky, and the "Wilderness Road" passed not far below the present-day lodge.

Built of wood and sandstone in the rugged Pine Mountain State Park, the lodge is operated by the Commonwealth of Kentucky. The lobby of this family resort has vertical log walls, beamed ceilings, and a huge stone fireplace. A piano for sing-alongs and an extensive collection of prints by wildlife artist Ray Harm are in the recreation room.

The comfortable guest rooms have private balconies overlooking the heavily forested mountains. In addition to the main lodge, well-furnished and nicely appointed cabins with screened-in porches are scattered along the mountainside.

The Mountain Laurel Festival is held in the park each May in celebration of the colorful flowering laurel that grows up the slopes and has been a showy event since 1935. Nearby stands the Clear Creek Baptist School and Pineville's looming Chained Rock. Hiking the many trails test the visitor's endurance, and old, abandoned farm settlements are part of the local heritage.

Meals are served in a dining room flooded with tree-top views. The menu includes Southern Fried Chicken, Kentucky Cured Ham with Red Eye Gravy, Lake Catfish and Hushpuppies.

Fresh Broccoli Salad

4 cups chopped fresh broccoli	**1 cup chopped nuts**
1 cup mayonnaise (or more)	**1 cup raisins**

Mix fresh ingredients thoroughly and chill before serving.

Pine Mountain State Resort Park
1050 State Park Road
Pineville, KY 40977
Tel (606) 337-3066

SOUTHEAST

HIGH HAMPTON INN

High Hampton Inn stands proudly at an altitude of 3600 feet in Cashiers Valley, North Carolina, an area where nothing changes much except the seasons. It was built nearly a century ago as the summer home of Confederate General Wade Hampton, governor of South Carolina and U.S. Senator, who hunted and fished on the estate with his friends. The Halsted Dahlia gardens testify to the love of High Hampton's next owner, Dr. William S. Halsted and his wife Caroline, niece of the general.

Its rustic architectural design has a mountain look that blends both the cottages and inn in harmony with the natural landscape. The lobby's huge chimney has four fireplaces, and the guest rooms are decorated with comfortable, sturdy furniture and walls of sawmill pine.

All outdoor sports abound, and High Hampton's 18-hole par 71 private course designed by internationally famous golf architect George W. Cobb reflects his statement: "I have yet to see a course, designed by me or by others, with greater natural beauty, or one more enjoyable to play."

Delicious meals are served in the dining room with outstanding views. The menu includes Country Ham, Homemade Breads, Garden Fresh Vegetables, and delicious desserts.

Black Bottom Pie

1-1/2 cups crushed Zwieback	6 tbs melted butter
1/4 cup powdered sugar	1 tsp cinnamon

Mix ingredients well and place in pie pan, patting along sides and bottom to make crust. Bake in moderate oven 15 minutes.

1 tbs gelatin	1 cup sugar
2 cups rich milk	4 tsp cornstarch
4 egg yolks, beaten lightly	1/2 tsp vanilla
1 1/2 oz melted chocolate	

Soak gelatin in 1/2 cup cold water. Scald milk. Combine egg yolks, sugar, and cornstarch. Stir in gradually milk and cook over hot water until custard will coat a spoon. Take out 1 cup custard and add chocolate to it. Beat until well blended and cool. Add vanilla and pour into pie shell. Dissolve gelatin in remaining custard, cool, but do not permit to stiffen, stirring in 1 tsp almond flavoring, 3 egg whites, 1/4 tsp salt, 1/4 cup sugar, 1/4 tsp cream of tartar. Beat egg whites and salt until blended, add cream of tartar and beat until stiff, gradually adding sugar, folding in remaining custard and covering chocolate custard with almond-flavored custard. Chill and set. Whip cup of heavy cream. Add 2 tbs powdered sugar and spread over pie.

Box 388
Cashiers, NC 28717
Tel (704) 743-2411

SOUTHEAST

HOTEL HILLTOP HOUSE

Hilltop House resides in a community which closely identified with the important Civil War battles of Monocacy and Gettysburg. Harper's Ferry was regarded as the key to Washington but was captured along with its 11,000 Union soldiers by Confederate General Stonewall Jackson in 1862.

On a hill overlooking the confluence of the Shenandoah and Potomac Rivers, this century-old hotel has large porches that provide views of three States and Harper's Ferry. Thomas Jefferson, in his notes on Virginia, said, "the scene is worth a voyage across the Atlantic", and Carl Sandburg wrote, "Harper's Ferry is a meeting place of winds and water, rocks and ranges." For years, artists and writers have been inspired by its beauty.

Hotel Hilltop House has been a favorite retreat of many famous people including President Woodrow Wilson and Mark Twain.

Family-style meals of Southern Fried Chicken, Virginia Style Ham, Choice Rib Steak, Stuffed Flounder with Deviled Crab, and Hot Biscuits are enjoyed by guests.

Hilltop House Chicken Salad

1 can pimientos
4 stalks celery, chopped fine
1-1/2 tbs vinegar
salt & pepper
about 3 cups diced, cooked chicken

3 tbs pickle relish
1 tsp ground mustard
2 tbs sugar
1 cup mayonnaise

Combine well and serve on pineapple ring with a bit of toasted coconut on top.

Harpers Ferry W. VA 25425
P.O. Box 930
Tel (304) 535-2132

SOUTHEAST

Hound Ears

Hound Ears Lodge offers golf, tennis, swimming, and snow skiing in a beautiful setting of streams, lakes, and waterfalls. This Mobil Guide four-season, 4-Star resort is named for a unique rock formation resembling huge ears and resides in a 900-acre luxury and residential community. Winter brings an average annual snowfall of 34 inches to the North Carolina mountains, where an average summer temperature of 68 degrees makes Hound Ears Lodge a most appealing retreat.

Riding stables are located within minutes of the community, as are several state and national parks. The Cone Estate and Price Park in Blowing Rock total over 7,000 acres and 55 miles of bridle paths, hiking trails, and trout streams. Pisgah National Forest, the scenic Blue Ridge Parkway, Grandfather Mountain (noted for its annual Scottish Highland Games), and the rugged Appalachian Trail are nearby. The Alpine lodge sits in a lush green valley that stretches its fingers into the folds of the mountains beyond.

Guest rooms are spacious and tastefully decorated. No two rooms are alike, and bed turn down completes the hospitality.

Gracious service is found in two dining rooms with superb cuisine.

Honey Dressing

1/4 cup lemon juice	1/2 cup sugar
1 tsp dry mustard	1 tsp paprika
1 tsp salt	1/4 plus 1 tsp honey
4 tbs celery seed	1 cup salad oil

Mix all ingredients together except oil. Add oil slowly, a little at a time, and serve on assorted fresh fruit.

Box 188
Blowing Rock, NC 28605
Tel (704) 963-4321

SOUTHEAST

Indigo Inn is awash in 18th century charm and resides in the delightful historic district of Charleston. This beautiful city of flowers, antebellum mansions, ancient trees, and walls of red brick invites leisurely tours that tell the story of its opulent days past. Steeped in history, Fort Sumter was the scene of the first shot that started the Civil War.

The elegant lobby's oriental motif and Sheraton sideboard dating to the 1700's are an indication of this 4-Star hostelry that has enjoyed very favorable comments in Time, U.S. News and World Report, and other prestigious publications.

A lush, tranquil courtyard filled with white lacey furniture is a private retreat for guests who revel in the luxury of 18th century antiques and reproductions, old chests, canopied and four-poster beds with down pillows, comforters, and colorful wallpaper.

The famous Hunt Breakfast is served each morning in the lobby from the sideboard or out in the courtyard. Homemade Pumpkin, Banana, and Blueberry Breads along with Ham and Biscuits, Fresh Fruit, and Coffee awaken the morning.

Prune Bread

5 eggs
1 cup oil
1-1/2 tsp cinnamon
3/4 cup nuts
3 cups sifted self-rising flour

3 cups sugar
1-1/2 tsp nutmeg
2 jars junior baby prunes
1-1/2 tsp cloves

Mix eggs, sugar, and oil. Measure spices in with flour. Add flour and prunes alternating. Mix well. Bake at 350º for about 1 hour. Makes 2 loaves.

1 Maiden Lane
Charleston, SC 29401
Tel (803) 577-5900

SOUTHEAST

Jarrett House

The Jarrett House is a hold-over from the days of the horse and buggy and steam passenger trains that once served as the official dining place for the Western North Carolina Railway. Built for the "comers and stayers" of the last century, the 1884 clapboard structure has large porches and dozens of rocking chairs. In the summer of 1886 it was recorded that two lady guests seen smoking cigarettes "set the countryside agog and gave zest to neighborhood gossip." The inn is now listed on the National Register of Historic Places. '

Although ownership has changed several times, it has never lost its reputation for a tradition of homestyle food, family-style service, and restful accommodations started by "Miss Sallie" nine decades ago. Eighteen guest rooms have been refurnished to reflect the style of the period.

The 125-seat dining room, known for its very tasty food, serves Fried Chicken, Trout, Country Ham with Red Eye Gravy, Hot Biscuits with Churned Butter and Sourwood Honey, and in season, Fresh Vegetables from the garden.

Country Ham with Red Eye Gravy

Cook slices of aged country ham in an iron skillet to which a very small amount of oil or shortening has been added. When ham is done, remove from pan. Turn up heat under the pan to get it very hot. Pour enough water in the very hot pan to cover the bottom. Let this boil a minute to get the drippings loose before pouring over ham.

P.O. Box 219
Dillsboro, NC 28725
Tel (704) 586-9964

SOUTHEAST

The Kenwood Inn

The Kenwood Inn was established in 1886 as a boarding house and is located between the Oldest House and the famous Castillo de San Marcos. According to local maps and early records the inn dates back between 1865 and 1885. The restoration was finally completed in 1984.

Guest rooms are decorated in themes that represent the different periods and styles from St. Augustine's varied past, ranging from the simple Shaker and country rooms to the more formal Colonial and Victorian.

Activities range from walking the cobblestoned streets, and wide sandy beaches to browsing through antique shops, historic homes, carriage rides, harbor excursions, and museums.

A Continental breakfast is served each morning in the dining room. Homebaked Cakes, Breads, Fruit, Juice and Coffee greet the morning.

Grandma's Cake

Mix together:

1-1/2 cup sugar	2 cups flour
1 tsp soda	1 tsp salt

Add:

2 eggs and 1 can No. 2 pineapple, crushed, in heavy syrup. Do not drain, and pour into greased 9 x 13 pyrex dish.

Spread over batter:

3/4 cup brown sugar	1/2 cup chopped walnuts

Bake at 325 degrees for 40-45 minutes. Just before cake is done, bring to boil:

1 regular can Pet milk	1/2 cup sugar
1 stick margarine	1 tsp vanilla

Pour over cake as soon as it comes from oven. Let stand before serving.

38 Marine Street
St. Augustine, FL 32084
Tel (904) 824-2116

SOUTHEAST

Loder House

Loder House was built high on a bluff overlooking the Ohio River sometime between 1790 and 1810. The location, in historic Petersburg, is convenient to downtown Cincinnati, shopping, theatres, and airport.

There are six well-appointed dining rooms furnished with antiques reflecting its warmth and gracious hospitality. Featured in the 1989 Travel Holiday Magazine, the Cincinnati Post Food Critics chose Loder House to be the friendliest restaurant in greater Cincinnati with the best country-style food.

Although there are no overnight lodging at this treasured old inn, a visit to Loder House is truly a step back to the days of good times and traditional Kentucky cuisine.

Blackberry Jam Cake

1 cup butter	3 cups flour	2 cups blackberry jam
1 cup white sugar	2 tsp. cinnamon	1 cup chopped nuts
1 cup brown sugar	1 tsp. nutmeg	1/3 cup Bourbon
1 cup buttermilk	1 tsp. allspice	(optional)
1 tsp. soda	1 tsp. vanilla	
5 eggs		

Cream butter with sugar thoroughly. Add soda to buttermilk and let set until ready to use. Sift all dry ingredients. Add eggs to creamed mixture. Alternate milk with dry ingredients and then add jam and bourbon.

Makes three 9-inch layers. Bake at 350° for 35 minutes. Can also be baked in tube pan at 300° for 15 minutes, then 325° for 95 minutes or until barely beginning to brown.

Icing

4 tbsp. butter	1/3 cup rich or	1/2 tsp. vanilla or
1/2 cup brown sugar	evaporated milk	1 tsp. Rum
1/8 tsp. salt	approx. 2 cups	1/2 cup chopped nuts
	confectioner's sugar	

Combine and heat in double boiler butter, sugar, salt, and milk. Cook until smooth. Cool slightly and beat in enough sugar to make spreading consistency. Add vanilla and nuts. Double for layer cake.

P.O. Box 130
Petersburg, KY 41080
Tel (606) 586-8092

SOUTHEAST

Maple Lodge, built in 1946, sits in the heart of Blowing Rock, an inviting spot that has welcomed guests in search of cool Blue Ridge summers for nearly a century.

Guests may enjoy the municipal park with tennis and swimming, or hiking and horseback riding over miles of mountain trails. There are countless attractions within easy walking distance of this mountain retreat that include specialty shops, restaurants, and the treasure-laden Blowing Rock Auction Gallery.

Inside, the inn is comfortable and tastefully decorated with antiques. There are two distinctive parlors. One has a fireplace and the other is home to a piano and pipe organ. Both offer the comforts of home along with old-fashioned hospitality. A complimentary fruit bowl welcomes each guest.

A Continental breakfast is served each morning on the sun porch overlooking the garden.

Lemon Cheese Cake

Combine:

1 box yellow cake mix   **1 egg**
1 stick melted butter or margarine

Mix until above ingredients form a dough ball. Spread into greased and floured 9x13 pan or pyrex dish.

Combine:

1 8-oz pkg cream cheese
3 eggs
1 box confectioner's sugar   **1 tsp (or more) lemon extract**

Spread above mixture over dough. Bake at 350° 45 minutes. Cool and slice into squares.

Box 66
Blowing Rock, NC 28605
Tel (704) 295-3331

The Martha Washington Inn

The Martha Washington Inn, both a museum and an inn with great charm and beauty with rocking chairs on the front porch and a $1.5 million restoration, is a fabulous repository of our nation's history. Built in 1832 as the home of General Francis Preston and his wife Sarah, niece of Patrick Henry, the mansion has been enlarged several times. It served as a college for many years and during the Civil War as a hospital for wounded soldiers. Stories abound from this period --- all a part of its colorful history.

The public rooms and halls are filled with 15th century Renaissance chests and other artifacts. Each guest room is furnished quite differently with antiques and some of the beds date back to the 1600's. Purchased in 1984 by the United Coal Company who committed itself to preserving its early historical and colonial atmosphere, the inn stands as a grand legacy to the past.

Across the street is the world-famous Barter Theatre.

Meals are served in the General Preston Restaurant.

Peanut Butter Custard

One 9'' pie shell or use Chef Gesser's Martha Washington Inn recipe, made with:

3 cups flour	**1 part shortening**
1 part water	**pinch salt**

Mix and roll lightly.

Filling:

1 cup peanut butter	**1 tsp real vanilla**
1-1/2 cups granulated sugar	**1/2 tsp salt**
2 eggs	**1-1/2 cups milk or cream**

On low speed, blend peanut butter and vanilla, then add sugar and salt. Add eggs, using medium speed, then add milk on low speed. Mix to smooth. Bake 45-50 minutes in 375 degree oven.

150 West Main
Abingdon, VA 24210
Tel (703) 628-3161

SOUTHEAST

Maryland Inn

The Maryland Inn is a handsome red brick structure, with Victorian additions, that offers a glimpse into the early life of the Annapolis community beginning with the Continental Congress since 1784. An origional Revolutionary period building, the inn is surrounded by several old landmarks including Reynolds Tavern, Governor Calvert House, Robert Johnson House and the State House Inn.

A Continental breakfast is offered each morning. Elegant meals of fine Continental cuisine are served in the Treaty of Paris Restaurant.

Crab Bisque-Maryland Inn

1/2 gallon milk	2 tbs chicken base
1/4 cup butter	1 tbs Old Bay Seasoning
1 tsp dry mustard	1 tsp celery salt
1/2 tsp white pepper	dash Worcestershire Sauce
1/4 cup Half & Half cream	1/4 cup cornstarch
3 oz dry sherry	1 lb backfin crabmeat

Heat milk and butter in sauce pan. Add all seasonings. Mix cornstarch and cream together and when milk has almost boiled, stir it in until thickened. Add sherry and crabmeat.

16 Church Circle
Annapolis, MD 21401
Tel (301) 263-2641

SOUTHEAST

Meadow Lane Lodge is a fine traditional resort situated on a 1600 - acre estate in the Alleghany Mountains. Hiking and bike trails lead from the front door and, for those who wish to bring their own mounts, stable facilities are available. A two-mile pastoral stretch of the Jackson River rolls right through the property where sparkling drinking water flows from a limestone spring at the rate of approximately one-million gallons each day. Guests often visit this secluded spot.

The spacious common room welcomes visitors with warming fires at either end along with beautiful antiques. Guests rooms and suites are cheerfully decorated, and some have screened-in porches. For additional lodging, one cottage stands in the Warm Springs Historic District built of logs hewn in 1820.

Breakfast is served daily from a 1710 oak sideboard.

Corn Meal Muffins

Mix together:

2 tsp baking powder
1/2 tsp salt
2/3 cup stone ground yellow corn meal

1/4 cup sugar
1 (scant) cup flour, all-purpose or unbleached

Blend until frothy 1/2 cup buttermilk, 3/4 cup sour cream, 3/4 tsp baking soda, 2 medium eggs. Mix wet and dried ingredients together thoroughly to get a sticky dough. Using a cast iron muffin pan, pre-heat pan with dab of butter, then fill 2/3 full. Bake 25 minutes at 325°.

Box 110
Warm Springs, VA 24484
Tel. (703) 839-5959

SOUTHEAST

Mentone Inn, an old fashioned two-story home, is best described as "a touch of yesterday". Draped with awnings and an inviting front porch to sit on, the inn is located on beautiful Lookout Mountain, next door to the oldest building in Mentone, and near the Sally Howard Memorial, a structure built into a huge rock. Drives to Sequoyah Caverns, Little River Canyon, Desoto Park, and many Civil War sites are pleasant outings.

A full complimentary breakfast includes Honey Apple Crisp, Corn Souffle, Rice and Asparagus Casserole, and Crab Shrimp Mold.

Honey Apple Crisp

4 cups sliced apples	1/2 tsp salt
1/4 cup granulated sugar	1/2 cup butter
1 tbs lemon juice	1/2 cup honey
1 cup flour	1/2 cup packed brown sugar

Spread apples in a 1-1/2-qt baking dish. Sprinkle with granulated sugar and lemon juice. Pour honey over all. Mix flour, brown sugar, and salt in bowl and work in butter, making a creamy mixture. Spread over apples and bake at 375° for 40 minutes, or until apples are tender and crust is crisp and brown.

Box 284
Mentone, AL 35984
Tel (205) 634-4836 or 634-4108

SOUTHEAST

Mill Farm Inn

Mill Farm Inn sits on three-and-a-half acres of lovely landscaped grounds that drop off into the Pacelot River. This quaint two-story building is located in Tryon, a favorite resort since the days of the Gay Nineties when South Carolinians discovered its beauty and delightful climate. The area has been a cultural oasis for years and it has never been more alluring than today.

An inn since 1982, guests enjoy the homelike atmosphere of traditional furnishings and decor. The spacious living room warmed by a glowing fire, comfortable guest rooms, sitting porches, and light summer breezes are all comforts that guests remember.

A complimentary breakfast is served each morning in the dining room. Specialty Breads, English Muffins, Dry Cereals, Juice, Preserves, Coffee, Tea, and Milk are offered.

Brown Breakfast Bread

3 cups honey and 3 cups molasses, to which add and beat:

14 cups wheat flour	8 tsp baking soda
4 dashes salt	8 cups milk
8 tsp each ginger, cinnamon, allspice	
4 cups raisins stirring in 1 small jar orange marmalade	

Combine ingredients and preheat oven to 350°. Bake 2 hours in greased loaf pans. Makes 8 loaves. (Recipe may be cut accordingly for fewer loaves.)

Tyron, NC 28782
Tel (704) 859-6992

SOUTHEAST

- 140 -

The Nu-Wray Inn

The Nu-Wray Inn has been owned and operated for four generations by the Garrett family and has served mountain travelers since it opened its doors in 1833. High in the mountains of western North Carolina with a commanding backdrop of Mt. Mitchell, portions of the original log structure are still intact.

History abounds at Nu-Wray Inn with antique furnishings that include turn of the century hanging lamps, old framed pictures, ticking clocks, rich velvet Victorian settees and warming fireplaces. Guests sleep every night in the cool mountain air under blankets. The inn is listed as a National landmark.

Meals are served "Southernboard" family style while listening to the Reginaphone music box and the Steinway Duo-art player grand piano. An extensive Southern menu headlines its nationally famous Country Ham and Fried Chicken dinners.

Nu-Wray Baked Beans

Parboil yellow-eyed beans in which a piece of salt pork has been added. Be sure to pour off first water, cooking in second water until soft. Drain off water and mix small amount of freshly chopped raw tomatoes, green pepper, and onions. Add molasses, salt, and pepper to taste. Let salt pork remain in baking dish and place in oven. Cook until done.

Box 156
Burnsville, NC 28714
Tel (704) 682-2329

SOUTHEAST

OLD STONE INN

Old Stone Inn can trace its beginnings back to the 1790's and to the days when it was a stagecoach stop on the line between Lexington and Louisville. The inn is an excellent example of Kentucky's early stone architecture with walls 2 feet thick and, according to artist-historian Robert A. Powell, the stone used in its construction was hauled by ox carts from miles away in Nelson County. Legend says the National Landmark once played host to General Lafayette.

Open year around, Old Stone Inn has a reputation for serving superb food in a land where farms are as well manicured as the best of parks.

Although no overnight lodgings are offered, the inn has a homelike setting with colonial and Victorian antiques, colorful wallpaper, fireplaces, and old cabinets lined with dishes and other interesting memorabilia.

Meals are served in five dining rooms appointed with crisp white linens. Well-known Kentucky fare such as Country Ham, Fried Chicken, Corn Pudding, Baked Fish, and Homemade Rolls await the guest.

Stuffed Eggplant

1 large eggplant	1/2 cup water
1/2 tsp salt	1/4 cup chopped onion
1 tbs butter	1 tsp Worcestershire sauce
1 tbs chopped parsley	1-1/2 cups water
1 cup fine butter-type cracker crumbs	
1 can (10-1/2 oz) condensed cream of mushroom soup	

Slice off one side of eggplant and remove pulp to within 1/2 inch of skin. Dice removed pulp and place in saucepan. Add water and salt, simmering until eggplant is tender. Drain. Saute onion in butter until golden brown. Stir onion, mushroom soup, Worcestershire sauce, and all of the cracker crumbs except 2 tbs into eggplant pulp. Fill eggplant shell with mixture. Place eggplant in shallow baking pan and sprinkle top with reserved crumbs and parsley. Pour water into baking pan, baking in preheated 375 degree oven for 1 hour or until piping hot.

Simpsonville, KY 40067
Tel (502) 722-8882

SOUTHEAST

®ld Talbott Tavern

Old Talbott Tavern was licensed under Patrick Henry and has welcomed guests to Bardstown since 1779. Believed to be the oldest western stagecoach stop in America that has remained in continuous operation, its outside walls are rare examples of handwork, and each stone is faced with over two hundred chisel marks.

The guest register of this old inn reads like a history of our country. During the American Revolution, the town of Bardstown and Old Talbott Tavern hosted King Louis Phillipe who was sent there by George Washington. General George Rogers Clark, Abraham Lincoln, John J. Audubon, Stephen Foster, Kentucky frontiersman Daniel Boone, Queen Marie of Romania, and General George Patton have enjoyed Old Talbott Tavern's hospitality. Jesse James stayed at the inn and, according to legend, used lovely old murals painted in 1797 for target practice. The bullet holes are still there.

The seven guest rooms are furnished with antiques.

The dining room's limestone walls, dark ceiling beams, and plank floors are the perfect setting for this inn that is beginning its third century. The same good food that has been served to America's past is still prepared for today's guests. Kentucky Country Ham is a favorite.

How To Cook A Country Ham

Soak ham 48 hours, change water often, and scrub thoroughly after each change. Line roaster with heavy duty wide foil (in order to fold into a tent around ham). Do not let foil touch ham. Place ham fat side down on foil and seal carefully. Put in oven with butt-end near door. Bake at 350° 18 minutes per pound. Check bone for looseness when time is up. Bone moves easily when ham is done. Take out of foil and turn over. Take skin off. Cut fat 1/2'' in square or diamond pattern. Put mixture of equal parts stale bread crumbs and brown sugar over the fat. Dot with cloves. Put in 300° oven to brown crumbs. Slice very thinly.

107 West Stephen Foster
Bardstown, KY 40004
Tel (502) 348-3494

SOUTHEAST

Planters Inn

Planters Inn opens into the 18th century city market and blends the warmth and charm of a small inn with that of a grand hotel. The historic district in which it resides is a festive extension of Charleston's gracious hospitality, and horsedrawn carriage rides with a coachman versed in the history of its colorful past and present complete the enchantment.

The lobby, beautifully decorated with polished wood floors warmed by an oriental rug, dentil moulding, and a handsome fireplace attests to the quality of this fine inn. Forty-six guest rooms and suites revel in high ceilings, equally tall windows draped in festoons and swags, fine fabrics, mahogany four-posters, and full-length mirrors. Each room, naturally, is different. Bed turn down and a chocolate on the pillow await the tired guest. Shoes are returned by morning, freshly polished, along with a complimentary newspaper.

The Silks Restaurant, named for its colorful collection of racing silks and fine equestrian paintings, serves elegant meals of Game, Beef, Lamb, and Seafood topped off with very tempting desserts.

Raspberry Chevre Cheese Cake

Crust:

1/2 cup finely ground granola or graham crumbs	1/4 cup butter 2 tbs flour

Mix until combined and flatten into greased 10'' round cake pan, using pressure to obtain an even layer.

Fruit:

1-1/2 cups raspberries	1 tbs flour

Take raspberries and flour in bowl and mix until berries are completely covered with flour; place on top of the crust in pan and set aside.

Filling:

2 lbs mild chevre (goat) cheese	
1 lb cream cheese	7 eggs
2 tbs vanilla	1/2 tsp salt
1 cup sugar	2 cups milk
rind and juice of 1 medium lemon	

Mix chevre and cream cheese until smooth with electric mixer; add eggs one at a time until smooth, then add vanilla, sugar, salt, and juice and rind of lemon. Mix smoothly, slowly adding the milk until thoroughly combined. Pour on top of crust and berries and bake in a water bath for one hour at 325° or until lightly browned and springs back to the touch in the center. (Any fruit can be used in place of raspberries as long as fruit is not too juicy.)

112 North Market
Charleston, SC 29401
Tel (803) 722-2345

SOUTHEAST

Shaker Village of Pleasant Hill

Inn at Pleasant Hill, "We make you kindly welcome" best describes this once-utopian community that has maintained its traditions of good food and hospitality since early days. The village started in 1805 and flourished with a membership of nearly 500 believers before closing in 1910. Known for their industry and celibacy, these dedicated workmen have made a lasting statement in Kentucky's Bluegrass region.

Twenty-four very handsome, yet austere, buildings have been restored and placed on the National Register. Owned and operated by a nonprofit organization determined to preserve the simplicity and graciousness of the village builders, this living museum shows the art of broom-making, spinning, weaving, quilting, and candle-dipping to its guests. An added attraction is a cruise on the historic Kentucky River aboard the "Dixie Belle" paddlewheeler.

Because of the very simple nature of the original inhabitants, all the buildings have two front doors - one for men, the other for women - and the buildings are noted for their simple designs, colors, and rows of pegs lining the walls.

Three hearty "Shaker" meals are served in the Trustees House. Country Ham, Fried Chicken, Hot Breads, Garden Vegetables, and very tempting desserts are savored by guests.

Bread Pudding

about 4 cups stale bread	3 eggs
1/4 tsp salt	3 cups warm milk
1 tsp vanilla	1/2 cup sugar
1/2 tsp nutmeg	

Crumble stale bread. Soak for 20 minutes in milk and salt. Combine eggs, sugar, vanilla, and nutmeg; beat very well. Pour mixture over the bread; stir lightly. Steam tightly covered with foil in pan set in hot water for about 45 minutes at 350°. Cover with meringue and bake at 300° 15 minutes. Serve with Brown Sugar Sauce.

Brown Sugar Sauce for Bread Pudding

1/2 lb brown sugar	1/4 cup butter
1/4 cup flour	1/2 tsp vanilla
1 cup boiling water	

Mix sugar and flour well. Add boiling water. Cook mixture until thick. Remove from fire and add butter and vanilla.

Route 4
Harrodsburg, KY 40330
Tel (606) 734-5411

The Red Fox Tavern
Est.h.c. 1728

The Red Fox Tavern is a handsome stone structure that has long served as a center for historical events of both local and national prominence. The roster of famous guests is studded with the names of George Washington, governors, senators, foreign dignitaries, and on one occasion President John F. Kennedy gave a press conference in the Jeb Stuart Room.

It was established in 1728 and the original stone walls and fireplaces were restored in 1976. Luckily, the random-width floor boards, deep window sills, and doorjambs that tilt and slant from the settling of time remain as they were.

The guest rooms are furnished with antiques, braided rugs, and canopied beds complemented by documented wallpapers, fabrics, and paint colors of the 18th century. All the rooms have working fireplaces. A Washington Post each morning and bedside sweets complete the hospitality. A complimentary breakfast is offered.

Meals are served in seven dining rooms appointed with beamed ceilings, Windsor chairs, tavern tables, and 19th century sporting art. In the dinner hours a collection of antique copper utensils and pewterware sparkle by candlelight.

Scallops Pernod

2 lbs scallops	1 or 2 tsp Pernod
2 leeks	2 cups cream

Reduce cream slowly. In separate pan, sweat leeks until translucent. When completed, in hot pan with butter saute scallops quickly. Do not overcook. Splash with Pernod. Add cream, leeks, salt and pepper.

Box 385
Middleburg, VA 22117
Tel (703) 687-6301

SOUTHEAST

The Lodge at Renfro Valley

Renfro Valley Lodge has welcomed returning visitors to the beautiful hills of Kentucky with old-fashioned hospitality and family-style dinners since 1939.

Built by John Lair, founder of Renfro Valley Barndance and his wife Virginia, the hand-hewn log structure is like a throwback to the pioneer days. It is made up of several log cabins and a modern motel nicely furnished.

Across the street the old barn stands as an old friend reminding visitors of its colorful past. The hearty greeting, "Howdy folks, welcome to Renfro Valley Barndance" can still be heard after more than 50 years. The Renfro Valley troupe once performed at a White House party given in honor of the King and Queen of England.

Today, a handsome new barn theatre that seats 1,500 is open nightly except Sunday and Monday. And Renfro Valley Village with its grist mill and Victorian-style shops filled with love-ly arts & crafts to take back home are a treat.

The lodge is situated at the very edge of both the Bluegrass and the Cumberland Mountains where many historical and scenic sites are within an hours drive. Seasonal festivals with colorful quilts, fine State Parks and Shrines, canoeing on the Rockcastle River, Bluegrass Horse Farms, and eastern Kentucky Mountains are regularly enjoyed.

Meals are served boarding house style in three dining rooms with polished wood and rock floors, stone fireplaces, and hanging lamps. The menu includes Kentucky Country Ham, Seafood, Fried Chicken, Vegetables and tempting Desserts.

This chicken and dumpling recipe of Mrs. Chloe Smith's, former owner, has been a favorite at the lodge for over 30 years.

Chicken and Dumplings

7-1/2 cups plain flour   1/2 cup lard
3 eggs   water
1/2 stick butter

Sift flour into bowl. Break eggs in cup and beat. Mix butter, lard, and beaten eggs together in flour. Add enough water to make a firm dough. Knead dough on floured board and roll out 1/4'' thick and cut into 2'' squares. Start chicken in gallon of water with salt to taste. Cook until tender, take out of pot and debone. After thoroughly deboned, drop chicken back into broth and add 1/2 tsp of yellow food coloring. Drop dumplings into bubbling broth and cook ten minutes. Occasionally stir so that dumplings do not stick together on a slightly lower heat. These dumplings can be made ahead of time and frozen.

Renfro Valley, KY 40473
Tel (606) 256-2638

SOUTHEAST

Richmond Hill Inn

Richmond Hill Inn, located on a steep slope in the Blue Ridge Mountains, is an outstanding example of Queen Anne-style architecture. Built as the home of congressman and ambassador Richmond Pearson, this nationally registered landmark with its distinctive gables, turrets and bays, has been handsomely restored to its turn of the century grandeur and luxury.

The impressive entrance hall has rich oak paneling and a portrait of Gabrielle Pearson, painted in Paris in 1888, hangs over the fireplace. Twelve guest rooms are elegantly decorated with canopy beds, Victorian furniture and oriental rugs.

In addition to its outstanding views, charming cottages with fireplaces, porches and rocking chairs surround a manicured croquet courtyard. The guest houses are named for trees found in Western North Carolina.

A full complimentary breakfast is offered. Excellent meals are served in the dining room, or the less formal sun porch with its wicker, ceiling fans and spectacular outside views.

Sunday Brunch is enjoyed with classical favorites played on a grand piano.

Mountain Apple and Vidalia Onion Soup
with Aged Gruyere & Parmesan Cheeses

2 cups of beef stock	1 tsp salt
3 cups apple cider	1 tsp granulated sugar
1 bay leaf	1-1/2 or 2 tbs sherry
1 tsp fresh thyme leaves	24 large garlic croutons
1 tsp coarsely ground black pepper	1/2 cup grated Parmesan cheese
Salt to taste	1/2 cup grated Gruyere cheese
3 tbs butter	1 cup diced chilled North Carolina
2 lbs 8 oz Vidalia onions,	red apples
thinly sliced	Fresh chives, chopped

In a large pot, combine the first six ingredients and bring to a gentle boil. Reduce heat to simmer and cook for 1 hour. In a large skillet, melt the butter and sauté the onions for 3 to 5 minutes. Add the salt and sugar and sauté for 4 to 5 minutes more, or until the onions are browned and thoroughly cooked. Deglaze the skillet with the sherry and add the onion mixture to the cider mixture. Simmer for 1 hour. Ladle the soup into small, ovenproof soup bowls and top each serving with 3 garlic croutons. Divide both cheeses among the servings and place the bowls in the oven. Brown under the broiler for 1 to 2 minutes. Garnish with the diced apples and the chives and serve immediately. Yields 8 servings.

87 Richmond Hill Drive
Asheville, North Carolina 28806
Tel 704-252-7313

Rokeby Hall

Rokeby Hall is located in the city's old residential section, the historic South Hill district of downtown Lexington. The late 19th century-style structure dates back to 1812 when it was built by Samuel Potter, son of an early settler at the cost of three Merino sheep (then valued at twelve hundred dollars apiece). Its next owner was the Hon. George Robertson, Chief Justice of Kentucky who named it Rokeby Hall in 1836. Rescued from time and neglect by Beth Hipp Clifton and Jenny Dulworth in 1984, the gracious inn is now listed on the National Register of Historic Places.

The original elaborately handcrafted stairway rises from the entrance hall to upstairs guest rooms individually decorated and tastefully furnished with antiques and reproductions. Lofty windows, armoires, four-posters, and polished wood floors warmed by rose-colored rugs lend to the genuine hospitality. All but one room has an open fire. In keeping with its rich Bluegrass traditions, scenes of race horses are hung throughout the inn.

Lexington, a world-class horse town, is surrounded by miles of white fences, rolling pastures, and unparalleled farmland. Historic homes, such as Mary Todd Lincoln's (wife of the president), Henry Clay's, and Cassius Clay's imposing White Hall (which is nearby) are but a few of the many houses, farms, and plantations open to the public. Directly across from Rokeby Hall stands the oldest house in Lexington, and both Transylvania University and the University of Kentucky call Lexington home.

A Continental breakfast is served each morning in the formal dining room. The menu, naturally, features old-fashioned Kentucky morning favorites.

Biscuits

1 pkg dry yeast
1/4 cup warm water
1/8 cup sugar
1/2 cup shortening
1 cup buttermilk
1/2 tsp baking soda

1/2 tsp salt
2-3 cups flour
1 1/2 tsp baking powder

Dissolve yeast in warm water, setting aside. Mix dry ingredients, cutting in shortening as you would for pastry dough. Stir yeast mixture and buttermilk, blending thoroughly. If dough is sticky, mix in more flour. The dough is now ready to make biscuits or to be refrigerated. Place dough on floured surface, roll out, and cut with biscuit cutter. Place on greased pan and let rise 10 minutes, then bake 12-15 minutes until brown and done. If dough is taken from refrigerator, let set a little longer to rise. Serve with honey or powdered sugar on top.

318 South Mill Street
Lexington, KY 40508
Tel (606) 252-2368

SOUTHEAST

Science Hill

Science Hill Inn stands amidst ancient oaks and an old iron fence in downtown Shelbyville, Kentucky. The handsome red brick building with pillars and porches was a finishing school for young ladies from 1825 - 1939. The original portion dates back to the 1790s with additions that resulted in an interior courtyard. Science Hill Inn now houses Wakefield-Searce Galleries, known for its fine collection of English antiques and decorative silver. Although no overnight lodgings are provided, the specialty shops that line the court yard make the inn an attraction in itself. It is listed as a National Registered Landmark.

The Georgian-style dining room hosts Kentucky Fried Chicken, Kentucky Trout, and Brown Sugar Pie and Biscuit Pudding with Bourbon Sauce. The Science Hill Inn "Hot Brown" appeared in the April '84 edition of Early American Life.

Science Hill Inn Hot Brown

4 slices toast
Mornay sauce
8 slices fried bacon

4 slices cooked turkey breast
4 slices tomato
grated Parmesan cheese

In four individual dishes, place a slice of toast, top with turkey and two bacon slices. Cover with sauce, sprinkle with cheese, and top with tomato slice. Bake at 400 degrees for 10 minutes, until brown and bubbly.

Mornay Sauce

Melt 3 tbs butter, remove from heat, stir in 3 tbs flour and 2 cups milk. Bring to a boil, stirring. Simmer 2 minutes, beating in ¼ cup grated Gruyere or Cheddar cheese. Stir in ½ tsp mustard and season to taste.

525 Washington Street
Shelbyville, KY 40065
Tel (502) 633-2825

SOUTHEAST

THE 1735 HOUSE

The 1735 House is located on the sandy shores of Amelia Island, close to historic Fernandina Beach. Painted white with black shutters, this quaint clapboard building is filled with interesting antiques and views of the Atlantic Ocean. The common rooms are decorated with wicker and rattan.

Adjacent to the main inn stands the "Lighthouse" with four floors of memories that bring back the spirit and feeling of the early seacoast adventure. Between the inn and lighthouse is a good spot to surf cast.

Nearby activities abound, including day trips to Georgia's Okeefenokee Swamp, America's oldest city, St. Augustine, Florida, and many miles of historic shoreline.

A complimentary breakfast is left in a basket beside the guest's door each morning along with the morning news.

Sour Cream-Cinnamon Loaves

2 cups all-purpose flour
1 1/2 tsp baking powder
1 tsp baking soda
1/2 tsp salt
1 cup sugar
1/2 cup shortening
1 1/2 tsp finely shredded
orange peel

1 tsp vanilla
1 cup dairy sour cream
1/4 cup milk
1/4 cup sugar
2 tsp ground cinnamon
2 eggs

In mixing bowl stir together flour, baking powder, soda, and salt; set aside. In large mixer bowl cream together 1 cup sugar and the shortening until light and fluffy. Add eggs and vanilla; beat well. Blend in sour cream and milk. Add flour mixture to sour cream mixture; mix well. Spread 1/4 of batter in each of two greased 7 1/2 x 3 12 x 2 inch loaf pans. Combine the 1/4 cup sugar, the cinnamon, and shredded orange peel. Sprinkle all but 1 tbs sugar-cinnamon mixture over batter in pans. Top each with half of remaining batter. Cut through batter gently with knife to make swirling effect with cinnamon. Sprinkle with remaining sugar-cinnamon mixture. Bake at 350° 35-40 minutes. Cool in pans 10 minutes, then remove and cool thoroughly on wire racks. Makes 2 small loaves.

584 South Fletcher Avenue
Amelia Island, FL 32034
Tel 1 (904) 261-5878

SOUTHEAST

Smith House, known for its family-style dining and old-fashioned hospitality, is a throwback to the friendly boarding house of 1922 when Henry and Bessie Smith charged $1.50 a day for room and board. The clapboard structure was built as the home of Captain Hall and sits right on top of a rich gold vein.

The inn has been enlarged over the years and is easily recognized by its old shade trees and inviting porches. Bountiful meals have been served to visitors from all over the United States and some foreign countries. Today, its rich tradition of operating as a simple mountain inn continues. The guest rooms are comfortable and have a pleasant nostalgic feel. Within walking distance, there is a museum that tells a story of the early gold rush days.

Meals are served family style at large tables laden with food from recipes dating back to the founding of Smith House. It is a "seeing is believing" experience. The varied menu includes huge platters of Fried Chicken, Sweet Baked Ham, Fried Steak, and twelve to fourteen different vegetables topped off wth a fruit cobbler.

Broccoli and Rice Casserole

2 pkgs frozen broccoli	1/4 cup water
1 can cream of mushroom soup	1/2 cup milk
1 cup cooked rice	1 onion, finely chopped
1/2 stick margarine	1/2 cup grated cheese or spread

Cook broccoli accordng to package directions; drain, cool, and chop. Saute onion in margarine. Mix broccoli with other ingredients and bake in greased casserole at 350⁰ for 30 minutes.

202 South Chestatee
Dahlonega, GA 30533
Tel (404) 864-3566

SOUTHEAST

St. Francis Inn

St. Francis Inn is a classic example of Old World architecture that has been a part of St. Augustine's history for more than 200 years. The Spanish-style entrance faces a courtyard filled with lush banana trees, bougainvillaea, jasmine, and other tropical flowers and shrubs. Guests enjoy the relaxed ambiance of the inn that has attracted visitors from far and near including artists, writers, and some nobility. Although several additions have been made, the atmosphere remains very old and the hospitality is great.

The foyer has a hand-carved stairway that sweeps to the second and third floors. Guest rooms are airy and decorated in a variety of styles. Some of the rooms offer balconies with rockers and swings overlooking beautiful gardens. A statue of St. Francis greets you as you enter the lobby.

St. Francis Inn Apple Butter

2 pecks apples	12 cups sugar
1 gallon sweet cider	2 tbs cinnamon
1/2 tsp ground cloves	

Quarter and core apples, cooking with cider to soften. Stir often. Put through sieve and place in an iron kettle or large pot. Add rest of ingredients and cook over outdoor fire for 3 or more hours to taste, stirring often. Seal in jars, serving on favorite bread.

279 St. George Street
St. Augustine, FL 32084
Tel (904) 824-6068

The Strawberry Inn

The Strawberry Inn is one of many fine Federal period architectural gems in New Market. The historic town was founded in 1793 and laid out by William Plummer and Nicholas Hall. From the very beginning, New Market made its living from travelers, and those services to travelers lasted until the end of the horse and buggy era. Today, referred to as the "antique capital of Maryland", New Market welcomes another type of traveler: the antique collector.

The inn has been restored to its former self, and the guest rooms are fittingly furnished with antiques, within easy walking distance of all antique shops. Mealy's home of fine food is just across the street and takes up residence in an old hotel that has served the town since the early 1880's. A Continental breakfast is served on trays at the guest's door at requested times.

Raisin Bran Muffins

4 eggs, slightly beaten	1 qt buttermilk
1 cup hot water	2 cups granulated sugar
1 15-oz box Raisin Bran cereal	1 cup margarine, melted

Mix in very large bowl until blended, combining with:

5 cups flour, white, whole wheat, or blend of both	
5 tsp baking soda	2 tsp salt

Bake at 400 degrees for 15-20 minutes. Store remaining batter tightly covered in refrigerator until needed (may be refrigerated for up to four weeks). Makes 4 to 5 dozen.

Box 237, 17 Main Street
New Market, MD 21774
Tel (301) 865-3318

SOUTHEAST

Casa de Solana

Casa de Solana is the fourteenth oldest house in this country's oldest city. It was built by Don Manuel Solana in 1763 of coquina with high ceilings, dark hand-hewn beams and pegged floors. The woodwork, doors, and window frames have been painted "haint blue," an old Southern custom believed to ward off evil spirits.

The rooms are filled with antiques, including cut glass, chandeliers, gilded mirrors, marble hearths, brass, and iron. Guest rooms have four-posters or brass beds, fireplaces, and balconies overlooking beautiful gardens or historic and colorful Matanzas Bay. The attached Carriage House provides bright and colorful lodging. Typical of old St. Augustine, a wall separates the grassy yard from the ancient, cobblestoned streets.

Breakfast is served each morning at 8:30. The formal dining room is furnished with a ten foot long mahogany table, elegant china, crystal, and flatware. Offerings include Eggs, Grits, Homemade Breads, Fresh Fruit, Juices, and Coffee.

Arroz con Langostinos
(Rice with shrimp)

2 lbs shrimp
2 cans chicken stock
1/2 cup celery tops, chopped
1 whole clove garlic
2 medium tomatoes
1/4 tsp cariander
1/2 tsp turmeric
1/4 tsp cummin
1 small can English peas
pinch seasoned pepper

1/2 tsp seafood seasoning
1/4 cup olive oil
4 green onions
1 bell pepper
1 1/2 cups white rice
1 can mushrooms
1 small jar pimientos
1/2 cup olives
2 bay leaves
salt & pepper to taste

Peel shrimp and put peelings in two cans chicken stock with celery tops, chopped clove of garlic, chopped tomatoes, adding cariander, cummin, bay leaves, seasoned pepper, and seafood seasoning. Bring to boil and let simmer at low heat while preparing in large frying pan 1/4 cup olive oil, green onions, and chopped bell pepper. Cook slowly until done. Add 1/2 cup white rice, stirring, and rest of rice, allowing to become clear looking. Add strained broth into rice mixture. Add 1 can mushrooms (no juice), pimientos, 1/2 cup chopped olives; add shrimp (leaving some of shrimp whole and with tail on for decoration) which have been cut up into large chunks. Add pinch of turmeric for color and can of English peas, salt and pepper. Allow to cook at low temperature for about 1/2 hour. Garnish with chopped green onions. With tossed green salad with light creamy dressing serves hearty portions to 6.

21 Aviles Street
St. Augustine, FL 32084
Tel 1 (904) 824-3555

SOUTHEAST

THE Tidewater Inn

The Tidewater Inn, where both the social and business affairs of friendly Easton revolve, is a handsome Federal-style structure, located in the historic district. Tree lined streets are filled with old homes and sites that date back to colonial times. The Third Haven Meeting House built by Quakers in 1682 and believed to be the oldest wooden house of worship in continuous use, is within walking distance.

Rich in history, the area also offers many outdoor sports. Just twelve miles away is one of America's deep water ports, and of equal distance is a maritime museum.

A warming fireplace, comfortable furnishings, and a sweeping stairway define the main lobby. A hundred and twenty rooms and suites await the guests with service and hospitality seldom found in today's busy world. Movies across the street and swimming in the outdoor pool are added pleasures.

An extensive menu of food of the Eastern Shore is presented in the seven dining rooms.

Crab Imperial

1 lb crab meat	4 tbs mayonnaise
3/4 tsp Worcestershire	1/4 tsp salt
dash Louisiana Hot sauce	1 egg
pinch each of thyme, oregano,	dry mustard, Accent

Mix all ingredients, adding crab meat last. Coat a casserole lightly with mayonnaise and fill with crab mixture. Spread a thin layer of mayonnaise over top and sprinkle with paprika and parsley. Bake at 350° for 15-20 minutes. Serves 4.

Escalloped Oysters

1 qt oysters	2 tbs butter
3 cups crushed saltines	salt and pepper
1 tsp chicken bouillon	(granulated type)

Mix crushed saltine with salt, pepper, and chicken bouillon. In a casserole, alternately layer cracker mixture and oysters making last layer of cracker mix. Melt butter and add with enough milk to cover. Sprinkle with parsley and paprika. Bake at 325° for 35 minutes. Serves 4-6.

Easton, MD 21601
Tel (301) 822-1300

SOUTHEAST

VICTORIAN HOUSE

Victorian House was built in 1890 as a boarding house. The two-story clapboard structure stands adjacent to the Carriage House, which also provides delightful accommodations. During the last century, St. Augustine was a haven for wealthy Easterners, and today the lure is greater than ever with visitors from around the world.

Once inside, the feeling is very old with its high ceilings, paddle fans, heart pine floors, oriental rugs, and stenciled walls, a complement to the antique furnishings. The living room's old fashioned organ, antique dolls, lace, and velvet are reminders of this home's Victorian past. Guests sleep in canopied beds under hand-woven coverlets and quilts and, upon rising, place their feet on hooked rugs.

Within walking distance of the old city's fine restaurants, shops, numerous museums, and the ancient water front, guests stroll down streets where first Spanish, then English, Confederate, and American soldiers patrolled so many years ago.

A complimentary breakfast is served each morning.

Victorian House Granola

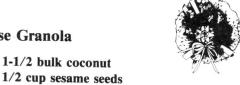

4 cups oatmeal	1-1/2 bulk coconut
1 cup chopped nuts	1/2 cup sesame seeds
1/2 cup bran	1 cup wheat germ
1 tbs cinnamon	1/2 cup corn oil
1 cup hulled sunflower seeds	1/2 tsp vanilla
1/2 cup honey	1/2 cup roasted & salted soybeans

Heat corn oil, honey and vanilla, adding to other ingredients and stirring well. Spread on oil sheets and bake at 325° for 30 minutes, stirring after 10 minutes. Add: raisins (light and dark), chopped dates and apricots. Store in air tight container or freeze.

11 Cadiz Street
St. Augustine, FL 32084
Tel. (904) 824-5214

SOUTHEAST

Vine Cottage Inn

Vine Cottage Inn is a Queen Anne-style house with gables and dormers near the Hot and Warm Springs in Virginia that date to 1761. The Allegheny Mountains are a sportsman's paradise abounding in deer, turkey, quail, bear and well-stocked trout streams. Hiking trails are steps away and so are carriage rides.

The inn has been almost entirely restored to the early 1900s period. Guest rooms are furnished in a variety of styles and some have sitting areas and private porches. Each reflects the quiet countryside.

A Continental breakfast is offered each morning. Homecooked meals are served in the dining room.

Zucchini Nibbles

1/2 cup Parmesan cheese	1/2 cup oil
1/2 cup finely chopped onion	3 tbs parsley
4 large eggs, slightly beaten	1 tsp salt
1/2 tsp baking powder	1/4 tsp oregano
1 clove finely chopped garlic	dash pepper
1 cup flour	3 cups grated zucchini

Mix all ingredients well. Spread in greased baking pan, baking at 350° 35 minutes. Cut into squares and serve warm.

Vine Cottage
Box 918
Hot Springs, VA 24445
Tel (703) 839-2422

SOUTHEAST

Von-Bryan Inn

Von-Bryan Inn can only be described as a lovely mountaintop retreat overlooking the agricultural landscape of Wears Valley and the Great Smokey Mountain National Park with majestic views at every turn.

Built as a private residence in 1986, the inn is made up of two authentic peeled log buildings. It welcomed its first visitors in the fall of 1988 and is open year round.

The main inn's living room is beautiful in a rustic setting of log walls, high open-beamed ceilings and a huge stacked rock fireplace. A piano for sing-alongs and a porch filled with rockers provide an atmosphere of old-fashioned hospitality.

Guest rooms are named after trees and furnished in eclectic styles accented with antiques and distinctive local works of art. The Red Bud is decorated in white and red featuring a large hot tub while the Blue Spruce is done in cool blues and beige. The Tulip Poplar is green and peach with a colorful quilt hanging on the wall. The White Oak is charming with wrought iron beds and white lacey wicker. Each spacious room has its own sitting area flooded with spectacular outside views. In addition to the Guest House, there is a swimming pool and library.

The area abounds in wildlife and hiking paths lead right from the front door. Nearby activities include golf, fishing, excellent restaurants and quaint shops in Pigeon Forge, Dollywood, and Gatlinburg. Just across the mountain puts the visitor on the Cherokee Qualla Indian Reservation and the drama,"Unto These Hills."

A full complimentary breakfast is offered each morning in the dining room.

Russian Chicken
2 whole chickens or 4 lbs. boneless chicken breasts
Wash and pat dry, place in shallow baking dish.
Mix together and pour over chicken:
1 bottle of 8 oz. Russian salad dressing
1 jar 16 oz. apricot preserves
1 envelope onion soup mix (dry)
Bake uncovered 325° for 1 1/2 hrs. or until done.
Serve over brown wild rice or any of the Country Inn rice dishes. Serves 12 to 14

Honey Mustard Dressing
1 cup mayonnaise (good grade)
1/4 cup honey
1/4 cup oil
1/4 cup Dijon style mustard
1 TBS red wine vinegar
dash onion salt
pinch of red pepper

Makes approximately 2 cups dressing.

Rt. 7 Box 91A
Sevierville, TN 37862
Tel (615) 453-9832

SOUTHEAST

Wayside Inn

Wayside Inn was best summed up by a traveling 19th century Englishman who noted in his diary, "Bless me, I must be in Virginia." Operated as a stagecoach stop and tavern, the inn has welcomed travelers with good food and lodging since 1797. Luckily, it was spared the ravages of Stonewall Jackson's famous Valley Campaign that swept close by.

In coaching days a young servant was sent to a nearby hill to wait for a cloud of dust. Rushing back with the news, a hot meal would be ready by the time the stage arrived. Except for these changes, expansions, and refurbishing, the inn remains much the same as when it attracted bounce-weary passengers long ago.

The guest rooms provide traditions of heritage with beautiful antiques, objects d'art, paintings, chests, and tables. Some of the rooms have canopied beds and fireplaces.

Meals are served in seven dining rooms. Waiters and waitresses in colonial costumes serve to reinforce the centuries-old charm. A favorite spot is the Old Slave Kitchen that dates back to 1742. The interesting menu serves up favorites of early travelers, including Peanut Soup, Pan Fried Chicken, and Spoonbread.

Wayside's Own Peanut Soup

1 stalk celery, cut up
1 cup creamy peanut butter
1 13-oz can evaporated milk or
light cream

1 medium onion, cut up
dash sugar
3-1/2 cups chicken broth
carrots, cut up

In large pan combine broth, celery, carrot, and onion. Bring to boil; reduce heat. Cover and simmer 15 minutes or until vegetables are tender. Strain, discarding vegetables. In same saucepan, gradually stir the hot broth into peanut butter. (Mixture may stiffen at first, but will become smooth.) Add evaporated milk and dash of sugar. Heat through, but DO NOT BOIL.

7783 Main Street
Middletown, VA 22645
Tel (703) 869-1797

SOUTHEAST

Wells Inn

Wells Inn, erected in 1894 by Ephraim Wells, grandson of the founder of Sistersville, West Virginia was operated by the same family for four generations. Sistersville was a booming oil town at the turn of the century, and during these flourishing times it played a rich part in hosting both the business and entertainment worlds. The inn was restored in 1965 to its former self and is now owned by the Spectrum Petroleum Corporation. It is listed on the National Register of Historic Places.

The interior has the original mahogany woodwork, colorful Victorian furnishings, and interesting memorabilia. A tall grandfather clock, an old-fashioned leaded phone booth, old pictures, a piano and a fountain in the center of the lobby lend credibility to its past. Guest rooms are at home with brass beds and period pieces.

Meals are served in the main dining room furnished with an old sideboard. Three hearty meals are prepared each day.

Wells Inn Chocolate Treat

1 cup flour
1 stick oleo

1 cup chopped nuts

Mix together. Pat down in long pyrex dish and bake at 350° for 20 minutes. Cool. Cream together:

1 cup Cool Whip
1 8 oz pkg cream cheese

1 cup powdered sugar

Spread on cooled crust. Next, mix together:

1 small pkg vanilla pudding
1 small pkg chocolate pudding

3 cups milk

Spread over second mixture and top with Cool Whip and grated chocolate. Chill before serving.

316 Charles Street
Sistersville, WV 26175
Tel (304) 652-1312

SOUTHEAST

Westcott House

Westcott House enjoys a spectacular view of the Bridge of Lions and the beautiful and historic Matanzas Bay with its colorful sailing vessels moored almost street-side. Built in the 1800s as the home of Dr. Westcott, prominent in establishing the St. John's Railroad and Intra-Coastal Waterway, this picture-book inn is painted a soft pink with blue shutters and provides lodging in the very image of grace and elegance.

Inside, furnishings include American and English antiques and reproductions. The colors of blue and white with splashes of rose accents are at once both cool and warm. Guest rooms with polished wood floors, oriental rugs, chandeliers, brass, china, and crystal have outstanding views of Americas's oldest city. Bed turn down with a chocolate on the pillow is an added touch.

A Continental breakfast is served each morning inside the Victorian porch or lush courtyard. Coffee, Juice, and Pastries are offered. Especially good are the Croissants and Wienerbrod, a Danish pastry.

Wienerbrod

1-3/4 cups milk
1/3 cup sugar
3 beaten eggs
1 tsp salt
2 cakes compressed yeast or 2 pkgs dry yeast
6 cups sifted all-purpose flour

1/4 cup warm water
1-1/4 cups butter
1 tsp ground cardamom

Heat milk to lukewarm. Add yeast to water, following package directions. Let stand few minutes, then stir until dissolved. Add yeast to milk with sugar, 1/4 cup melted butter, eggs, seasoning, and 2 cups flour. Beat very well, then mix in remaining flour and knead until smooth. Let rise until doubled in bulk, about 1 hour. Punch down and roll into rectangle. Knead 1 cup butter until smooth but not too soft; form into a flat, square cake. Put in center of dough and fold each side over it, pressing down at the edges to seal. Give dough a half turn, again rolling into rectangle, and fold as before. Repeat. Wrap in plastic or foil and chill 15 minutes. (Do not let butter get too hard or it will break through dough when rolled.) Roll, fold, turn, and chill three more times. Dough is now ready to be used. Roll 1/8" thick, and cut as desired, either into crescents, turnovers, or bear claws. For crescents, cut into 5" squares, cut into halves diagonally, and put a spoonful of jam, preserves, almond paste, or applesauce on each triangle; roll, starting at the long side. Turn ends in slightly to form crescent and put on greased cookie sheet. Chill for couple hours before baking. Brush with beaten egg and put in preheated hot (425°) oven, reducing heat at once to moderate (350°). Bake 15 minutes, or until nicely browned.

46 Avenida Menendez
St. Augustine, FL 32084
Tel (904) 824-4301

SOUTHEAST

Williamsburg Lodge is a rambling building with shaded verandas and restful gardens bordering the historic area of Colonial Williamsburg. And it stands directly across from the Golden Horseshoe Golf Course.

To visit Williamsburg is to take a step back to the days of the 18th-century with its warm red brick walks, carriage rides, and faithfully restored buildings. Thanks to the Colonial Williamsburg Foundation, ''that the future may learn from the past'', these handsome old structures include Court House 1770, Chowning's Tavern 1773, King's Arms, and the Williamsburg Inn.

Meals are served in the Bay Room. The menu includes Eastern Shore Chowder, Chicken Tetrazzini, Pumpkin Soup, Blueberry Crisp, and Hot Fruit Compote. The famous Chesapeake Bay Feast is offered on Fridays and Saturdays.

Gravad Lax

1 side North Pacific Fresh Pink Salmon	1/4 cup Pernod (for aniseed flavor)
2 tbs finely chopped fresh dill	1 qt vegetable salad oil
1/2 cup wine vinegar	1 tbs coarse salt
1 tsp crushed black pepper	1 tbs finely chopped fennel

Rub into both sides of salmon the dill, fennel, salt, and pepper. Blend other ingredients and cover salmon with mixture. Marinate under refrigeration (38⁰) for 48 hours. Slice thinly. Serve with Danish Pumpernickel, Cream Cheese, Capers, and finely chopped Bermuda Onions.

Box 13
Williamsburg, VA 23187
Tel (804) 229-1000

SOUTHEAST

Anchuca, a stately two-story mansion, is where confederate president Jefferson Davis delivered a speech from the front balcony. Built in 1830 and within walking distance of the Old Courthouse Museum and downtown historic Vicksburg, the inn is a classic example of Greek Revivalism, a style that was prevalent in the pre-Civil War South.

Now on the National Register of Historic Places and simply filled with magnificent antiques and gas-burning chandeliers, Anchuca can only be described as a repository for rich, ornate, colorful furnishings not often found in homes today. Anchuca is, without a doubt, an historical and romantic antebellum mansion.

Although there are no overnight lodgings in the main house, accommodations are provided in the original slave quarters and in the turn-of-the-century Guest Cottage located on the grounds. A tour of beautiful Anchuca is given the guest.

A complimentary breakfast is served in the dining room of this 4-diamond inn with lots of Southern friendliness.

Overnight Coffee Cake

1 cup sugar
1 8-oz carton sour cream
1 tsp baking powder
1/2 tsp salt
1/2 cup chopped pecans
3/4 cup butter, softened
3/4 cup firmly packed brown sugar

2 eggs
2 cups all-purpose flour
1 tsp soda
1 tsp ground nutmeg
1 tsp ground cinnamon

Combine butter and sugar, cream until light and fluffy. Add eggs and sour cream, mixing well. Combine next 5 ingredients, adding to batter and mixing well. Pour into greased and floured 13 x 9 x 2 baking pan. Combine brown sugar, pecans and cinnamon, mixing well and sprinkling evenly over batter. Cover and chill overnight. Uncover and bake at 350 degrees for 35-40 minutes until cake tests done.

1010 First East
Vicksburg, MS 39180
Tel (601) 636-4931

SOUTHCENTRAL

Annies

Annie's, an elegant Victorian inn with decorative porches, balconies, handcrafted touches, and seven magnificent gables, is truly a step back in time. It was named after prominent Big Sandy citizen George Alexander Tohill and is known by the locals as The Tohill House.

The original structure, built in 1901 by W.B. Mask for his wife, Annie, remains intact and houses the parlor and dining room. Painted blue with white trim, the house is surrounded by beautiful flower and rock gardens and a white picket fence.

Inside, ornate chandeliers, elegant wallpaper, and over 13-ft. ceilings grace the old-fashioned home. Guest rooms are colorful and decorated in a variety of styles that include antique iron, brass, and wooden beds. Other amenities are handmade quilts, armoires, sofas, and a small refrigerator that doubles as a nightstand. A bouquet of fresh flowers welcomes each visitor.

Afternoon tea is served along with a tempting dessert. Waitresses in turn-of-the-century costumes serve fine country cuisine each day in Annie's Tea Room on delicate china.

Stuffed French Toast

1 8-oz pkg softened cream cheese
1 16-oz loaf French bread
1 cup chopped pecans
1 tsp ground nutmeg
1/2 cup orange juice
12-ozs (1½ cups) apricot preserves

1 cup crushed pineapple
4 eggs
1 cup whipping cream
1/2 tsp vanilla

Beat together cream cheese and pineapple until fluffy. Stir in nuts and set aside. Cut bread into 10 1½-inch slices; cut a pocket in the top of each. Fill each with 1½ tbs cheese mixture. Beat together eggs, whipping cream, vanilla, and nutmeg. Using tongs, dip the filled bread slices in egg mixture, being careful not to squeeze the filling. Cook onlightly greased griddle until both sides are golden. Mix together the preserves and juice and heat. To serve, drizzle the apricot/juice mixture over the hot French Toast.

107 North Tyler
Big Sandy, TX 75755
Tel (214) 636-4952

ASPHODEL PLANTATION

Asphodel Plantation, called by Lysle Saxon "the jewel of Louisiana", is an elegant example of the Greek Revival period and was built in 1820-1833 by Benjamin Kendrick as a gift to his wife, Caroline.

Although Asphodel is a museum open for tours only, several guest houses scattered along the 500-acre estate providing lodging are a realization of a dream that took the Couhigs 15 years to achieve. Two of the buildings are very old, and the Inn, which dates back to the 1780s, was moved from Jackson in three pieces. The film "The Long Hot Summer" was shot on the grounds.

The area is filled with antebellum mansions, historic sites, flowering magnolias, and egrets, which are characteristic of its varied wildlife. Nearby stands a Civil War memorial and site of the longest battle in American history.

A full complimentary breakfast is offered each morning, and meals served at the Inn revolve around Cajun and Creole cooking.

Crab Corn Soup

1 pkg frozen hard crabs or frozen king crab
1/2 lb crab meat (clay or white lump,) canned or fresh
1 cup chopped green onions, including tops
2 cups water
2 cups whole milk
2 cans cream-style white corn
1/4 cup flour

1/2 stick butter
salt & pepper

Rinse crab and break into small pieces. If using king crab, cut into inch-long pieces complete with shell. Boil in 2-3 cups seasoned water. Melt butter in heavy saucepan. Add flour and cook until it is softened. Add milk and stir until sauce thickens. Add the hard crabs and water in which they were boiled. Add corn, salt, and pepper. Cook and stir until well blended. Before serving, add crab meat. Heat to boiling and serve in heated bowls with a sprinkling of chopped parsley for garnish.

Route 2, Box 89
Jackson, LA
Tel (504) 654-6868

BORGMAN'S BED & BREAKFAST

Borgman's Bed and Breakfast is a comfortable 19th century home located in historic Arrow Rock, a bustling river town during the 1880s. At this old-fashioned inn, there are four spacious cheery guest rooms from which to choose.

The sitting room is an ideal place to relax and features a wind-up Victrola, games, puzzles, and a library. And grandma's trunk holds all kinds of handcrafted items just waiting to be discovered.

Within easy walking distance to all points of interest, guests enjoy the quiet village that tells the story of days past.

A complimentary breakfast is served each morning that includes Fresh Baked Breads, Juice, Fruit, Coffee and Tea.

Divinity Candy

Have ready 4 egg whites at room temperature. Beat stiff. When eggs are foamy add ½ tsp cream of tartar. Boil to 250 degrees the following mixture:

4 cups sugar
1 cup water   **1 cup white syrup**

Beat egg whites continuously as you slowly add ½ of the above boiled mixture. Boil the rest of the syrup mixture to 280 degrees. Again beat egg white mixture as you slowly add the rest of the boiled syrup mixture and add vanilla. Let set until cool. Beat occasionally, and should lose glossy look. Drop with spoon on waxed paper.

Highway 41
Arrow Rock, MO 65320
Tel (816) 837-3350

SOUTHCENTRAL

The Burn has a fine history as well as exceptional architecture. The front porch of the Greek Revival Mansion is supported by huge Doric columns and the paneled doorway is framed in sidelights of early glass.

Once the headquarters for Federal troops and later a hospital for Union soldiers, horses trod where a priceless collection of antiques and fine paintings now reside. The entrance hall's unusual spiral stairway, New York Empire furnishings, and a shimmering chandelier attest to the elegance of The Burn.

Rooms are lavishly furnished with carved four-poster canopied beds, fireplaces, crocheted bed spreads, Aubusson carpets, velvet chairs, and draperies of Belgian fabrics. The formal dining room is appointed with matching Regency servers, and the table is adorned with old Paris china.

In all its splendor and charm, overnight guests are pampered with a seated plantation breakfast, private tour of the home, and lots of Southern hospitality.

Breakfast Cake

1 pkg yellow cake mix	3/4 cup corn oil
1 pkg vanilla instant pudding	3/4 cup water
1 tsp butter extract	4 eggs
1 tsp vanilla	1/2 cup chopped pecans
1/2 cup raisins	

Grease pan and sprinkle with nuts. Combine cake mix and pudding. Add oil and water. Mix well. Add eggs, one at a time, mixing well after each addition. Add flavorings. Beat 6 minutes at high speed. Layer batter in thirds, with nut-raisin-cinnamon-sugar filling between, starting and ending with batter. Make first layer just a little thicker than the other two. Bake at 350 degrees for 40-45 minutes. Remove from oven and cool 10 minutes. Turn out and glaze with 1/2 cup powdered sugar, 2 tbs milk, 1 tbs butter, and 1/2 tsp vanilla.

Nut-Raisin-Cinnamon-Sugar Mixture

1/2 cup sugar	2 tsp cinnamon
1/3 cup nuts	1/3 cup raisins

712 North Union Street
Natche, MS 39120
Tel (601) 442-1344

The Columns can trace its beginnings back to 1883 when it was built as the home of a wealthy tobacco merchant. Its history as one of the finest small hotels in New Orleans actually began sometime during the 1940's and until 1915 the building was a private residence before converting to an exclusive boarding house. Near other pre-Civil War mansions constructed by early settlers, this National Landmark is located in the heart of the city's finest residential section: the fashionable historic Garden District on St. Charles Avenue. The St. Charles streetcar that rolls in front transports passengers within minutes of the famous Old French Quarter, Canal Street, parks, universities, and elegant shopping.

A Victorian lounge, carved mahogany stairwell, magnificent stained glass panels, skylights and windows bring back memories of the Victorian days of New Orleans in the 1880's.

A Continental breakfast and newspaper is offered each morning.

Eggplant St. Claire

4 eggplant halves, peeled and hollowed

Oyster Sauce made with:

**8 oysters
1 pint heavy cream
chicken base to taste
1 tsp Worcestershire sauce
garlic to taste
pinch of thyme**

**4 peeled shrimp
1 pint oyster water
chablis to taste
2 ozs chopped green
onions
3 tbs cornstarch**

Crabmeat filling made with:

**2 ozs crabmeat
7 ozs chopped parsley
pinch Seafood Seasoning**

**1 tbs whipped cream
pinch garlic**

Seafood Seasoning:

**10 oz salt
4 oz thyme
4 oz oregano
3 ozs black pepper**

**8 oz paprika
8 oz granulated garlic
2 oz cayenne**

Preheat fryer to 320 degrees. Flour, eggwash, and roll eggplant in bread crumbs. Deep fry 5 minutes (2-1/2 minutes on each side). Mix all ingredients of crabmeat filling and heat in sauce pan until hot. Heat heavy cream and oyster water to boil. Add white wine, chicken base, thyme, green onions, Worcestershire sauce. Add water to cornstarch until thickened. Add oysters and shrimp to sauce and remove from heat. Set deep-fried eggplant on individual plates. Fill each portion with hot crab filling and top with oyster sauce. Sprinkle with chopped parsley. Serves 4

3811 St. Charles Avenue
New Orleans, LA 70115
Tel (504) 899-9308

SOUTHCENTRAL

Crystal River Inn

Crystal River Inn was built in 1884 as the home of Judge William Daniel Wood and his wife, Jane. Elegantly restored, this Victorian mansion has served as a gracious inn since 1984. During the following decade two nearby buildings were also restored, and a rose garden centers the complex.

The original four guest rooms, named after Hill Country rivers, are decorated in class and style. The Pedernales is warm and folksy, filled with antiques and done in blue and peach, while the Frio is spacious with a fireplace, wicker and primitives decorated in shades of blue and white. The Colorado is warmed with desert colors and Indian rugs. The most elegant is the Medina room (honeymoon suite) with white on white and has fourteen foot ceilings, fireplace, and rich antique satins. Fresh flowers and potpourri complete the hospitality.

Visitors to Crystal River Inn may select from two options: non-stop activity, or doing nothing. The hammock beside the fountain in the courtyard is a good spot to relax, while nearby activities include antique hunting, fishing, and tubing and canoeing on the San Marcos River.

Southwestern Brunch Eggs

10 eggs	1/2 cup flour
1 tsp baking powder	1 tsp salt
1 lb Monterey Jack	1-1/2 cups cottage cheese
8 oz chopped green chilis	1 stick melted butter

Beat eggs well, whisk in salt, baking powder, and flour. Fold in shredded Monterey Jack, then cottage cheese and chilis. Finally, stir in melted butter and bake in greased and floured 9 x 13 casserole at 350 degrees for 35-40 minutes. We serve topped with Pico de Gallo (salsa) and a sprig of cilantro.

326 West Hopkins
San Marcos, TX 78666
Tel (512) 396-3739

SOUTHCENTRAL

Dairy Hollow House is a charming 4-star inn where guests enter through an old-fashioned flower garden. The small Ozark farmhouse, expanded a little and restored by the innkeepers, was built sometime around 1880 and opened its doors to visitors in 1981.

The large open beamed parlor has a stone fireplace and lots of comfortable sofas and chairs to relax in. Seven guest rooms are furnished with antiques appropriate to the style of the house. The original two rooms are the Rose Room, which is decorated in warm tones of rose, pink and raspberry, while the Iris Room is filled with shades of blue. Each guest room is quite different with fresh flowers lending an added touch..."the height of unpretentious luxury," wrote Ted Parkhurst of Little Rock, Arkansas.

A delicious breakfast "unmatched anywhere" said the Arkansas Gazette, is served each morning at 9 in the comfort of the summer parlor. Dinner for guests are a feast. The innovative and original cuisine that blends the best of French and New America includes Mushrooms Diablo in Filo, Chicken Fricasee with Herbs, Apricot-Glazed Cornish Hen, Supreme of Vegetable and Olive Soup Eureka, Poke Salat, and a Chocolate-Mocha Dream Torte that was featured in CHOCOLATIER MAGAZINE.

Dairy Hollow House Gingerbread Muffins

Preheat oven to 375 degrees and combine:
> **1-1/2 cups unbleached flour**
> **3/4 cup sugar**
> **2 tsp ginger**   **1 tsp cinnamon**

Cut in until crumbly:
> **1/2 cup butter or shortening, setting aside 1/4 of this mixture for topping, adding 3/4 cup chopped walnuts. To the remaining flour-shortening mixture, add 1 egg and 3 tbs blackstrap molasses.**

Dissolve:
> **1 tsp baking soda and 1/2 tsp salt in 1 cup buttermilk. Stir buttermilk mixture into molasses-flour mixture and, when blended, stir in 1/2 cup raisins.**

Spoon batter into well-greased muffin tins, filling two thirds full. Sprinkle with reserved topping. Bake 15 minutes. May be served with ice cream or whipped cream.

Rt 2, Box 1
Eureka Springs, AR 72632
Tel (501) 253-7444

In Continuous Operation Since the 1850's

EXCELSIOR HOUSE

ACCOMMODATIONS FIRST CLASS.

SAMPLE ROOMS FOR COMMERCIAL TRAVELERS.

Excelsior House served the sprawling lusty river town of Jefferson when it was built by Captain William Perry and has been in continuous operation since the late 1850s. A colorful figure of early Jefferson, Perry's daughter Lucy was the first white child born in the town.

During Jefferson's heyday, many of the famous Mardi Gras-type "Queen Mab" balls were held in the beautifully appointed drawing and dining rooms. Notables who have been the hotel's guests include Presidents Rutherford B. Hayes and Ulysses S. Grant, industrialists John Jacob Astor and W.H. Vanderbilt, Oscar Wilde, and Jay Gould, who signed his name in the register with a jay bird sketch.

The brick and timber structure was restored in 1954 by Mrs. Estella Peters and is now operated by the Jessie Allen Wise Garden Club. Guest rooms are furnished with maple, cherry, and mahogany marble-topped dressers and spool beds.

The Jay Gould family's private railroad car "Atalanta" stands just across the street.

Excellent meals are served from recipes handed down from generation to generation. Chicken Excelsior House, Shrimp Creole, Swedish Ham Balls with Brown Sauce, and delightful desserts are part of the available fare.

Beets in Orange Sauce

2 tbs cornstarch	3tbs sugar
2 tbs beet juice	1/2 tsp salt
1 cup orange juice	2 tbs grated orange rind
4 tbs lemon juice	2 tbs vinegar
2 cans (1 lb 4 oz each) baby beets, drained	
1/4 cup butter or margarine	

Mix cornstarch with beet juice in sauce pan. Add orange juice, lemon juice, and vinegar. Cook, stirring constantly, until clear and thickened. Stir in butter, sugar, salt, and orange rind. Add beets. Heat. Serves 6.

Jefferson, TX 75657
Tel (214) 665-2513

SOUTHCENTRAL

Laborde House

Laborde House is one block from the river in Rio Grande City, Texas. It was designed in Paris by French architects in 1893 and completed in 1899 as the home of Francoise Laborde.

The handsome structure was once the stop over for wagon and river-boat travelers, visitors to political events, cattle barons, and military officers on their way to California.

Today, authentically restored and richly decorated with period furnishings, oriental rugs, and English Axeminster carpets, Laborde House offers both historical importance and continental elegance. Listed on the National Register of Historic Places, it is truly; "a gracious tradition . . . reborn."

The 21 guest rooms are Victorian in style and beautifully furnished with antiques. Many of the wallpapers and fabrics used are the same as in the Texas Governors Mansion.

A short trip puts visitors in the South Texas Valley and Padre Island National Seashore. Monterrey, Mexico, with its famous waterfalls and crystal factories is an easy days drive away. For the outdoorsman, there is excellent hunting and fishing. All water sports abound.

The inn's restaurant, Che's, serves border cuisine that includes "true" Mexican food as well as Steaks, Catfish and Vegetables grown on nearby farms.

Chicken Cilantro

12 chicken breasts cut into
 1/4 in. pieces
 deboned and skinned
1 cup butter or margarine
1/2 cup vegetable oil
6 lg. clove garlic, minced

3 med. onions, chopped
1 cup cilantro, chopped
1/2 cup lemon juice
 salt and pepper to taste

In large frying pan melt butter, add oil. Add onions, garlic, cilantro, lemon juice and saute until onion is tender. Add cut up chicken, salt, pepper and cook for about 5 minutes. Pour over steamed rice, about 6 cups rice.

Makes 12 servings.

601 E. Main St.
Rio Grande City, Texas 78582
Tel (512) 487-5101

SOUTHCENTRAL

LAMOTHE HOUSE

Lamothe House provides a glimpse into an early 19th century home that for many years entertained Creole aristocrats. The French-style mansion was built around 1800 by a wealthy sugar planter, Jean Lamothe.

Elegantly restored and recommended by Mobile Guide, AAA, and other prestigious publications, Lamothe House is located on Esplanade Avenue within walking distance of antique shops, museums, the French Market, and historic Jackson Square.

The entrance hall's twin-winding stairways have mahogany rails that sweep to the second floor reception area and third floor suites. Guest rooms are furnished with priceless antiques; some have canopied beds and huge armoires. The patio is filled with the sweet scents of magnolia and olive trees. Steeped in tradition, a pecan praline is placed on the pillow at bed turn down.

The Creole's "Little Breakfast" is served complimentary each morning in a well-appointed dining room. Coffee is served from a 200-year-old Sheffield urn.

Lamothe House Pecan Pralines

1-1/2 cups white sugar
1/2 stick butter
1 tsp vanilla
1/2 cup chopped or whole pecans

1/2 cup brown sugar
1/2 cup evaporated milk
pinch baking soda

Cook sugar and milk over medium heat, stirring until it starts to boil. Add butter, pecans, and soda. Cook, stirring occasionally until soft ball stage (238 degrees). Remove from fire and beat with spoon until creamy and mixture begins to thicken. Drop by teaspoonfuls on buttered flat surface or waxed paper. If mixture becomes too hard, return to heat and add a little water.

621 Esplanade Avenue
New Orleans, LA 70116
Tel (504) 947-1161

LE
RICHELIEU

Le Richelieu, hailed by United Press International as being "one of the city's most lavish," and by Business Week "A Creole Williamsburg...the South's most luxurious suite," is the result of a handsome restoration that combined a macaroni factory with an old row mansion. The hotel is centrally located within walking distance of several historic landmarks. Both the French Market and the romantic 1826 Beauregard Keys House, home of novelist Francis Parkinson Keys, are nearby.

The guest rooms and suites are luxuriously appointed. Each room is different and many have private balconies. The lobby is characteristic of this city's wealth of small hotels.

Visitors to the city may enjoy the River Plantation and Battlefield Cruise aboard an authentic paddlewheeler, the "Creole Queen," in addition to the world-renowned jazz center.

Continental and American breakfasts are available in Terrace Cafe. Try the homemade biscuits!

Roquefort Dressing LeRichelieu

ONE QUART SIZE		ONE GALLON SIZE
20 oz or 1 1/4 lb	blue cheese	5 lbs
2 cups or 16 oz	mayonnaise	1/2 gallon
1/2 cup	olive oil	2 cups
1/4 cup or 2 oz.	white vinegar	1 cup
1/4 cup or 2 oz.	water	1 cup
3/4 tsp	white pepper	1 tbs
3/4 tsp	salt	1 tbs

Blue cheese should be reduced to reasonably moderate chunks. Wire whip ingredients until well mixed then chill thoroughly prior to serving. This dressing is so good that some of the regular patrons fondly refer to it as "Rochefort" (pronounced "Rockfort") Dressing, after the owner, Frank Rochefort.

1234 Chartres Street
New Orleans, LA 70116
Tel 1-800-535-9653

SOUTHCENTRAL

Linden

Linden, a lovely Southern mansion noted for its outstanding collection of Federal-style furnishings, is home to the sixth generation of Conners. Built in 1792 by James Moore and listed on the National Register of Historic Places, several additions have been made that include a very magnificent 98-foot gallery. The exquisite fanlight over the front door was made famous in the film, "Gone With The Wind". Sheraton and Chippendale are used throughout the public rooms, and the banquet room has Hepplewhite with a beautiful white cypress punkah hanging over the table. On the walls are three Havell edition John James Audubon prints.

Guest rooms in the wings provide overnight lodging in great style, and a Sheraton bed with four handsomely carved posts believed to have been made around 1800 by Samuel McIntyre occupies the master bedroom. The east wing bedrooms overlook a manicured courtyard and garden. The two-story west wing, built by Mrs. Conner in the 1850s, was used for schoolrooms for her thirteen children. These rooms today await guests.

Open daily throughout the year, Linden's guests are partakers of the hospitality, charm, and history which are heritages of the Deep South. A delicious Southern breakfast of Ham, Grits, Eggs, Biscuits, Orange Juice and Tea greet the morning riser.

Sausage-Egg Souffle

l lb milk bulk sausage	1/2 tsp dry mustard
5 slices toasted bread	salt & pepper to taste
6 eggs	2 cups milk
1 cup grated cheddar cheese	

Brown the sausage and drain. Cut each slice of toast into 4 pieces. Beat together eggs, milk, and seasonings. In casserole, layer half the toast, half the sausage, and sprinkle on half the cheese. Pour half the custard over the layers, repeating layers once more. Cover and bake at 325° for 45 minutes to 1 hour (or until souffle has puffed-up). Let set 5 minutes before serving, although the souffle is best when made 24 hours ahead and refrigerated until ready to bake. Serves 6.

1 Linden Place
Natchez, MS 39120
Tel 1-601-445-5472

OAK ALLEY PLANTATION

Oak Alley Plantation is truly an outstanding example of Greek-Revival architecture, and has appeared even in encyclopaedia. Built in 1839 for the bride of wealthy sugar planter Jacques Telesphore Roman, Oak Alley was spared the torch during the Civil War and was the first Great River Road plantation to be saved from the ravages of time and neglect during the post-Civil War era. Through the generosity of Josephine Stewart, this monument to the pre-war South was left so that others might enjoy the opulence and grandeur of the region's past. Today the mansion is open for tours only, and is a national historic landmark with turn-of-the-century guest cottages situated on the grounds.

Oak Alley Plantation Restaurant is quaint, informal, and Cajun. Specialties are recipes handed down from generation to generation.

Oak Alley Plantation Chicken and Andouille Gumbo

1-1/2 cups all-purpose flour
2 cups onion, chopped
1 cup green pepper, chopped
1/2 cup green onion, chopped
3 lbs smoked sausage, cut
2 whole chickens, boiled and deboned
2 gal chicken stock (use broth from boiled chicken and water to make 2 gallons)

1-1/2 cups vegetable oil
1 cup celery, chopped
2 bay leaves
1/4 cup parsley, chopped
1 lb andouille, cut
salt, black pepper, cayenne to taste
filé powder to taste

Make a roux by slowly browning flour in hot oil. This is a slow process and must be stirred constantly. When roux is medium brown, add onions, celery, green pepper, green onions, and parsley. Cook on low flame until vegetables are soft, adding 1-1/2 gallons hot stock to roux. Boil 15 minutes. Add smoked sausage and andouille. Cook over medium-low flame for 4 hours. Add more chicken stock to get desired consistency and stir in salt, pepper, and cayenne. Add cooked chicken and cook another hour. Just before serving, stir in filé. Serves 20.

Great River Road
3645 Hwy. 18
Vacherie, LA 70090
Tel (504) 265-2151 or 800-44ALLEY
www.louisianatravel.com/oak_alley

Oak Square

Oak Square is a grand legacy to those turbulant days when General U.S. Grant referred to Port Gibson as "the town too beautiful to burn." Built in 1850 as the home of a cotton planter, the front gallery of this Greek Revival mansion has six corinthian columns 22 feet tall with terracotta capitols that were made in England. Besides the beauty of the structure itself, the grounds are enhanced with a courtyard, gazebo, fountain, and giant oaks...qualities that exemplify the grandeur of South Antebellum days.

Upon entering, one is immediately taken into a period of gracious living with local history and the inn's outstanding collection of heirloom antiques. Also on display is a rare collection of Civil War memorabilia with many original family documents.

Adjacent to this impressive home is the guest house that provides comfortable accommodations. Tours of Oak Square with rooms of rosewood Victorian furniture, beautiful French Rococo Revival pier and mantle mirrors, the library and music room accented by a rare Chickering piano, and graciously appointed dining room await the visitor.

A Southern Continental breakfast is served each morning from such specialties as Porcupine Meat Balls, Rice Casserole, Lime Gelatin, and Cottage Cheese Salad.

Porcupine Meat Balls

1 lb ground beef	1 lb ground pork
1/2 cups uncooked rice	1/2 pkg onion soup mix
1 egg	salt and pepper

Put rice in pan of boiling water and leave 1 minute. Drain and cool. Add to ground meat. Add package soup mix, salt and pepper, and egg. Shape into large balls and brown in 1 inch of fat. Arrange balls in shallow, rectangular pan. Pour gravy made of cream of chicken or mushroom soup and 1 soup can water, blended and heated, over meat balls. Cover with aluminum foil and bake at 250⁰ for 1 hour.

1207 Church Street
Port Gibson, MS 39150
Tel (601) 437-4350

The Pontchartrain Hotel

The Pontchartrain Hotel, located in the historic Garden District on St. Charles Avenue, was built by the Aschaffenburgs and has been in continuous operation by the same family since it opened its gracious doors in 1927. The hotel's Spanish-style architecture and imposing red canopy distinguish this New Orleans landmark. Gas standards along the sidewalk are duplicates of those in the Place Vendome in Paris, and the Georgian gate was transported from London. The Pontchartrain Hotel has entertained many famous celebrities over the years.

The lobby's vaulted ceiling, marble walls, crystal chandeliers, comfortable chairs, and fresh flowers are a statement of class. The soft pink oriental rugs blend harmoniously with the pink in the ceiling.

Guest rooms and suites are very elegant. Furnished with Chippendale, rare antiques, Italian marble, paintings, mirrors, plush velvet and silk fabrics, one suite boasts a grand piano. Each room is quite different.

Meals are served in four dining rooms. The internationally famous and winner of the coveted Holiday Award, The Caribbean Room is richly appointed with pink velvet and a huge mural by New Orleans artist Charles Reinike.

Crawfish Etouffe

1/2 lb all-purpose flour
1 bell pepper, chopped fine
1 medium white onion, chopped
1/2 bunch green onions, chopped
1 1/2 tsp salt
1/4 cup chopped parsley
2 tsp green pepper sauce
1 gal shrimp or crawfish stock
1/4 tsp white pepper

1/2 lb butter
3 lb crawfish tails
4 bay leaves

1 tsp thyme
1 tsp sweet basil
1 1/2 tsp chicken base
1/2 tsp caramel coloring

In saute pan place 1/2 lb butter, 1/2 lb flour. Cook 5 minutes. Add chopped bell pepper, onion, green onions, and cook 10 minutes. Add crawfish, bay leaves, white pepper, salt, thyme, sweet basil, parsley, chicken base, green pepper sauce, caramel coloring, and 1 gallon stock. Mix. Cook 15 - 20 minutes more. Serve with steamed rice.

2031 Saint Charles Avenue
New Orleans, LA 70140
Tel (504) 524-0581

SOUTHCENTRAL

Salmen-Fritchie House

Salmen-Fritchie House is a fine example of the grand old homes found in the deep South at the turn of the century. Built in 1895 by Fritz Salmen, the house has remained in the same family ever since.

Elegantly restored and richly decorated with family antiques, Salmen Fritchie House has welcomed visitors from around the world since opening as an inn. It is now listed on the National Register of Historic Places.

Each guest room is decorated differently. The Honeymoon Room offers a small Victorian sitting room. The Poster Room has a warming fireplace. All the rooms are magnificently furnished reflecting the era.

The formal dining room looks out on a large oak tree. A full southern complimentary breakfast is served at a huge oak table.

Bread Pudding

1 10-oz. loaf stale french bread crumbled (or 6-8 cup any type bread)	2 tbs vanilla
	1 cup raisins
4 cups milk	1 cup coconut
2 cups sugar	1 cup chopped pecans
8 tbs butter, melted	1 tbs cinnamon
3 eggs	1 tbs nutmeg

Combine all ingredients; mixture should be very moist but not soupy. Pour into buttered 9 x 12 or larger baking dish. Place in non-preheated oven. Bake at 350° for approximately 1 hour and 15 minutes, until top is golden brown. Serve warm with sauce.

Whiskey Sauce

1/2 cup butter (1 stick, 1/4 lb.)	2 egg yolks
1-1/2 cup powdered sugar	1/2 cup bourbon (to taste)

Cream butter and sugar over medium heat until all butter is absorbed. Remove from heat and blend in egg yolk. Pour in bourbon gradually to your own taste, stirring constantly. Sauce will thicken as it cools. Serve warm over warm bread pudding.
NOTE: For a variety of sauces, just substitute your favorite fruit juice or liqueur to compliment your bread pudding. Makes 16-20 servings.

127 Cleveland Avenue
Slidell, LA 70458
Tel 504-643-1405

SOUTHCENTRAL

the Schwegmann house

The historic town of Washington was a leading river port during the early 1800s, attracting both European immigrants and American pioneers. Listed on the National Register of Historic Places, Schwegmann House which overlooks the Missouri River was beautifully built in the 1850s with bricks made on the grounds.

This stately Federal-style structure was the home of John F. Schwegmann, a miller, and his wife Mary. Over the front door an impressive double frosted transom bears the initials J.F.S.

There are two parlors with fireplaces and nine guest rooms attractively decorated and furnished with antiques and colorful handmade quilts.

Visitors may stroll the gardens with river views or relax on the patio shaded by a hundred year old pecan tree.

A full complimentary breakfast is offered.

German Apple Pancake

5 medium apples
 peeled, cored and sliced
3/4 cup brown sugar
2-1/2 tsp cinnamon
1-1/4 cup flour
1/2 teaspoon salt
5 eggs
1-1/4 cups milk
4 tbs of butter for pan

Preheat oven at 425°. Mix apples, brown sugar and cinnamon in bowl and set aside. Combine flour, milk, eggs, and salt, and beat until smooth. Place butter in pan and put into oven until butter melts. Then tilt pan to distribute butter evenly. Pour batter into hot pan. Spread apples over batter and bake 25 to 30 minutes. Serve with powdered sugar sprinkled on top. Easy and delicious!

Variation: omit apples. Bake as directed. Garnish top with fresh fruit of the season.

438 West Front Street
Washington, MO 63090
Tel 314-239-5025

WILLIAMS HOUSE
BED & BREAKFAST INN

Williams House Bed and Breakfast Inn was built with the finest materials of its day and is now listed on the National Register of Historic Places. Within walking distance of downtown Hot Springs and historic Bath House Row, the Victorian stone building has wrap-around porches, gables, and an unusual corner turret. Decorated with family furniture, plants, and cherished antiques, the reception hall lends a romantic atmosphere with its piano and fireplace. Guest rooms are comfortable and furnished in a variety of charming styles with outside views of towering shade trees.

A full breakfast is served in an old-fashioned dining room with linens and warm hospitality. Varied offerings include Stuffed French Toast with Raspberry, Creative Egg and Sausage Dishes, Homemade Biscuits, Jelly and Jam.

Baked French Toast Almondine

Vienna French Bread that has been left out overnight, dip in following egg mixture:

1 egg for every 2 slices bread	**splash milk**
1 tsp liquid brown sugar	**1 tbs melted butter**

Place in glass, preheated cake pan with 2 tbs melted butter. Arrange bread in pan and bake at 400° for 20 minutes, turning after 10 minutes. Top with almond syrup made of:

1/2 cup sliced almonds sauteed in 2 tbs butter	
1-1/4 cups liquid brown sugar	**tsp almond extract**

Store remainder in refrigerator.

420 Quapaw
Hot Springs National Park, AR 71901
Tel (501) 624-4275

Arizona Biltmore

Arizona Biltmore is nestled at the base of Squaw Peak Mountain and its history is as colorful as the beautifully landscaped grounds that surround it. Inspired by the late famous Frank Lloyd Wright and commissioned into reality by Albert Chase McArthur and the McArthur Brothers, this world-renowned Weston resort has hosted famous people for over half a century.

The hotel is an architectural wonder. Built of decorative block tiles that were made right on the site and called the Jewel of the Desert, its custom-woven carpets, draperies and stained glass windows are a reflection of its elegant style. It was under the ownership of the Wrigley family of Wrigley Chewing Gum for 43 years. With 500 luxuriously appointed guest rooms and suites offering striking views of the Camelback Mountain, the expansions over the years have not sacrificed its early traditions of fine service and warm hospitality. The Arizona Biltmore is rated 5-Star by Mobil Travel Guide.

In addition to the two 18-hole PGA golf courses, 17 lighted tennis courts, lawn games, and swimming pools, guests may enjoy day trips to the Painted Desert, the Grand Canyon, Ghost Town of Jerome, Mexico, and Tombstone.

Meals are served in four dining rooms. The Gold Room with its famous gold leaf vaulted ceiling offers excellent Continental dining.

Poached Pears with Almond Raisin Stuffing and Raspberry Sauce

6 Bartlett Pears, cored and peeled
5 oz almond paste
1-1/2 cups white wine

1 cup maple syrup
3 oz raisins

Raspberry Sauce:

1 cup poaching liquid
2 cups red wine

2 pints raspberry puree
lemon juice to taste

Poach pears in liquid until pears are soft. Remove when finished and let cool. Mix almond paste with raisins and stuff pears.

For sauce: Puree raspberries and cool poaching liquid. Add red wine and lemon juice. Strain. If sauce is too tart, adjust with small amount of sugar. Arrange pears on glass plate and cover with sauce. Serves 6.

24th Street and Missouri
Phoenix, AZ 85016
Tel (602) 955-6600

SOUTHWEST

The Apple Blossom Inn

The Apple Blossom Inn, located in the heart of the historic district, was the home of A.V. Hunter, prominent businessman who owned interests in various lead mines such as the Little Jonney.

Built in 1879, this handsome frame house with its gables and porches is a classic example of Victorian architecture. The eight guest rooms are beautifully furnished with reminders of an earlier age. There are four posters, feather beds, lacy pillows and rockers. Estilla's room has a fireplace and sitting area.

Properly restored, the inn offers a charming environment with its fireplaces, crystal with brass chandeliers and fine woodwork. As part of its old-fashioned hospitality, baked goodies, teas and lemonade are offered all day.

Just minutes away activities include hiking, biking, museums, skiing and a scenic train ride.

A full complimentary breakfast is served.

Hominy Grits Cheese Casserole

1 cup quick-cooking hominy grits	1 cup shredded cheddar cheese
3-3/4 cups milk (divided)	1/2 cup butter
1 tsp salt	1/4 cup chopped chives
2 beaten eggs	

Preheat oven to 325° F. Bring grits, 3 cups milk, and salt to a boil. Add eggs and 3/4 cup milk, and cook until thickened. Stir in cheese, butter, and chives, and blend well. Bake in buttered baking dish for 45-50 minutes. Serve hot. Makes 6 servings.

Cocoa Kisses

1 cup sugar	1 tsp vanilla
3 egg whites	3 tbs cocoa
1/8 tsp salt	3/4 cup chopped pecans
2 tsp water	

Preheat oven to 250°F. Sift sugar. Whip egg whites and salt until stiff but not dry. Gradually add half the sugar. Combine water and vanilla. Add the liquid a few drops at a time alternately with the remaining sugar, whipping constantly. Fold in cocoa and pecans. Drop the batter onto a lightly greased cookie sheet and shape into cones. Bake until kisses are firm to the touch, but soft inside. Remove from pan while hot. Makes 40 - 1" meringues.

120 West 4th Street
Leadville, CO 80461
Tel 800-982-9279

SOUTHWEST

The Awahnee

The Awahnee stands in Yosemite National Park where nature shows off its handiwork through spectacular waterfalls, ice-shaped granite, peaks, and domes. Wildlife and outdoor activities abound.

The Awahnee is a world-renowned hotel that has hosted American presidents, foreign dignitaries, and hundreds of thousands of park visitors since 1927. Listed as a National Registered Landmark, the architecture is outstanding. The hallways have Indian-style borders along the tops of the walls, and each doorway is decorated in an Indian pattern. Open the door, and the guest walks into a room created from Indian motifs. Colorful tapestries hang throughout the public rooms. Twenty-four wooden cottages shaded by trees are directly behind the main building.

Excellent meals are served in the surroundings of the main dining room with its 34-foot ceilings, huge beams, columns, and spectacular views.

Famous Awahnee Pancakes

2-1/3 cups flour
1 tbs baking powder
3 eggs, lightly beaten
1 tsp vanilla

1/2 cup sugar
1/8 tsp salt
1/3 cup melted butter
1-1/2 to 2 cups Half & Half

Stir together flour, sugar, baking powder, and salt. Combine eggs, butter, vanilla, and 1 cup cream. Add all at once to flour mixture, stirring until blended. Add additional cream to desired consistency. Bake pancakes on hot, lightly greased griddle or in large heavy skillet. Makes 24 4-inch pancakes.

Yosemite National Park, CA 95389
Tel (209) 372-1435

SOUTHWEST

The Baldpate Inn

The Baldpate Inn has a collection of over 20,000 keys started in 1923, and according to Denver historians, the rustic establishment was family operated for over 70 years.

Inspired by Gordon and Ethel Mace in a pine forest overlooking Rocky Mountain National Park, the inn opened its doors in 1917 hosting famous Hollywood celebrities and other well-known personalities. Earl Derr Biggers, author of "Seven Keys to Baldpate" and the Charley Chann mysteries, was a frequent visitor.

Inside, the library and comfortable lobby, each with its own massive fireplace, is a good spot for friendly get togethers. The guest rooms are decorated with handsome colorful quilts and ginghams reflecting its mountain setting. With a front porch commanding striking views of the country side and a world-renowned Key and Photograph Collection, Baldpate Inn is truly a step back to the days that Estes Park and other early guests came to know.

Offerings in the dining room includes a delightful Soup and Salad Buffet, Homemade Breads and a tempting array of Homemade Pies and Desserts.

Mastery Key-Ch of Baldpate
1 lb Jimmy Dean sausage, browned and drained
1/2 pkg. Knorr vegetable dry soup mix
1 cup Swiss cheese, shredded

2 cups milk
1 cup Bisquick baking mix
4 eggs

Mix together drained sausage, dry soup mix and cheese; spread evenly in a greased 9" glass pie pan. Stir together milk, Bisquick and eggs until blended; pour over sausage mix. Bake at 400° for 30-40 minutes until golden. Serve warm with fresh fruit garnish.

P.O. Box 2778
Estes Park, CO 80517
Tel (303) 586-3415

SOUTHWEST

Benbow Inn

Benbow Inn is a picturesque Tudor-style structure that has attracted guests since it opened its doors in 1926. It was designed by famous architect Albert Farr and is listed on the National Register of Historic Places. Lovingly restored to its former elegance, there have been several owners of this charming old inn.

The common rooms are furnished with antiques, paintings, needlepoint, and objects d'art. The terrace and garden levels are newly constructed with country decor, antiques and woodburning fireplaces. A basket of mysteries is placed in each room and a bellman is always on duty. English tea and scones are served each day at 2:00 p.m.

Meals are served in the dining room offering the finest meat and fresh produce available. Breads and pastries are baked daily.

Creamy Berry Royal

Combine and heat in heavy sauce pan (do not boil):

2-1/2 cups heavy cream	1-1/4 tsp gelatin
1 cup sugar	

Let above mixture cool, then add:

1 lb sour cream	1 tsp vanilla

Mix until smooth, pour into glasses, and let solidify in refrigerator for around 8 hours. Top with fruit.

445 Lake Benbow Drive
Garberville, CA 95440
Tel (707) 923-2124

SOUTHWEST

CAMPBELL RANCH INN

Campbell Ranch Inn is a fine example of contemporary architecture designed to blend harmoniously with its California landscape. This delightful hilltop inn is surrounded by 35 rolling acres.

Located in the heart of Sonoma County wine country, the inn is made of old brick and wood, and painted grey with white trim. The doors are wedgewood blue. Inside, the beautiful living room provides a warm and friendly atmosphere.

The four guest rooms are nicely decorated and some have balconies. All have spectacular outside views of gardens and countryside. In addition to the main house, there's a guest cottage on the grounds. Fresh fruit and flowers are the added touch.

Open year round, activities include tennis, swimming, hot tubs, bicycles, horseshoes and ping pong.

A full complimentary breakfast is served on the terrace overlooking lovely flower gardens.

Raspberry Cream Cheese Coffee Cake

2-1/2 cups flour	1/4 tsp salt
3/4 cup sugar	3/4 cup dairy sour cream
3/4 cup butter	1 egg
1/2 tsp baking powder	1 tsp almond extract
1/2 tsp baking soda	

Filling:

1 8-oz. pkg. cream cheese	1 egg
1/4 cup sugar	1/2 cup raspberry jam

Topping:

   1/2 cup sliced almonds (2 oz. pkg.)

Preheat oven to 350°. In a large bowl, combine flour and sugar; cut in the butter using a pastry blender until mixture resembles coarse crumbs. Remove 1 cup of crumbs for topping. To remaining crumb mixture, add baking powder, baking soda, salt, sour cream, egg and almond extract. Blend well. Spread batter over bottom and 2 inches up sides of a greased and floured 9 inch spring form pan. Batter should be 1/4 inch thick on sides. In small bowl, combine cream cheese, 1/4 cup sugar and egg; blend well. Pour over batter in pan. Spoon jam evenly over the cheese filling. In a small bowl, combine 1 cup of reserved crumbs and almonds; sprinkle over top. Bake at 350° for 55-60 minutes or until cream cheese is set and crust is a deep golden brown. Cool 15 minutes, remove sides and cool completely. Can be served warm or cold but I prefer this at room temperature.

1475 Canyon Road
Geyserville, CA 95441

SOUTHWEST

Hotel del Coronado

Hotel Del Coronado is a grand example of Victorian architecture located between the sparkling Pacific and Glorietta Bay across from San Diego. Since opening in 1888, this historic and majestic resort has been a cultural center for European charm and cuisine.

Many U.S. presidents, foreign dignitaries, celebrities and other famous people have been guests, including Thomas A. Edison who supervised the work of his incandescent lamp installation, and it is alleged that the famous inventor pulled a switch on the hotel's first electrically-lighted Christmas tree.

The magnificent features of "The Del" include rich wood paneling, crystal chandeliers, and luxurious appointments. It has never been more alluring than it is today.

Meals are served in several dining rooms. The Crown Room has been the scene of many state functions and greatly admired as an architectural masterpiece. An extensive menu noted for distinctive cuisine offers many specialties.

Leek and Potato Soup

1 cup finely chopped onions
2 cups diced potatoes
6 cups chicken stock
salt & pepper to taste

1 cup chopped leeks
1/4 lb butter
2 cups Half & Half

Saute onions and leeks in butter; add potatoes, stock, seasoning to taste. Add Half & Half at the very last minute. Serves 12.

1500 Orange Avenue
Coronado, CA 92118
Tel (619) 435-6611

SOUTHWEST

The Gingerbread Mansion

The Gingerbread Mansion is an outstanding example of the Victorian style. Surrounded by English flower gardens and painted a colorful peach and yellow, little wonder this architectural beauty is northern California's most photographed inn. Located in the historic district, the inn was built as a doctor's home and dates back to 1899.

Many changes have been made over the years and at one time it housed a hospital. Elegantly restored, the mansion now welcomes visitors with charm and gracious hospitality.

There are four parlors and nine guest rooms. The rooms are lavishly appointed. Private baths — some are very unusual. As part of the hospitality, early morning coffee is served in your room.

A full complimentary breakfast of homemade delights is offered.

Pumpkin Gingerbread

3 cups sugar	1/2 tsp baking powder
1 cup salad oil	2 tsp ginger
4 eggs	1 tsp cinnamon
3-1/2 cups all purpose flour	1 tsp nutmeg
2 tsp baking soda	1 tsp cloves
1-1/2 tsp salt	1 tsp allspice
2/3 cup water	1 16-oz. can pumpkin

Cream together sugar, salad oil and eggs. Sift together all dry ingredients. Add water and mix into creamed mixture. Beat in pumpkin. Pour into two (2) greased 5 x 9 loaf pans. Bake at 350° for 1 hour. Note: When doubling recipe, use a 1 lb. 13-oz. can of pumpkin and pour batter into five loaf pans.

P.O. Box 40
400 Berding Street
Ferndale, CA 95536
Tel 707-786-4000

SOUTHWEST

The Grey Whale Inn origionally housed a hospital when it was built in 1915 and its weathered outside look hasn't changed much since that time. Central to all of the north coasts historic sites and only two blocks from the famous Skunk Train Depot, the inn offers splendid views of the Pacific Ocean.

Huge double doors welcome the guests to the privacy of wide hallways and large rooms individually furnished. Some of the rooms have ocean views, and one room features an old gimballed surgery lamp, a reminder of the room's earlier use. From the Sunset Room guests may view the picturesque town of Fort Bragg or watch the annual grey whale migration (December - March) beyond the surf. A magnificent whale, hand-carved by artist and whale protectionist Byrd Baker, graces the front lawn.

A Continental breakfast is served. Fresh Fruit, Juices, and Homemade Coffee Cakes can be expected.

Fresh Lemon-Nut Bread

2 cups sugar
1 cup butter or margarine
4 eggs, separated
1 tsp salt
3-1/4 cups unsifted all-purpose flour

2 tsp baking powder
1-1/4 cups milk
1 cup finely chopped nuts
grated peel of 2 lemons

Topping:

juice of 2 lemons

1/2 cup sugar

Cream sugar and butter well. Beat in egg yolks. Alternately add sifted dry ingredients with milk. Mix well. Add nuts and lemon peel. Fold in stiffly beaten egg whites. Pour into greased 10-12 cup tube pan. Bake at 350° 60-70 minutes or until done. Remove from oven, spoon topping over top and leave in pan 1 hour. Cool completely on cake rack.

615 North Main
Fort Bragg, CA 95437
Tel (707) 964-0640

SOUTHWEST

HARBOR HOUSE

Harbor House, an enlarged replica of a model displayed in the 1915 Pan American Exposition in San Francisco, commands a rugged bluff overlooking Mendocino Coast and Greenwood Landing. This 10-room inn was designed by Louis Christian Mullgardt and was built by the Goodyear Redwood Lumber Company as an executive residence and for the entertainment of its guests.

The lounge is very fitting to the house with a vaulted ceiling and virgin redwood from the Albion forest. Guest rooms are comfortable with either fireplaces or Franklin stoves. Some have private sundecks.

Striking outside coastal views complete with delicious four-course dinners, including fresh regional specialties. Dinner and full breakfast are included in your room rate.

Tomato-Basil Soup

2-1/2 lbs tomatoes, peeled, seeded,
   and cut up (about 6 cups) or
   two 16-ounce cans tomatoes
1/4 cup lightly packed fresh basil leaves
   or 1 tbs dried basil, crushed
1 cup chicken broth

1 tbs sugar
Dash to 1/4 tsp salt
Dash ground red pepper
Dash ground black pepper
Dash bottled hot pepper sauce
Desired fresh herb (optional)

In a blender container or food processor bowl place about half of the fresh or undrained canned tomatoes and all of the basil. Cover and blend or process till smooth. Transfer pureed tomato mixture to a medium saucepan. Repeat blending or processing with remaining tomatoes. Stir chicken broth, sugar, salt, red and black pepper, and hot pepper sauce into the tomato mixture. Bring to boiling, then reduce heat. Cover and simmer for 30 minutes. Serve immediately or transfer to a covered container and refrigerate. To serve, ladle warm or chilled soup into small bowls. If desired, garnish each serving with a fresh herb. Makes 6 (3/4-cup) servings.

5600 S. Highway 1, Box 369
Elk, CA 95432
Tel (707) 877-3203

the Hearthstone Inn

The Hearthstone Inn is made up of two handsomely restored buildings joined together with a charming carriage house. One is a Queen Anne style, built in 1885 by a paper manufacturer named Bemis. The other is Victorian with its dormers, porches and railings. Located on a a tree-lined street, both are painted grey and lavender, together with eight colors including lilac, peach, plum and magenta.

Listed on the National Register, there are three floors elegantly furnished with antiques of walnut, oak, cherry and other beautiful woods. No two rooms are alike. All have striking outside views and Victorian art.

Activities abound in Colorado Springs. Within walking distance guests may visit the Fine Arts Center, public tennis courts, churches, restaurants and all downtown stores and gift shops.

A delicious gourmet breakfast is served each morning, such as eggs served in a creamy Florentine sauce with fresh melon wedges and spicy apple cake.

Chocolate Bread with Vanilla Butter

1 cup milk	1 tsp vanilla extract
2 tbs butter	1 package dry yeast dissolved in 1/4 cup
2 eggs, beaten	tepid water (100°) with 1 tbs sugar
3-1/2 cups all-purpose flour	2/3 cup sifted cocoa
1/2 cup sugar	1 cup chopped walnuts (optional)

Scald milk, remove from heat and add butter, stirring until it melts. Add 1/2 cup sugar and vanilla. When mixture is cool, add yeast mixture, which should be good and frothy. Add beaten eggs and stir. Measure flour and cocoa into a large bowl. Add nuts if desired. Add milk-and-yeast mixture and stir vigorously. Turn out onto a floured board, and butter the bowl. Knead dough 5 minutes, adding flour if necessary to yield a smooth dough. Put into bowl, cover, let rise 1-1/2 hours. Punch down, let rise again. (If you are not in Colorado, where the altitude is near 6,500 feet above sea level, you need let it rise only once.) Punch down, knead 10 times. Shape, place in 9 x 5 loaf pan, let rise again 30 minutes. Put sugar on top of the loaf, bake 30 minutes. Put sugar on top of the loaf, bake 30 minutes at 350° or until it sounds hollow. Cool 10 minutes in pan. Serve with lots of vanilla butter.

Vanilla Butter

12 tbs butter	3/4 cup powdered sugar
2 tbs vanilla	

Beat all together until smooth and fluffy.

506 North Cascade
Colorado Springs, CO 80903
Tel 719-473-4413

MEADEAU VIEW LODGE

Meadeau View Lodge enjoys the company of tall pines, aspens, and cool breezes at an altitude of 8,400 feet inside a triangle made by Cedar Breaks, Zion National Park, and Bryce Canyon. The lodge is a restful, comfortable retreat with miles of trails leading from the front door into forests and meadows. Utah's famous powder light snow makes the area the choice of color country snowmobiles.

The lounge is typical with a circular fireplace and tall windows overlooking a vast expanse of meadows where many movies have been filmed. All the guest rooms have fine views.

Guests may join local groups for rides to Navajo Lake, Tippits Valley, Strawberry Point, or Cedar Breaks. Moonlight trail rides are a must.

A complimentary breakfast each morning awaits the guest. Meals are served in the dining room.

Mexican Eggplant

1 large eggplant	1/4 cup vegetable oil
1 cup grated cheddar cheese	6 ripe olives sliced
1 cup sour cream	

Sauce:

1 15 oz can tomato sauce	1/2 tsp ground cumin
1/2 tsp garlic salt	1/4 cup chopped green onions
1 4-oz can chopped mild chilis	

Peel and slice eggplant. Brush both sides of eggplant with oil. Place in a single layer on a greased sheet and bake at 450 degrees for 20 minutes. Combine sauce ingredients and simmer uncovered for 10 minutes. In greased 9 x 13 casserole, layer eggplant, sauce, and cheese. Top with sour cream and olives. Bake uncovered at 350 degrees for 20 minutes.

Box 356
Cedar City, UT 84720
Tel (801) 682-2495

SOUTHWEST

The Old Milano Hotel

The Old Milano Hotel was originally built in 1905 by Bert Lucchinetti as a rest stop and tavern along the railroad tracks. For many years it was a private home.

The hotel has been restored and its doors are open once again to travelers amidst views of the Pacific, tall cedars and flower gardens. There are two guest cottages, one drowned in colorful scarlet blossoms for which it is named and the other, an authentic caboose tucked among cedar trees.

The main inn's music room has a collection of art books and designs on the walls by William Morris. Six comfortable upstairs guest rooms have either ocean or garden views. The suite where the Lucchinetti family lived has a sitting room, spectacular views, and a hand-painted bed with a Hollywood career.

Guests enjoy quiet walks along the beach, and nearby is the Sea Ranch Golf Course.

A Continental breakfast is served each morning.

California Orange Raisin Loaf

1/4 cup sherry	8 eggs
juice of 8 oranges (save rind)	1/4 cup sour milk
4 cups currants	1 lb sweet butter
2 cups whole wheat pastry flour	4 tsp soda
5 cups brown sugar	orange liquer
6 cups unbleached white flour	

Combine currants, orange juice, butter, and sherry. Bring to boil and cool. Blend sugar and eggs. Combine with dry ingredients. Add currant mixture. Add 3 tbs orange liquer. Add milk and 1/4 cup orange rind. Mix well. Bake at 350° 35-40 minutes. Top with blend of:

3/8 cup orange juice	1/8 cup sugar
1/8 cup orange liquer	

Pour topping over warm loaves. Should make 13 small loaves.

38300 Highway 1
Gualala, CA 95445
Tel (707) 884-3256

SOUTHWEST

The Old Miners' Lodge housed local miners seeking their fortunes in the silver mines back in 1889, and today it is still a delightful place to stay. Overlooking the peaceful Park City basin and convenient to shops, ski lifts, and restaurants on Historic Main Street, the inn has been restored to reflect the frontier air of long ago. One of America's Favorite 25 inns in 1997.

The parlor provides a library, games, and a cozy fire on chilly days. Each guest room is named for a historical person from Park City's colorful mining days. A hot tub, down comforters and pillows, and bed turn down complete the hospitality. Nearby activities of skiing, golfing, tennis, fishing, hiking, horseback riding, and art galleries make a memorable visit.

A full complimentary breakfast is prepared each morning. This third-generation family recipe has never before been published.

Daniels Family Waffles

1/2 tsp salt	1 tbs sugar
4 tbs oil or melted shortening	1-1/2 cups milk
3 tsp baking powder	1-3/4 cups finely ground wheat flour
2 eggs beaten separately (room temperature eggs only)	

Sift and mix dry ingredients. Mix milk and egg yolks. Bring mixtures together and stir until smooth, adding oil. Fold in easily beaten egg whites and pour mixture into seasoned waffle baker. Serves 6.

615 Woodside Ave
P.O. Box 2639
Park City, UT 84060-2639
Tel (801) 645-8068

SOUTHWEST

The Pelican Inn

The Pelican Inn captures the spirit of 16th century England's West Country in a setting of pines, alders, and sweet fragrances of honeysuckle and jasmine.

The dining room has a massive fireplace with a secret hiding hole and chamber for smoking hams - things not needed in today's homes, but gentle reminders of our past. Guest rooms are snug and cozy with English antiques, heavily draped half-teester beds, and floors warmed with Turkish rugs. Fresh flowers add the finishing touch.

Elegant meals are served from a menu that includes succulent Meat Pies, Bangers, Fresh Fish, Meats, Salads, Homemade desserts. On special occasions, Elizabethan Feasts that last an evening with merrymaking await the guest in the flickering firelight reflected on dark, rough-hewn beams.

Bread Pudding

5 cups fresh cubed French Bread	1 cup amaretto
(approximate 1/2" x 1/2")	1 cup raisins
1-1/2 cups sugar	1/2 cup almonds (sliced)
2 cups milk	2 tsp cinnamon
5 whole eggs	1/2 tsp nutmeg

Preheat oven at 350 degrees. Mix all ingredients together except bread. After ingredients are well mixed, mix bread until soaked. Pour mixture in a 9 x 12 inch pan. Dip pan in bigger pan and fill with water. Place pan in oven for 25 to 30 minutes until golden brown.

Muir Beach, CA 94965
Tel (415) 383-6000

RANCHO de los CABALLEROS

Rancho De Los Caballeros is an elegant working/guest ranch surrounded by 20,000 acres of rolling hillsides and flowering Arizona desert. Typical of the Southwest's architecture, the low rambling adobe structure provides a variety of spacious accommodations in themes of the colorful Southwest. Many of the rooms have fireplaces.

The Bradshaw Mountain, the resort's newest lodging, is furnished with Indian rugs, Mexican tiles, has large patios, and enjoys great views of the golf course and mountain ranges.

Guests at this family resort enjoy skeet and trap shooting, golf, tennis, swimming, horseback riding, leisurely strolls, and joining wranglers on cattle roundups.

Meals are served each day in the dining room.

Chicken Enchilada Pie

3 - 4 lbs chopped chicken or turkey
2 lbs shredded cheddar
l pkg flour tortillas
2 cans (small) diced green chillies
enough gravy to make chicken moist

Mix chicken, gravy, and chillies together and spread 1/3 of mixture on bottom of casserole dish. Cover with layer of tortillas. Spread another layer of meat mixture over the tortillas, sprinkling cheese on top. Cover with tortillas. Spread last 1/3 of meat mixture on top of tortillas and cover with remaining cheese. Bake at 325 degrees for 45-60 minutes.

Wickenburg, AZ 85358
Tel (602) 684-5484

SOUTHWEST

The Seal Beach Inn

The Seal Beach Inn is one block from the beach and within walking distance to Main Street activities. The guest's first impression of the inn as they enter the flower-laden courtyard is of being transported to a European-style wonderland. An old Parisienne iron fence, ornate antique lamp posts, British phone booths, window boxes, shutters, and smart blue canopies complete the picture.

The inn is filled with antiques brought by the proprietress and her husband from their many trips to Europe. Each guest room is furnished with Early American, French, and Victorian styles set off by Bentwood rockers, ruffled eyelet cafe curtains, and art nouveau pieces. John Barrymore's four-poster bed sits in one suite, and another room has a wooden, stained glass door from Universal Studios.

A complimentary breakfast is served each morning. The menu includes Croissants, Whole Wheat Raisin Nut Bread, Freshly Squeezed orange juice and Viennese and French Roast Coffee.

Whole Wheat Raisin-Nut Bread

3 cups whole wheat flour
1/4 cup toasted wheat germ
1 tsp salt
1/2 cup honey
1/2 cup chopped walnuts

2 tsp baking powder
1-1/4 tsp soda
1-1/2 cup buttermilk
1/4 cup salad oil
1/2 cup raisins

In a 6-to-8 cup bowl, stir together flour, wheat germ, baking powder, soda, and salt. In separate bowl, combine buttermilk, honey, and oil, pour all a once into flour mixture, stirring just until all ingredients are combined. Add raisins and nuts, being careful not to overmix the batter. Pour into greased 5 1/4 x 9 1/2 loaf pan; bake for 1 hour 15 minutes at 325 degrees or until done. The loaf top should be lightly pebbled and evenly browned. Let cool in pan 10 minutes, turning out on rack and cool thoroughly. Makes 1 loaf.

212 5th Street
Seal Beach, CA 90740
Tel (213) 493-2416

Sutter Creek Inn

Sutter Creek Inn has been a local landmark in the historic town of Sutter Creek since 1859. Located on main street about 35 miles from Sacramento, the inn is the very first of its type to be established in the west. It is rated 4-Star by Mobil Travel Guide.

Lush lawns are filled with garden furniture and hammocks in addition to a huge grape arbor. The spacious old living room is one of informality and relaxation with books and games. All the guest rooms are individually and tastefully furnished. Some have fireplaces, private patios and delightful swinging beds.

A complimentary breakfast is served each morning in an old-fashioned kitchen warmed by a fireplace.

Jane's Potatoes

1-1/4 cups grated jack cheese
3 tbs minced green onion
1 large tomato, diced
salt, pepper, garlic to taste
4 potatoes, unpeeled, boiled, and diced

3 tbs butter
1 diced avocado
1-1/4 cups grated cheddar cheese
1/2 cup sour cream at room temperature
3 tbs minced onion

Melt butter in large skillet over medium-high heat. Add diced potatoes and cook until brown and crisp. Add cheese, tomato, and onion, stirring occasionally until cheese melts. Season well with salt. Gently mix in avocado and spoon onto platter. Top with sour cream. Sprinkle with finely chopped parsley.

75 Main Street, Box 385
Sutter Creek, CA 95685
Tel (209) 267-5606

SOUTHWEST

Tanque Verde Ranch has an authentic history of pioneering, cattle rustling, and Indian battles at an altitude of 2,800 feet in the foothills of a triangle made up of three mountains: the Tanque Verde, Rincon, and Catalina ranges.

It was built in the 1880s by Raefael Carillo on the site of an old Spanish land grant and has gradually expanded from a cattle ranch to a dude ranch.

Miles of unfenced trails, rocky canyons, and spectacular views at every turn provide the setting for Tanque Verde. Because of its unusual history, the ranch has been featured in many fine publications, such as **Esquire, Sports Illustrated,** and **Better Homes and Gardens.**

The lobby's huge stone fireplace, beamed ceiling, colorful Indian rugs, and artifacts make the visitor realize the special past and present of the Southwest. Swimming, tennis, pack trips, and breakfast rides are added pleasures. The cottage-casitas are delightfully furnished with antiques and original art. Most of the lodgings have fireplaces and private patios.

Elegance in dining is to be expected at Tanque Verde. The colorful and well-appointed dining room with its wall of windows provides striking views of the mountains. The menu offers Continental and American cuisine.

Ranch Hickory-Smoked Beef Brisket

2 tbs liquid smoke
1/3 cups white vinegar
2 tsp hickory smoked salt
1 tsp freshly ground black pepper
6 lbs boneless beef brisket, well trimmed
3 cups hickory flavored barbecue sauce

2/3 cup oil
4 bay leaves
1 tsp garlic salt

Rub liquid smoke over entire surface of brisket. Place meat in shallow pan. Blend oil and vinegar and pour over meat. Add bay leaves. Refrigerate 2 hours, turning occasionally. Before cooking, remove brisket from marinade and pat dry. Blend seasonings and rub into both sides of beef. When mesquite or charcoal fires are ready, toss in layer of dampened hickory chips and position grill 6 inches above coals. Sear brisket 6 to 8 minutes on each side. Remove brisket from grill. Place on 2 layers of heavy duty aluminum foil, cover with 3/4 cup hickory flavored barbecue sauce, large Spanish onion, thinly sliced. Seal foil, place on grill, and roast 50 minutes on each side or until done. Serve with crusted homemade bread and warm barbecue sauce. Excellent as cold leftover.

14301 E. Speedway
Tucson, AZ 85748
Tel (520) 296-6275

SOUTHWEST

THE
WINE COUNTRY INN

The Wine Country Inn is a New England-style inn that extends a warm welcome to travelers in the beautiful agricultural landscape of Napa Valley. With its restful surroundings of century-old stone bridges, houses, barns, rock buildings, and pump houses, the perfect setting for artists and photographers is captured.

Guest rooms are colorful and individually decorated with country antiques. Some of the rooms have patios, others have intimate balconies. Most all the rooms have fireplaces and outside rural views. Nearby, guests may enjoy tennis, hot air balloons, and several Robert Lewis Stevenson memorial sites.

A buffet-style Continental breakfast is served each morning.

Strawberry Nut Bread

2 10-oz pkgs frozen, sliced strawberries

4 eggs	**1 cup cooking oil**
2 cups sugar	**3 cups all-purpose flour**
1 tbs cinnamon	**1 tsp baking soda**
1 tsp salt	**1 1/4 cups chopped nuts**

Defrost strawberries. Beat eggs in bowl until fluffy, add cooking oil, sugar, and berries. Sift together flour, cinnamon, soda, and salt into mix bowl; add strawberry mixture and mix well until blended. Stir in nuts. Pour into two greased and floured 9 1/2 x 5 x 3 loaf pans. Bake in 350° oven for 1 hour 10 minutes. Cool in pans for 10 minutes, then turn out of pans and cool on racks. This bread slices best when chilled. May be sliced and warmed to serve with butter, whipped cream cheese, fruit salad, or for sandwiches.

1152 Lodi Lane
St. Helena, CA 94574
Tel (707) 963-7077

SOUTHWEST

The Captain Whidbey

The Captain Whidbey Inn is the very image of an old inn by the sea greeting visitors with good food and lodging just as it did nearly a century ago when towns people arrived to the remote location by steamer. It is built of madrona logs and enjoys one of the northwest's most beautiful areas between Seattle and Vancouver.

The downstairs sitting room has a beach stone fireplace, and the upstairs guest rooms are furnished with antiques. A well stocked library is at hand to entertain guests who like to slip into a good book on dark nights and listen to the water lapping the shore. Rustic cottages with large rooms, fireplaces, and waterfront views continue the privacy.

Hospitality is the main ingredient of this old inn where good food is served in the dining room overlooking the cove. Specialties include Salmon Bisque and Cream of Broccoli Soup.

Captain Whidbey Washington Apple Cake

3 eggs	1 tsp baking soda
2 cups sugar	1/2 tsp salt
1 tsp vanilla flavoring	1 cup vegetable oil
2 cups flour	1 cup chopped walnuts
2 tsp cinnamon	4 cups thinly sliced, pared, tart apples

Beat eggs with mixer until thick and light, combining sugar and oil. Pour in eggs with mixer on medium speed. Stir flour, cinnamon, soda, and salt together; add to egg mixture. Add vanilla. Beat until thoroughly mixed. Stir in walnuts, spread apples in buttered 9 x 13 pan. Pour mixture over apples, spreading the batter to cover apples. Bake at 350 degrees for 1 hour. Cool, spread with cream cheese icing.

Cream Cheese Icing

Soften 2 3-oz pkgs cream cheese. Beat until fluffy. Beat in 1/4 cup melted butter, adding 2 cups powdered sugar and 1 tsp lemon juice. Spread over Apple Cake and refrigerate until served.

2072 West Whidbey Island Inn Road
Coupeville, WA 98239
Tel (206) 678-4097

NORTHWEST

Columbia Gorge Hotel

Columbia Gorge Hotel quickly became the get-a-way for the rich and famous when it was built by lumber baron Simon Benson in 1921. Looking over the mighty Columbia River Gorge with snow-capped Mt. Hood looming in the background, the exquisite hotel has been restored to reflect the 1920's jazz era into which it was born and enjoys one of the world's most inspirational locations.

Close to a 200-foot cascading waterfall, there is river rafting on the White Salmon River, world class skiing on Mt. Hood, cross-country skiing, fishing, hiking, tennis, water sports on the Columbia River, and sternwheel excursion trips. For the less active, simply magnificent scenery lies with every turn of the head.

Of the hotel's 46 guest rooms, no two are alike. Some have canopied beds, gooseneck rockers, and fireplaces. Garden or river views fill the windows.

A world-famous complimentary breakfast whose menu originated over a quarter century ago is served every morning and was once featured in LIFE magazine.

The Columbia River Court dining room offers the very finest Northwest cuisine such as Fresh Columbia River Salmon, Dry-Aged Eastern Prime Beef, Roast Rack of Lamb Provenciale, and Hood River Apple Pie.

Warm Spinach Salad with Smoked Duck

5 bunches spinach	4 tbs crisp bacon bits
1 hardboiled egg, chopped	
1 breast of tender smoked duck, cut into strips	

Dressing

1 tbs dry mustard	1/8 cup sugar
2 tbs Worcestershire sauce	1 cup olive oil
1/2 cup red wine vinegar	

Heat bacon bits and smoked duck, add pre-mixed dressing and simmer. Pour dressing over salad and toss. Heat retained duck and bacon again, flame with 2 tbs cognac and smother on spinach to wilt. Sprinkle chopped eggs on top. Toss gently and serve. Serves 2.

4000 West Cliff Drive
Hood River, OR 97031
Tel (503) 386-5566

NORTHWEST

Favorite Bay Inn

The Favorite Bay Inn (Whalers Cove Lodge) once served as the general store for Angoon which lies about halfway between Juneau and Sitka on the west side of Admiralty Island. Built as the home of Elvira Maurstad, foreman of the Civilian Conservation Corps, the inn is accessible by the Alaska Marine (ferry) and is served daily by float plane air-taxis. Excellent views of the boat harbor and towering spruce provide the rustic retreat a most pleasant spot.

The area abounds with marine and upland wildlife. In addition to excellent fishing for salmon, trout, halibut, clams, shrimp, guests frequently hear the sounds of whales, sea lions, Bald eagles, and drumming grouse.

A complimentary breakfast is served each morning and family style dinners upon request. Favorites are Halibut and Rice Casserole and Halibut Caddy Ganty.

Halibut and Rice Casserole

3 cups halibut cubes
1 tbs soy sauce
1 cup crushed pineapple
1/4 medium green pepper, crushed

1/4 cup butter
2 tbs prepared mustard
1/4 cup honey

2 cups partially cooked long grain rice

Preheat oven to 350 degrees. Put butter in large casserole dish and set in oven to melt. Remove and add honey, soy sauce, and mustard. Stir in until well mixed. Add remaining ingredients and toss lightly. Cover and bake 45 minutes to 1 hour.

Box 101
Angoon, AK 99820
Tel (907) 788-3123

NORTHWEST

Lone Mountain Ranch

Lone Mountain Ranch was homesteaded by Clarence Lytel in 1915 as a working cattle and hay ranch. Located 20 miles from Yellowstone National Park, many of its native log buildings were built by the Butlers and Kilburns. It was a showplace for Mrs. Butler's Indian artifacts and friends would find their way up to the reverse B bar K, as it was then called, to view Yellowstone and admire her extensive collection.

The fifty-year-old cabins are furnished with handmade tables and chairs, fireplaces for warmth, and porches that provide spectacular sights near a rushing stream. Planned activities at this all-season resort include horseback riding, sleigh rides, and cross-country ski trails that lead from the cabin door. Deep powder snow makes Lone Mountain Ranch an outstanding center for Nordic skiing.

At the sound of a bell, excellent meals are served family style in an old-fashioned Western dining hall. Specialties include Oatmeal Bread, Spinach Salad with Hot Bacon Dressing, and desserts that are baked daily from "scratch."

Spinach Salad with Hot Bacon Dressing

Salad:

1 bunch cleaned spinach	4 oz sliced mushrooms
2 hardboiled eggs, sliced	
2 tomato wedges or cherry tomato halves	

Arrange first spinach, then mushrooms, and tomatoes along edge and top with sliced egg.

Dressing:

4 egg yolks	1 oz white sugar
1 oz stone ground mustard	1 oz white vinegar
3 strips bacon cut into thin strips	
1 tbs dill weed	1/2 cup salad oil
1 tsp fresh cracked black pepper	
salt, Worcestershire, Tabasco to taste	
onions	

Saute bacon and onions together. Mix all other ingredients together except salad oil. Add salad oil slowly, as in making mayonnaise, mixing with wire whip. When bacon is browned slightly, cool for only a few minutes. Bacon fat should still be warm when added. Add slowly to oil and other ingredients, mixing with wire whip. To adjust consistency, add salad oil to thicken or vinegar to thin.

Box 145
Big Sky, MT 59716
Tel (406) 995-4644

NORTHWEST

PARADISE RANCH INN

Paradise Ranch Inn is warm and friendly with the natural beauty of Oregon everywhere. Outside Grants Pass in the scenic Rogue River Valley, this working-guest ranch has welcomed visitors since 1969. The white painted fences against the green countryside, swans floating on willow-lined ponds, trout fishing, and walks along beautiful trails that encircle the ranch provide it with a fitting name. Additional activities include two lighted tennis courts, golf, horseback riding, and float trips on the rugged Rogue River, one of the last truly wild rivers in the country. An occasional cattle roundup recalls the days of the Old West. Guest rooms are warm and homey with colorful touches.

Meals are served in the dining room with traditional regional dishes and the menu includes Breast of Chicken Cacciatore, Veal Cordon Bleu, Rack of Lamb, Stuffed Scampi, and a selection of tempting desserts.

Chicken with Garlic Sauce

Seasoned flour	2 tbs butter
2 tbs oil	1-1/2 cups dry white wine
1-1/2 cups chicken broth	1/2 cup parsley, chopped
1 tsp dried tarragon	boneless breasts of chicken for 6

15 to 20 garlic cloves, peeled and cut in length-wise halves
Do not be afraid to use this number of cloves).

Assemble all ingredients. In seasoned flour, dredge chicken. In casserole, heat butter and oil and brown chicken. Remove. To casserole, add any remaining flour, stirring to blend well. Add wine and deglaze casserole. Add broth and cook, stirring, until sauce thickens. Stir in garlic, parsley, and tarragon. Bake covered at 350° 1 hour or until chicken is tender.

700 Monument Drive
Grants Pass, OR 97526
Tel (503) 479-4333

NORTHWEST

LAKE
QUINAULT
LODGE

Lake Quinault Lodge is bordered by the lush Olympic National Forest and has welcomed visitors to the south shore of Lake Quinault since 1926. The spacious lobby of the large cedar structure is warmed by a massive brick fireplace, old-fashioned wicker furniture, stenciled beams, and windows flooded with spectacular views of the mountains and lakes. Each guest room is comfortably furnished and some have fireplaces. Open the year 'round, activities include an indoor swimming pool, boating, hiking, fishing, and hunting. The inn is rated AAA.

The dining room is cheerfully decorated with colorful Indian art and artifacts of the Northwest. Regional seafood entrees and a selection of other dishes are served as part of the hearty menu. This recipe was seen earlier in *America's Country Inn Cookbook.*

Salmon Papillote

6 salmon fillets, 5 to 6 oz each
salt & French's Pepper
parchment paper
2 tbs melted butter or margarine
1 lemon (6 wedges)

Newburg Sauce
French's Paprika

Lightly season salmon with salt and pepper. Cut 12 pieces parchment paper 2'' larger in diameter than salmon fillets, rounding corners. Generously brush centers of papers with butter. Prepare Newburg Sauce; spoon 2 to 3 tbs onto each of 6 paper centers. Top each with 1 salmon fillet. Spoon about 1 tbs sauce over each fillet; sprinkle with paprika. Cover with remaining parchment, buttered side down. Roll up edges of paper and press to seal. Place on baking sheet and bake at 400 degrees for 12-15 minutes, until parchment is lightly browned and puffed. Serve fillets in parchment cases garnish with lemon wedges. Serves 6.

Newburg Sauce

2 tbs butter or margarine
2 tbs plus 1 tsp flour
dash French's Cayenne Pepper
2 tsp French's Vive la Dijon Mustard

1/2 cup chicken broth
1/2 cup Half & Half
1 tbs dry sherry

Melt butter in small saucepan. Remove from heat; add flour, mustard, and cayenne pepper. Cook over low heat, stirring, 1 minute. Gradually add chicken broth. Bring to boil, stirring constantly; simmer 1 minute. Stir in Half and Half and sherry. Simmer 1 minute.

P.O. Box 7, South Shore Road
Quinault, WA 98575
Tel (206) 288-2571

NORTHWEST

Shoshone Lodge

Shoshone Lodge is surrounded by lofty pines and the incomparable beauty of Shoshone National Park. Only four miles from Yellowstone with an elevation of 6,700 feet, the rustic resort is truly an exciting place for the outdoorsman.

Inside, the lobby sets the pace for true Western hospitality with its large fireplace, walls lined with hunting trophies, colorful Navajo Indian rugs, and piano for sing-a-longs. Each guest room is comfortably furnished in western decor and tempered with cool, pine scented nights. Several log cabins are hidden among the pines and firs.

Pack trips into the adjacent wilderness area and big game hunting with a licensed outfitter are what Shoshone Lodge guests expect.

Delicious homecooked meals are served in a warm, Western fashion beside an open hearth.

Old Fashioned Bread Pudding

1 cup sugar	4 eggs slightly beaten
1 tsp cinnamon or nutmeg	1/2 tsp salt
1 cup raisins	2 tsp vanilla
4 cups milk scalded with 1/2 cup	margarine
6 cups soft bread crumbs (8 cups for	firmer pudding)

Heat oven to 350°. Place bread crumbs in 3-qt baking dish. Blend in remaining ingredients. Place dish in pan of hot water 1'' deep. Bake 40-45 minutes or until knife inserted 1'' from edge comes out clean. Serve warm with orange sauce. Serves 12-16.

Orange Sauce

1 cup sugar	2 tbs cornstarch
2 cups boiling orange juice	4 tbs butter
3 tbs lemon juice	few grains nutmeg
few grains salt	

Mix sugar and cornstarch. Add juice gradually, stirring constantly. Cover and boil 5 minutes, stirring occasionally. Remove from heat and add other ingredients. Makes 2 cups.

Box 790
Cody, WY 82414
Tel (307) 587-4044

NORTHWEST

STEAMBOAT INN

Steamboat Inn is a welcome retreat for those who love the sport of fishing for fighting Steelhead Trout. Surrounded by a fortress of towering Douglas Firs and views of North Umpqua, the building was constructed of cedar and stone in 1954 by Clarence Gordon, an expert fly fisherman, and named for an old gold camp fraud: when a speculator sold a worthless claim under false pretenses, he "steamboated" down the river. Fishermen from around the world have been attracted to North Umpqua including Zane Grey, who spent several summers in the cascade wilderness.

Eight rustic cabins are secluded among the sights, sounds, and scents of forest and river. Each guest room is carpeted, pine paneled, and opens onto a spacious deck facing the river.

Dinner is served at sundown by candlelight before a blazing fire to inn guests only. An expansive table hewn from a single slab of sugar pine is graced with colorful appointments. Specialties include Vichyssoise, Smoked Salmon, Chicken Breast with Proscuitto, Mushroom Souffle, Pork Loin with Sour Cream Sauce, and Lamb and Spinach with Phyllo.

Steamboat Coffee Cake

Cream together:

1/2 cup butter	1/4 cup sugar
1/4 cup date sugar	1/4 cup honey

Add:

1 tsp vanilla	3 eggs, beaten

Sift and add to above alternately with 1/2 pt sour cream:

1 cup sifted flour	1 tsp baking powder
1 cup whole wheat pastry flour	1 tsp baking soda

Cream:

6 tbs butter	1/3 cup brown sugar
2 tsp cinnamon	1 cup chopped nuts

Grease a 10-cup bundt pan, pour in 1/2 batter and sprinkle nut mixture over batter. Cover with remaining batter and bake 50-60 minutes in 350⁰ oven.

HC60 Box 36
Idleyld Park, OR 97447
Tel (503) 498-2411 or 496-3495

NORTHWEST

Inn of The White Salmon is nestled on a bluff above the mighty Columbia River providing striking views of snow-capped Mt. Hood and great hospitality. Its location is ideal for the outdoorsman. While cross-country skiers enjoy the Mount Adams wilderness area, downhill skiers love the groomed slopes of Mt. Hood.

The handsome red brick structure dates back to 1937 and has changed very little since it was built except for refurbishing the 19 Victorian-style guest rooms. No two are alike with their brass beds and antique dressers. The unhurried atmosphere is complete with hostesses dressed in long skirts and old fashioned blouses.

The Columbia Scenic Gorge Excursions offer all-season activities, wilderness pack trips with malamute dogs carrying supplies, and Mt. St. Helen tours.

The famous "Loretta's Inn Breakfast" is served buffet each morning on lovely, delicate china. Offerings include an array of seasonal Fresh Fruits, Hot Egg dishes, Cream Cheese and Raisin Strudel, Hungarian Love Letters boasting a cream cheese, butter and nut filling, German Beer Bread, and Baklava.

Artichoke Frittata

2 18-oz cans non-marinated artichoke
hearts (20-25) cut into quarters, enough to
cover bottom of 9 x 13 pan
2 tbs butter
1/2 cup Parmesan cheese, divided
1-1/2 cups Half & Half
20 eggs
3 cups shredded jack cheese

Saute artichoke hearts and butter in skillet for a few minutes, then add 1/4 cup Parmesan cheese. Place in pan. Mix eggs and Half & Half together and pour over artichokes. Top with jack cheese and bake 25 minutes at 350°. Top with 1/4 cup (or more) Parmesan cheese, enough to cover top of casserole. Bake 5 minutes longer. Serves 12 people very generously. Recipe can be cut in half.

172 Jewett Boulevard
White Salmon, WA 98672
Tel (509) 493-2335

THE WINCHESTER INN

The Winchester Inn, once the site of the first hospital in southern Oregon, is a fine example of a Queen Anne style house. The parlor and six guest rooms are furnished with handsome period pieces that create a pleasant country style. An easy stroll to the Shakespearean theatre and the Lithia Park enhance the visit to the inn. A complimentary breakfast is offered on the patio or in the dining room each morning.

Evening meals are served to guests and the public alike in a room overlooking tiered gardens.

Chocolate Raspberry Cake

6 oz pastry flour
2 oz coco butter
1/2 cup hot coffee
2 oz butter
2 tbs apricot jam
1 lb semi-sweet Belgian chocolate
1 cup almonds toasted and ground with
berries for garnish

2 pts fresh raspberries
8 eggs
1/3 lb sugar
1 cup cream
2 oz melted butter

Sift together flour and cocoa. Whisk eggs with sugar over hot water until thick and has reached temperature of 100 degrees. Remove from heat and whisk until cool. Mixture should be light and thick, three times greater in volume. Carefully fold in flour and cocoa mixture, adding butter. Bake in two well-greased 9 x 12 cake pans about 40 minutes. Tops should spring back when pressed. Turn cakes out and when cold, slice off top third. Carefully scoop out insides to form a container with sides and bottom 1/2'' thick. Melt jam and combine with berries. Fill cake with raspberries and jam. Return top slice and chill. Melt chocolate, coffee, and butter together. In another pan bring cream to boil. Whisk all together lightly until completely combined. When chocolate mixture has cooled, spread on top and sides of cake. Mask sides with almonds and garnish top with a few berries. Serves 10-12.

35 South Second Street
Ashland, OR 97520
Tel (503) 488-1113

NORTHWEST

THE ARCHER HOUSE

Archer House's opening was described in the Rice County Journal as a grand event in the history of Northfield. Built by James Archer in 1877, this stately French Second Empire-style hotel is bordered on the west by Cannon River and on the east by bustling Division Street.

After a colorful century of sheltering travelers and a succession of innkeepers, Dallas Haas in 1981 rescued the structure from the ravages of time. A building contractor, he used his expertise to properly restore the old landmark where the greeting, "Welcome Friends" still stands.

The elegant lobby has a stained glass portal, pressed tin ceiling, carved wingbacks, and an open stairway sweeping to upstairs guest rooms. Old fashioned, the rooms are furnished with crafted pine, quaint wallpaper, handmade quilts, tiebacks and collectibles.

A short stroll leads to the Northfield Historical Society Museum headquartered in the former bank where the notorious Jesse James and his gang attempted a robbery in 1876. Stopped by local townspeople, the gang that had raided banks and trains for a decade came to a bitter end.

A Continental breakfast is offered each morning. Meals are served in the restaurant.

Galatoboureko
(Greek Custard Dessert with Lemon Syrup)

3 cups milk
1/2 cup sugar
1 tbs vanilla
3/4 cup melted butter
1/2 cup plus 1 tbs Quick Cooking
Farina Cereal

3 cups heavy cream
7 egg yolks
1/2 lb phyllo leaves

Preheat oven to 375° and grease a 9 x 13 x 3 baking pan. Combine milk and cream in a heavy 3-qt sauce pan, heating just to a boiling point on medium high, stirring occasionally to prevent scorching. While milk and cream are heating, combine sugar and farina in small bowl. In large mixing bowl beat egg yolks and vanilla well. When milk and cream come to boil, reduce heat to medium low and slowly sprinkle sugar/farina mixture into sauce pan, stirring constantly 5-10 minutes until mixture is slightly thickened. Remove from heat and pour into egg yolks and and stir until mixed. Lay one phyllo leaf into greased baking pan, allowing the extra dough to slope up the sides of the pan, carefully brushing with melted butter. Repeat procedure for 5 more layers of phyllo. Now pour custard mixture into pan and with sharp knife trim remaining phyllo to fit 9 x 13 pan exactly. Place a layer of dough on custard mixture, brushing with melted butter, repeating until 5 more layers are added. With sharp knife cut TOP LAYER OF DOUGH ONLY into 2" squares. DO NOT CUT BOTTOM. Bake 35 minutes. While still hot, pour lemon syrup over top of baking pan. Cool on rack for at least 1 hour before cutting. May be served warm or cold.

Lemon Syrup:
3/4 cup sugar
1/3 cup water
1/4 tsp finely grated lemon peel

1 tbs lemon juice

Combine sugar and water in sauce pan and heat until boiling. Reduce heat and simmer 8-10 minutes until thickened slightly. Remove from heat and add lemon juice and lemon peel.

212 Division Street
Northfield, MN 55057
Tel (507) 645-5661

The Blackfork Inn

The Blackfork Inn is a handsome mansard roof mansion with dormers, bays and porches, built in 1865 and is listed on the National Register of Historic Places.

The Amish lend the dominating atmosphere of this hill area location that abounds in prime orchards that Johnny Appleseed established in the late seventeen and eighteen hundreds. In addition to the quaint pastoral countryside, activities include skiing and more.

A Continental breakfast is graciously served in the dining room where Amish foods are made by local families. Apple Butter, Raspberry Jam, Spicy Chutney, and Trail Bologna are enjoyed.

Chutney

15 large, very ripe tomatoes, peeled, cored, and chopped
5 large tart apples, cored and chopped
3 green peppers, seeded and chopped
4 cups firmly packed brown sugar
1 large onion, chopped
3 cups cider vinegar
2 tsp ground ginger
¼ tsp cayenne

2 tsp salt
1 tsp allspice
1 tsp dry mustard

Combine all ingredients in large kettle. Simmer uncovered two hours or until thickness desired, stirring often during last half-hour. Ladle boiling hot mixture into hot pint jars leaving ¼-inch head space. Process in boiling water bath 10 minutes. Makes about nine pints.

303 North Water Street
Loudonville, OH 44842
Tel (419) 994-3252

NORTHCENTRAL

Botsford Inn

Botsford Inn, established in 1836, recalls the days of the stagecoaches and cattle drovers. The inn is located on the Grand River Trail and is Michigan's oldest operating hostelry. It was bought in 1924 by Henry Ford as a romantic gesture to his wife Clara, whom he had met at a square dance in the ballroom.

The historic inn has been enlarged several times and today it has the look of a 19th century plantation home. Brick paths in the courtyard lead to the fragrance of many colorful flowers and shrubs.

Inside, the inn is filled with antiques. Some of the Ford furnishings include a lovely Swiss music box, a chickering grand piano, and a 100 year old melodian. All the guest rooms are decorated in the Early American style. One room still has the same period furnishings that were used by Thomas A. Edison when he visited the Fords.

Greenfield Village and Henry Ford Museum, Ford Fairlane Estate, golf courses, Franklin Village, and Plymouth are all within a 30 minute drive.

Waitresses in long calico dresses add to the atmosphere in the Early American dining room that serves Roast Turkey with Giblet Gravy, other Midwestern fare, and tempting desserts.

Raspberry Gem Tarts

1/4 cup unblanched almonds
1/2 cup fine, dry bread crumbs
1/4 cup flour
1/2 tsp baking powder
1/4 tsp salt

1/2 cup butter
3/4 cup sugar
2 eggs
1/2 tsp vanilla extract
1/4 tsp almond extract

Combine finely chopped almonds, bread crumbs, flour, baking powder, and salt. Cream together butter, sugar, and eggs, and mix in vanilla and almond extracts. Add dry ingredients a little at a time, combining lightly but thoroughly. Line tart pans with thinly rolled pie crust, spooning a small amount of good raspberry jam into each, being certain to cover the bottom of each tart completely. Spoon batter over jam and bake 20-25 minutes or until golden brown at 375°. Yields approximately 2 dozen tarts.

28000 Grand River at Eight Mile Road
Farmington Hills, MI 48024
Tel (313) 474-4800

Cascade Lodge

Cascade Lodge is a large wood and stone structure overlooking Lake Superior with an endless forest of resting aspen in the background. The lodge blends perfectly with its rustic surroundings that abound with birds, deer, bear, moose and other wildlife.

A cozy fire, piano for sing-alongs, good conversation, and Christian fellowship make this a memorable place to visit. The guest rooms are comfortable with either lake or forest views. There are also log cabins with fireplaces.

The lodge offers all-season outdoor sports and planned activities for all ages including miles of groomed cross-country ski trails that lead right from the front door. Everyone enjoys watching and feeding the deer.

The North Shore Restaurant is home to meals. Burgers, steaks, seafood, and pasta dinners are part of the fare.

Cascade's Homemade Split Pea Soup

1 ham bone	2 cups chopped onion
1 lb split peas	1-1/2 cups diced ham
2 cups chopped celery	1 cup diced or shredded carrots
1/2 tsp Lawry's seasoned salt	2 tbs ham base or stock from roast ham
1/4 tsp marjoram	(not if it has been glazed with anything
5 qts water	sweet)

In large kettle add water, ham bone, ham base, peas, onions, and celery; simmer until vegetables are very tender. Remove ham bone. Strip any meat from bone; dice and use as part of the 1-1/2 cups diced ham. Add diced carrots, ham, seasoned salt, marjoram, and celery salt. Cook until carrots are tender. Makes 1-1/2 gallons.

3719 W. Hwy. 61
Lutsen, MN 55612
Tel (218) 387-1112

NORTHCENTRAL

The Cider Mill

The Cider Mill recalls the days when it served the religious community of Zoar as an old mill. Built in 1863 and completely renovated in 1972, the building still plays a rich part in Zoar, once the summer retreat of President McKinley.

Inside, the character of the inn's construction has been well preserved. The custom handmade, three-story spiral stairway, original ceiling beams, and fireplace complete with stone hearth are fitting complements to the old structure. Tastefully furnished with antiques, cozy guest rooms reflect the charm of the country.

Zoar's museum is composed of eight historic buildings that take visitors on a journey into the past. Besides other nearby activities such as river trips, antique and craft shops, hiking trails, fishing, and golf, the inn has its own gift shop with handcrafted items by local craftsmen. A complimentary breakfast is offered each morning.

Favorite family-style meals are served in the country restaurant.

Hot Spiced Cider

1 gal apple cider
2 tsp whole allspice
2/3 cup sugar

2 tsp whole cloves
2 sticks cinnamon (3" each)
2 whole oranges

Tie spices in cheese cloth or place in tea ball. Add to cider along with sugar and whole oranges. Heat to boiling; cover and simmer 20 minutes.

198 Second Street
P.O. Box 438
Zoar, OH 44697
Tel (330) 874-3240

Duneland
Beach Inn

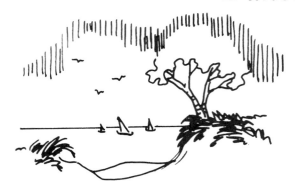

The Inn At Duneland Beach offers gracious hospitality and fine food in a secluded residential area surrounded by trees and wildlife. An ideal vacation spot, and open all year, ten cozy guest rooms lead to sandy white beaches that stretch along clear Michigan waters.

Winter activities bring cross-country skiing, snowmobiling, popcorn and apple cider in front of a blazing hearth. Just a short trip away, guests enjoy tennis, horseback riding, and charter fishing.

A hearty complimentary country breakfast is served each morning.

Pate

For each pound of chicken livers, barely cover with water and simmer 20 minutes. Drain and grind up. Blend into livers:

1 stick margarine
1 small onion, minced
1 tsp salt
dash cayenne

1/4 tsp ground cloves
1 tsp dry mustard
dash nutmeg

Best prepared day ahead.

3311 Pottawattomie Trail
Michigan City, IN 46360
Tel (219) 874-7729

Fort Robinson State Park's colorful past has undoubtedly stamped an indelible mark into the fabric of American Indian history.

The Fort was the site where famed Sioux warrior Crazy Horse surrendered to the cavalry in 1877. The Cheyennes, led by Chief Dull Knife, were also captured at the Fort. The Cheyennes escaped in 1879 and within two weeks the last escapee was killed or captured at the Battle of Wounded Knee. In 1890 Fort Robinson served as a supply point and in 1943 it was a prisoner of war camp for German soldiers.

Today, the Enlisted Men's Barracks, 1887 Officer's Quarters, and Bachelor Officers's Quarters provide accommodations amidst the 22,000-acre wildlife preserve situated near the confluence of Soldier Creek and White River. Activities include tennis, swimming, games, hunting, horseback riding, and museums.

Buffalo Stew and Cornbread are served every evening at the fort's cookout along with entertainment.

Buffalo Stew

30 lbs cooked buffalo stew meat
3 large onions chopped small
10 bay leaves
1-1/2 qts tomato soup
5 tbs basil
3-4 gals vegetable stew mix, drained
2 large cabbage heads, chopped small

Add stew meat broth to cover mixture of meat, cabbage, basil, onions, and bay leaves and cook at 375 degrees for 2 hours. Add vegetables and tomato soup. Turn down heat to 250 degrees and simmer for approximately 1 hour. Serves 60.

Box 392
Crawford, NE 69339
Tel (308) 665-2660

The Golden Lamb

The Golden Lamb has provided a warm welcome from the very beginning. In the early days, travelers and coachmen unable to read were told to look for "the sign of the golden lamb and stop for the night". Established as Ohio's oldest continuous business, the inn was liscensed to Jonas Seaman in 1803.

The two-story Federal brick structure was built in 1815 to replace the original log tavern that houses the lobby. Notables who have enjoyed its hospitality include Mark Twain, Charles Dickens, William Henry Harrison, Ulysses S. Grant, and Kentucky statesman, Henry Clay. The Golden Lamb is listed on the National Register of Historic Places.

The inn is a museum in a sense, filled with an extensive collection of Shaker pieces and Currier and Ives prints. On the fourth floor is Sara's room, named for Sara Stubbs who lived there as a child around the turn of the century. The room is decorated with nostalgic furnishings and toys reflecting her early childhood. Each of the 19 guest rooms is comfortable with antiques and named for a famous visitor. No two rooms are alike, and in its old-fashioned atmosphere, the Lamb Shop has gifts to take back home.

Meals are served in four public and five private dining rooms furnished with antiques. The Lebanon Dining Room dates back to 1825. A wide variety of Mid-Western favorites in addition to seafood entrees are served.

Celery Seed Dressing

1/2 cup sugar
1 tsp dry mustard
1 tsp salt
1 tsp celery seed

1/4 tsp grated onion
1/3 cup vinegar
1 cup salad oil

Mix all dry ingredients. Add onion. Add small amount of oil and mix well. Add vinegar and oil alternately, ending with oil.

Lebanon, OH 45036
Tel (513) 932-5065

Grand Hotel

Grand Hotel, the "Dowager Queen of Mackinac Island", aptly describes the world's largest summer hotel. It was built by a railway company and has dominated the island since 1887. The hotel is undoubtedly the showpiece on this island that was a famous resort long before the Civil War. The atmosphere is further enhanced by the total absence of gasoline powered vehicles.

The adventure begins with a 30 minute ferry trip and the trek to the hotel is turned into a charming story book classic by a horse-drawn coach whose driver is dressed in immaculate attire. Many U.S. presidents, ambassadors, generals, and royalty from around the world have been its guests. Activities abound with golf, tennis, swimming, music and walks through 500 acres of woods and gardens. Shops, restaurants, and natural and historic sites are at every turn.

The guest rooms, individually and pleasantly decorated, overlook landscaped grounds with bright geraniums and the sparkling deep blue waters of the Straits of Mackinac.

The menu includes European fare and the best of American dishes such as Shrimp Madagascar, Raspberry Cheesecake, and Grand Hotel Brownies.

Bamboo Peach

1 lb. 4 oz. canned peached   **13 oz bamboo shoots**

Sauce:

1 cup sour cream
1 tsp cinnamon   **1/4 cup sugar**
1/2 tsp curry   **1 tsp mace**
                         1 tsp nutmeg

In stainless steel bowl, mix peaches and shoots together. Mix ingredients of sauce by hand to smooth. Combine with the peaches and bamboo shoots. Serve in champagne glass or other suitable glassware. Serves 4.

Mackinac Island, MI 49757
Tel (906) 847-3331 or (517) 487-1800

THE HERITAGE HOUSE

The Heritage House has a reputation for fine dining that has been a tradition in the Cincinnati area since the turn of the century. In those days this fashionable restaurant was known as Kelly's Roadhouse.

Sports celebrities, politicians, newspaper writers, and all sorts of famous people were frequent guests. It also played a part in the prohibition era and it was the hub for John Robinson's Circus performers who wintered nearby. Stories abound from this period. . .

Built by Edgar Scott as a home in 1827, the Colonial style structure has been completely renovated and under new ownership since 1959. As part of its hospitality and charm, an extensive collection of Indian artifacts is on display that tells the story of still another era. A walk through delightful herb gardens is an added treat. No overnight lodgings are provided.

Meals are served in seven dining rooms, and some have wood-burning fireplaces and beam ceilings. The menu includes authentic Cajun Foods, Medallion of Beef, New York Cut Sirloin, Rack of Lamb with Rosemary and Garlic Sauce, Wild Game in season, Fresh Vegetables, and a delightful array of tempting desserts.

White Chocolate Mousse with Antlers

1/2 lb real white chocolate (with cocoa
butter content)
1 cup sugar
3 cups whipping cream

6 eggs, separated
white cream de cocoa

Melt chocolate in double boiler. In saucepan, heat egg whites and sugar over low heat, stirring until sugar has melted. Transfer to mixing bowl. Whip egg whites until stiff. Whip chilled cream until it is almost stiff (soft peaks). Beat egg yolks slightly. Add creme de cocoa. Blend well. Transfer melted chocolate to large bowl. Add egg yolk mixture. Blend. Add 1/3 of whipped egg whites. Blend well. Fold whipped cream into remaining whipped egg whites. Add chocolate mixture to cream and egg whites, folding carefully until well blended. Spoon into serving dishes and chill, or chill in mixing bowl and then, using an ice cream scoop, serve in a cookie shell. For something extra special, the cookie shell could be coated with melted semi-sweet chocolate before placing the mousse in the shell. Top with Melba sauce. Yield: about 10 servings.

Chocolate Antlers

6 oz semi-sweet chocolate, cut in small pieces
1 tbs vegetable shortening

Tempered chocolate produces a beautiful satin sheen on the antlers. Place chocolate and shortening in top of double boiler over medium heat. Stir until chocolate is melted and is blended with the shortening. Remove from heat. Cook until chocolate starts to thicken. Line a baking sheet with parchment paper. Using a pastry bag with a writing tube, pipe chocolate onto parchment in the shape of antlers. Cool completely. Remove from parchment. To serve, insert antler into center of each serving of White Chocolate Mousse.

Marinade (Variation)

Chocolate Cups

6 oz semi-sweet chocolate, cut in small pieces
1 tbs vegetable shortening

Cool chocolate mixture until it is cool enough to handle. Fan out cupcake liner, place a tbs of chocolate in the center of the liner. Use a small spatula or back of a spoon to spread the chocolate evenly inside the liner. Place the chocolate cup in a muffin tin. Repeat the procedure with the remaining liners. Refrigerate until chocolate is hardened. Carefully remove foil liners before serving. The cups should be kept in the muffin tins in the refrigerator until ready to serve. Yield: 8 cups.

Grilled Duck Breast With Raspberry Barbeque Sauce

This recipe of Jerry Hart's has been requested by Gourmet Magazine. Raspberry Barbeque Sauce can also be served with grilled pork or chicken.

8 duck breasts, boned and   salt and pepper
skin removed

Grill duck breasts over a hardwood fire, (2-3 minutes on each side for medium rare). Serve with Raspberry Barbeque Sauce. Yield: 8 servings.

Raspberry Barbeque Sauce

1 cup onion, chopped
1/2 cup celery, chopped
1/2 cup green pepper, chopped
2 tbs olive oil
2 garlic cloves, crushed
pinch of cayenne pepper
1/4 tsp thyme
1/4 cup brown sugar

1/4 cup molasses
1 tbs. German style mustard
1 bay leaf
1/4 cup red wine or raspberry vinegar
2 cups chicken stock
1/8 tsp salt
2 cups raspberries, fresh or frozen

In a large saucepan, heat oil and sautee onion, celery and green pepper for 3 minutes. Add garlic, cayenne, thyme, brown sugar, molasses, mustard, bay leaf, vinegar, stock and salt. Stir to mix. Simmer over low heat for 20 minutes. Add raspberries and simmer 15 minutes. Puree sauce in food processor or blender in small batches. Strain. Serve hot with grilled duck breast, pork or chicken. Yield: 4 cups.

7664 Wooster Pike
Cincinnati, OH 45227
Tel (513) 561-9300

Lowell Inn - and the Palmers have welcomed guests with treasured traditions that have become a national hallmark of family innkeeping since 1930. Today, a third generation continues to pamper guests in that same spirit of hospitality.

The stately red brick structure has white columns, colorful flags, and verandas filled with cozy little tables and chairs. Lowell Inn, a "Crown Jewell" of American inns, is to be enjoyed every season for all occasions.

The impressive living room is furnished with period pieces and other interesting memorabilia. Guest rooms and suites feature the soft touch of French Provincial. Each is a strong reflection of the innkeeper's taste.

Meals are served in three well-appointed dining rooms. The George Washington, the Garden Room, and the Matterhorn Room present a menu that has remained the same for nearly a quarter century. Family recipes for Swiss Pear Bread and Fruit Salad Dressing have been served to patrons now for over 50 years.

Old-Fashioned Maple Frango

3/4 cup maple syrup

4 egg yolks

1/4 cup alaga syrup

3 cups whipped cream

Warm syrup slightly before adding to warm egg yolks. Boil gently until thick. Cool. Whip cream and fold in maple mixture. Pour into pan 3-4'' deep. Serves 8-10.

Lowell Inn
102 North Second Street
Stillwater, MN 55082
Tel (612) 439-1100

MICHILLINDA BEACH LODGE

Michillinda Beach Lodge greets returning visitors year after year from a wooded bluff overlooking Lake Michigan. In a setting of thick green lawns, pines, and flower gardens, this 1904 estate has gradually expanded to include a variety of charming cottages.

The main inn, furnished with many period pieces and a fireplace, is a favorite gathering spot for old friends to meet and to make new ones. Guest rooms are large and comfortable.

A family resort with planned activities for children, tennis, miniature golf, swimming, shuffleboard, volleyball, and lawn games are all part of the fun at Michillinda Beach Lodge. With outstanding views of the lake, meals are served three times a day in the dining room.

Michillinda Fruit Cocktail Torte

1 cup flour	1 cup sugar
1 tsp baking soda	1 egg
1/2 tsp salt	6 oz fruit cocktail
2/3 cup chopped walnuts	3 tsp brown sugar

Blend flour, sugar, baking soda, and salt. Add eggs and fruit cocktail by hand. Pour into greased pan and sprinkle with brown sugar and chopped walnuts. Bake 30-45 minutes at 350 degrees.

5207 Scenic Drive
Whitehall, MI 49461
Tel (616) 893-1895

THE NATIONAL HOUSE INN

The National House Inn undoubtedly served as a link in the charitable Underground Railroad. These secret stations protected runaway slaves from the South on their way to Canada during pre-Civil War days. Built in 1835 as a stagecoach stop in the village of Marshall, known for its hospitality and fine 19th century architecture, National House is Michigan's oldest operating inn. In 1878 it converted to a windmill factory and later on to an apartment building. Open once again to travelers, this National Register Landmark is restored and filled with antiques.

The guest rooms are named for historic Marshall personalities and range from the elegant Victorian Ketchum suite to pleasant country styles. Mary Daniels of the Chicago Tribune, wrote, "Today, National House is picture book cozy and could serve as a movie set of a by-gone era".

The dining room, with authentic salmon-hued woodwork, oak tables and chairs, is a reflection of our country's heritage. A Continental breakfast of homebaked goods is served each morning.

Sam Hill Breakfast Cake

A delicate cake shell filled with luscious, sweetened sour cream and topped with fresh strawberries.

Cake:

1 cup all-purpose flour	3/4 cup sugar
1/4 tsp salt	3/4 tsp baking powder
1/3 cup butter	1/2 cup milk
1 egg	1 1/2 cups graham crumbs

Filling:

1 16-oz container sour cream	3/4 cup sugar
fresh strawberries, Mandarin oranges,	
or other fruit	

Sift together dry ingredients. Cream butter until fluffy. Add egg and beat until light yellow. Add dry ingredients alternately with milk. Beat until well mixed and somewhat thin. Grease two shallow cake pans with depressed ridge inside rim. Sprinkle 1/2 cup graham cracker crumbs on each cake pan and shake to distribute evenly. Divide batter between two pans. Sprinkle remaining crumbs on top of cake batter and bake at 350 for 10 minutes or until done. Mix sugar with sour cream and fill the center of each cake after they are cooled. Arrange fruit in decorative pattern on top of sour cream. Chill until serving.

102 South Parkview
Marshall, MI 49068
Tel (616) 781-7374

THE NEW HARMONY INN

The New Harmony Inn, composed of a unique collection of contemporary buildings, is in the historic community of New Harmony, founded in 1814 by Lutheran dissenters. These include an Entry House, Chapel, Residence, and a greenhouse swimming pool that overlooks a pastoral scene.

The Entry House has vaulted ceilings, highly polished wood floors, contemporary furnishings, and provides a "retreat" setting for educational and business meetings.

Guest rooms are comfortable yet austere, reflecting the early heritage of the inn. Many of the rooms have balconies and wood-burning fireplaces, and some have spiral stairways that lead to sleeping lofts. All blend harmoniously with the cultural traditions.

Two restaurants offer pleasurable dining. The Red Geranium and the Shadblow serve specialties of Shaker Ham, Red Geranium Shaker Ham Glaze, and Crabmeat stuffing for Shrimp and Fish.

Shaker Ham

Pour over ham:

1 gal. apple cider
1 tsp cloves

1/4 cup chopped onion
1 lemon, quartered

Bake at 300 degrees for 1 hour. Next, pour Red Geranium Shaker Ham Glaze over ham, returning ham to oven and baking 30 minutes longer. Take ham from oven, strain liquid into sauce pan, and return to stovetop. Add to saucepan mixture and heat until thickened.

2 cups cornstarch

1 cup water

Slice ham and serve thickened over ham.

Red Geranium Shaker Ham Glaze

Mix well:

1 lb brown sugar
1/4 cup French's Dijon Mustard

1/2 cup fruit juice

Heat in saucepan until melted, pouring over ham.

New Harmony, IN 47631
Tel (812) 682-4491

NORTHCENTRAL

Old Rittenhouse Inn

Old Rittenhouse Inn was built in 1890 as a summer home for Allen C. Fuller, Adjutant General for the state of Illinois during the Civil War. Except for a change in color, expanded kitchen, and an added solarium, the Queen Anne style mansion remains much the same as it did in Fuller's day.

The interesting structure has welcomed visitors with twenty-six rooms and twelve working fireplaces since 1976. All of the guest rooms are furnished with antiques, and breezes sweeping the front porch on lazy afternoons draw visitors to comfortable chairs.

Elegant six course dinners are served in the Victorian dining room. Specialties are fresh Lake Superior Trout Aux Champagne, Cordon Bleu with Wild Rice Dressing, Prime Roast Leg of Lamb, Crepes de la Mer, and Scallops Provencal.

Strawberry Consomme

1 pt fresh strawberries	1 - 3 inch stick cinnamon
1-2/3 cups fresh cut rhubarb	2 cups water
3/4 to 1 cup sugar	1/2 cup burgundy wine
1/2 cup soda water	sour cream

Set aside about six strawberries; cut up remaining berries and put in saucepan with rhubarb, cinammon stick, sugar and water. Bring to boil, reduce in heat, and simmer until rhubarb is tender, about 5 minutes. Pour into strainer and press out juice (there should be 3 cups rosy-pink juice). Add burgundy and soda. Slice remaining berries. Serve or hot or chilled, garnished with sliced berries and dollops of sour cream. Serves 4 to 6.

Box 584
Bayfield, WS 54814
Tel (715) 779-5765

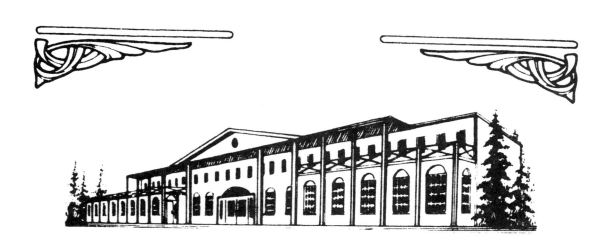

PINE EDGE INN

The Pine Edge Inn was called the Elks Hotel when it hosted Charles Lindburgh's hometown return with a glittering banquet in tribute to his historic flight in 1927. It has long been the center of the town's social affairs. Other well-known personalities who have been entertained at the inn include Hubert Humphrey, General George C. Marshall, Jack Benny, Sinclair Lewis, Fred Waring, and Van Cliburn.

The guest rooms are large and comfortable with newer accommodations across the street. Cross-country skiing, snowmobiling, and an excursion boat ride are just minutes away. Wild game and excellent walleye fishing are at hand.

Hearty meals, all from "scratch" are served in the New England colonial dining room. The menu includes Meat and Potatoes, Roast Veal Bourguignon, Veal Bird with Mushroom Sauce, Leg of Lamb, Beef Stroganoff, and Smoked Beef Tongue. To top off the meal, the guest should treat himself to Caramel Walnut Pie.

Caramel Walnut Pie

3 eggs
1 cup white syrup
1/2 tsp maple flavoring
3/4 cup chopped walnuts

1/2 cup sugar
1/2 cup milk
1 9-inch pie crust
whipped cream

Mix eggs, syrup, flavoring, sugar, and milk into regular unbaked pie crust. Sprinkle ¾ cup chopped walnuts on top and bake 45 minutes at 350 degrees or until done. Cool. Serve topped with whipped cream.

308 First Street SE
Little Falls, MN 56345
Tel (612) 632-6681

Sherwood Forest is a charming Victorian home built in 1905 and located 1/2 block from the beautiful sandy beaches that stretch along the eastern shore of Lake Michigan. Painted a deep farmhouse red, Sherwood Forest offers a delightfully relaxed atmosphere.

Hardwood floors, leaded glass windows and an oak paneled staircase add to its ambiance. The guest rooms are furnished in a compatible mixture of traditional and antique pieces, wingbacks and Oriental rugs. One room boasts a hand-painted mural that transforms the room into a canopied loft high in the tree tops. There's a fireplace in this room. In addition there's a cottage with a fireplace on the grounds.

Nearby activities include sailing and canoeing, summer theater, golf, art galleries and restaurants.

Breakfast is served in the dining room or on the wraparound porch.

Temptations are lemon yogurt bread, blueberry muffins, sour cream coffee cake with fresh fruit, juice and gourmet coffee.

Vanilla Yogurt — Granola Dish

32 oz Dannon Vanilla Yogurt	1/2 lb apricots (dried)
1 small box Kellogg's® Low-fat Granola	1 kiwi
1/2 lb dried cranberries - sweetened	1 8-oz can Dole® pineapple chunks

Using an 8-ounce or 1-cup Pyrex® bowl, spoon in 4 to 5 ounces of vanilla yogurt. Sprinkle granola to cover yogurt. Sprinkle dried cranberries on top. Cut apricots in half and circle them around the middle (cut side in). Put a slice of kiwi in the middle. Put 4 chunks of pineapple in between apricots. Makes 10 individual dishes.

Lemon Yogurt Bread

3 cups flour	3/4 cup vegetable oil
1 tsp baking soda	1-1/2 cups sugar
1/2 tsp baking powder	2 cups lemon yogurt
1 tsp salt	2 tbs lemon juice (real lemon)
3 eggs	

Sift the dry ingredients, put in separate bowl. Lightly beat the eggs in a large bowl. Add oil and sugar; mix well. Add yogurt and lemon juice and add dry ingredients —mix well. Pour into two well-greased loaf pans. Bake at 325° for one hour.

938 Center Street, Box 315
Saugatuck, MI 49453
Tel 1-800-986-1999

Skoglund Farm

Skoglund Farm, the two-story clapboard structure with front and screened-in porches, was built on the prairie in 1917. Furnished with some antiques, the guest rooms are comfortable to visitors at this working/guest farm where cattle, horses, barn fowl, and peacocks reside in harmony with the pastoral landscape. The inn is an excellent place to see first-hand a house and farm on the American prairie, and the area is very popular with pheasant hunters in the fall of the year.

A Continental breakfast is prepared each morning for the guests, and American fare of Roast Beef, Fresh Garden Vegetables, Chicken, Fish, and Steak are on the menu.

Squash Casserole

6 cups sliced summer squash
1 can condensed milk
2 cups shredded carrots
1 8-oz herb stuffing mix

1/4 cup chopped onion
1 cup sour cream
1 can water chestnuts, sliced
1/2 cup melted butter

Cook onions til tender. Mix all ingredients except stuffing mix with squash. Put stuffing mix in bottom of 12 x 7 pan, saving some for top layer. Place squash mixture over bottom layer of stuffing mix and top with stuffing. Bake for 25-30 minutes until lightly browned in 350° oven.

Box 45
Canova, SD 57321
Tel (605) 247-3445

Stafford's Bay View Inn

Stafford's Bay View Inn suggests an earlier time of architectural beauty and is one of Michigan's oldest hostelries. The inn has played a part in the rich history of the area since before the turn of the century when it catered to summer visitors traveling to Petosky and Bay View by steamship. Crowned by a spiraling cupola, Stafford's Bay View Inn is listed on the National Register of Historic Places.

The lobby's furnishings with period antiques include an elegant French mantel clock dating back to 1887. Each of the 22 guest rooms have fine pieces such as writing tables, rocking chairs, antique beds, and one room is home to a massive mahogany sleighbed. The cheery sunroom is filled with lacey wicker.

Besides sailing and canoeing, guests may enjoy Nordic skiing right from the front door along the lake.

Meals are served in three dining rooms that accommodate 300. The Garden Room faces the bay. Its exceptional cuisine is known throughout the area.

Hot Bacon Dressing

10 cups vinegar cider	10 cups water
2 cups sugar	5 tsp salt
7 tsp white pepper	20 tsp dry mustard

Cut up and cook enough bacon to get 2 cups fat. Separate. Add 2 cups flour to bacon fat and bring to boil, adding bacon and other ingredients. Remove from heat, slowly adding 40 whipped eggs. Bring to boil for 1 minute. Recipe may be cut by 3/4.

U.S. 31
North Petoskey, MI 49770
Tel (616) 347-2771

Welshfield Inn

Welshfield Inn is an old landmark known from coast to coast that dates back to the 1840s. When it opened as the Nash Hotel by Alden J. Nash, it served as a stagecoach stop on the run from Cleveland to Pittsburgh. It was also the center for social and cultural affairs including a singing school, spelling matches, jigs and reels.

The historic inn was a link in the charitable Underground Railroad during the Civil War. David Nash, son of the landlord, recalled seeing his mother send food in a basket to the barn where runaway slaves were hiding in a load of hay.

Over the years the establishment has changed hands, been renamed, and the building itself reworked. Although no overnight lodgings are available at this treasured old inn, meals are pleasantly served in a manner that preserves the traditions of Welshfield.

Melon Soup

flesh of 1 choice, diced melon
(cantaloupe)
grated rind of 1 lemon
2 cups milk
lemon juice

dash of salt & ginger
6 tbs butter
rum

Combine melon with sugar, salt and ginger. Saute in butter in saucepan. Stir in 2 cups milk and simmer at low temperature, stirring occasionally for 10 minutes. Let cool. Place in blender until smooth stirring in a hint of lemon juice and rum. Serve chilled, garnished with mint leaves.

Route 422
Burton, OH 44021
Tel (216) 834-4164

NORTHCENTRAL

The White Gull Inn was established in 1896 as part of a larger resort bought by Dr. Herman Welcher and it was moved across the frozen waters of Green Bay by teams of horses and sleds.

In the beginning visitors arrived to the coastal village by steamboat to enjoy its quiet ambiance and bill of fare. Today, sailboat masts and motor yachts are a part of the local scene. Open year round, activities abound in Fish Creek and Door County.

Three cottages, in addition to the main inn, have been refurbished and decorated in styles that recall their earlier use. Furnished with iron and brass beds, wicker chairs, walnut and oak dressers, some of the rooms have fireplaces and pieces that date to the original owner.

Three meals are served daily. Selections of Beef, Fish and Fowl are prepared from original recipes. A specialty is the Door County Fish Boil as prepared by the Scandinavians over a hundred years ago.

Door County Fish Boil

12 small red potatoes	**cheesecloth**
8 qts water	**1 lb salt (2 cups)**
melted butter	**lemon wedges**
12 1" thick whitefish steaks	

Wash potatoes and cut a slice from each end. Tie potatoes in cheesecloth bag. Put water in large pot, preferably one with removable basket and bring to boil. Add potatoes and half the salt; cook 20 minutes. When potatoes are almost done, wrap fish in cheesecloth and add to pot with remaining salt. Cook 10 minutes. Skim fish oils from surface of water. Lift cooked potatoes and fish from cooking water and drain. Serve with melted butter and lemon. When cooking over open fire, fish oils are boiled off by tossing a small amount of kerosene on the fire, causing the water to boil up and over.

Box 159
Fish Creek, WI 54212
Tel (414) 868-3517

Wickwood Inn

Wickwood Inn, inspired after a visit to the Duke's Hotel in London by Sue and Stub Lewis, is in the delightful setting of Saugatuck Village with its sailboat masts, tall shade trees and quaint Victorian homes . . . reminders of a New England coastal town.

Inside, the inn is furnished with family and antique pieces which reflect its early shipping port days. The spacious and sunny living room has a warming fireplace flanked by a pair of crewel wingbacks and on the floor is an old Chinese rug that provides the color scheme of navy, tan, and rust. French doors lead into the relaxing atmosphere of a plant-filled room with vaulted ceilings, cedar walls, shutters, and brick floors.

Ten guest rooms and suites are furnished in a variety of charming styles. Brass headboards, canopied beds, armoires, lacey wicker, and a marble-topped writing desk are complemented with flowered wallpaper and fabrics by Laura Ashley. Crabtree and Evelyn of London are added amenities.

A Continental breakfast is served each morning of freshly squeezed Juice, Hot Rolls, Coffee, and Tea.

Spinach Dip

1 pkg frozen, chopped spinach
1/2 small onion, chopped
mayonnaise to make a smooth consistency

Mix all together and chill for 1 hour. Serve with crackers or bread cubes.

510 Butler Street
Saugatuck, MI 49453
Tel (616) 857-1097

NORTHCENTRAL

Auberge HANDFIELD

Auberge Handfield Inn is a family business whose innkeepers take great pride in extending charm and hospitality to their many guests. Located on the Richelieu River amidst graceful trees, the inn was renovated in 1984 leaving intact the originality of the home that was built more than 160 years ago.

The guest rooms have horizontal logs and exposed ceiling beams that are quaint and comfortable with some antiques. In addition, several rustic accommodations surround the inn. During the summer months, receptions are held on the terrace, and banquets and meetings are held aboard the showboat "Escale."

Meals are served in a dining room filled with warmth and sunshine. Both Continental and New French Canadian cuisine tempt the diner.

Rillette of Goose in White Wine

1 large goose	8 lbs rich pork stock
4 big onions	3 cups white wine
salt, pepper, thyme, laurel, and cinnamon to taste	

Stew the goose and pork stock in pan with water. Add onions cut into pieces and all spices, cooking for 2 hours. Take off the meat and grease, passing liquid through a sieve and putting back to boil to reduce. Cut all pieces of goose into big pieces and then mince. Add reduced cooking liquid with white wine, then add goose and grease. Spread in pan and refrigerate.

St. Marc-sur-le-Richelieu
Quebec, Canada JOL 2EO
Tel (514) 584-2226

CANADA

Blomidon Inn sits on 2-1/2 acres of terraced lawns shaded by century-old elms, chestnuts, and maples. The front veranda of this Victorian mansion overlooks a small garden and the Minas Basin beyond. Built in 1877 as the home of Capt. Rufus Burgess, the magnificent wood used in its construction was brought back as ship's ballast. Much of the finish work was created by shipwrights, including the impressive stairway and entrance hall. The plaster cornices, dados, and marble fireplace were fashioned by Italian craftsmen.

The formal Blue Room and Rose Room are beautiful examples of Victorian elegance. Guest rooms are furnished with mahogany poster beds, handcrafted quilts, wingbacks, hardwood floors, and rich carpeting.

Meals are graciously served in two dining rooms. The main dining room is furnished with Chippendale chairs, a warming fireplace for cool evenings, and a bay window. The Library Dining Room is smaller and more intimate. An extensive menu presents traditional English Trifle, Succulent Scallops, Prime Rib, Chilled Strawberry Soup, and Aigby Scallops in Green Sauce.

Scottish Oatcakes

3 cups rolled oats
1 cup white sugar
1 tsp soda

3 cups white flour
2 tsp salt
1-1/2 cups lard

Combine oats, flour, sugar, salt, and soda, working in the 1-1/2 cups lard. Moisten and add cold water to roll out on a rolled oat-covered board (not flour) and cut into diamond shapes. Bake 10-15 minutes in moderate oven.

Strawberry Butter

Cream 2 tbs butter and 2 tbs cream cheese until fluffy. Add 4 tbs strawberry jam and sprinkle with nutmeg. Serve with Scottish oatcakes or scones.

Box 839
Wolfville, N.S. BOP 1X0
Tel (902) 542-9326

CANADA

Gray Rocks

Gray Rocks is as enchanting during the summer and autumn months as it is in winter, making it an inn for all seasons. It sits at the very edge of the lake like a medieval fortress, and its red roof accents the colorful sailboats in summer, while skiers glide down slopes right to the door in winter. All water sports, golf, tennis, horseback riding, and a stroll along the beautiful sun-washed lakeside bordered with white birches make unforgettable memories. Home of the famous Snow Eagle Ski School, the resort drops dramatically into the clear waters of Lac Quimet.

Excellent full course meals, prepared by Executive Chef Jean Labelle, are served in the dining room. Filet Mignon with Boneless Stuffed Quail, Osso Busso Milanaise, and Cold Grand Marnier Souffle are among the many temptations.

Osso Busso Milanaise

**12 veal shanks, 2-inch slicesbroken in-
to bits**

2-3 tbs flour	**4 tbs butter**
2 tbs oliver oil	**salt & pepper to taste**

Dredge veal in flour, saute, remove, and set aside. Add and saute:

1/3 cup diced onions	**1/2 cup diced mushrooms**
1/4 cup diced ham	**1/2 cup diced carrots**
1/2 cup diced celery	**2 cloves garlic, chopped**
flour as needed	

Dust, cooking until roux becomes brownish. Remove fat and add:

1 cup dry white wine	4 cups beef stock
2 tsp tomato paste	bouquet garni

Heat to boiling point, adding veal previously set aside. Cover partially and simmer for 1 1/2 hours. Serve with rice. Yield: 6 servings

Mont Tremblant
B.P. 1000 St. Jovite JOT2HO
Quebec, Canada
Tel (819) 425-2771

CANADA

MARATHON INN

Marathon Inn, completely surrounded by the sea and historic charm of a picturesque Maritime fishing community, was built over a century ago by a retired seaman, Captain Pettis, and to this day, visitors arrive by ferry. The island lies in the world-famous Bay of Fundy known for its extreme tides and is a naturalist's and bird watcher's paradise. When John J. Audubon visited the island in 1833, he found more than 275 species of birds. He would still be impressed: they haven't moved away.

The inn makes no pretense of being elaborate, it is, nevertheless, inviting and provides a welcomed respite for those who want to steal away for a quieter moment. Many of the guest rooms enjoy views of the harbor.

Excellent meals are served in the dining room with fresh-from -the-ocean plates topped off with Raisin and Walnut Pie.

Raisin and Walnut Pie

In an unbaked 9'' pie shell, spread 3/4 cup raisins and 3/4 cup walnut pieces. In a bowl, mix:

3 eggs, well beaten	1/3 cup white sugar
1/2 stick butter	1 cup corn syrup
1/2 tsp cinnamon	1/2 tsp nutmeg

When well mixed, pour over raisins and walnuts and bake at 350 degrees for about 40 minutes or just until center of pie starts to be firm. Very nice served with ice cream.

North Head
Grand Manan, NB E0G2MO
Tel (506) 662-8144

CANADA

The Oban Inn is one of the oldest buildings in the historic town of Niagara-on-the-Lake. The Victorian structure was built as the home of Duncan Milloy and has served mainly as a hostelry, but during World War I it was an officer's mess. Restored to capture its former charm in this pretty town on the lake, the inn is recognized along with the Shaw Festival as a Niagara landmark, and George Bernard Shaw's portrait hangs above the fire in the lounge.

Guest rooms are colorful and nostalgic with lake breezes and views that, more than a hundred years ago, held steamships and sailing vessels gliding through the waters offshore.

In addition to strolling through the quaint village, it is only a few minutes drive from Niagara Falls, shops, and beautiful botanical gardens.

Meals are served in cozy, well-appointed dining rooms with the soft touch of candlelight and fresh flowers.

Chicken Breasts with Pistachio Nut Dressing

Chicken breasts boned, skinned, and pounded with meat tenderizer until quite flat, and make dressing of:

1 loaf white bread, broken into bits   **1 onion chopped**
chopped parsley   **chopped celery tops**
coarsely chopped nuts
salt, pepper, little garlic, melted butter little milk heated with butter

Saute lightly in butter:
   onions and celery

Add hot milk and toss very lightly. Add chopped nuts, salt, pepper, and garlic to taste. Place on chicken breasts and roll up. Put in roasting pan cut side down, dot with butter and cook 1 hour at 350°. When completely cold, cut into 1/2 inch rounds. Colorful on buffet table.

Box 94
Niagara-on-the-Lake, Ontario LOS IJO
Tel (416) 468-7811 or 2165

CANADA

Index of Recipes

APPETIZERS

Apple Dip 43
Country Ham Balls 118
Dilled Cheese Cubes 78
Hot Broccoli Dip 126
Pate 218
Sauteed Mushrooms 28
Smoked Eggs 38
Spinach Dip 235
Zucchini Nibbles 158

BEVERAGES AND SALADS

Chicken Salad 129
Fresh Broccoli Salad 127
Hot Spiced Apple Cider 43
Hot Spiced Cider 217
Lemonade 41
Spinach Salad with Hot Bacon Dressing 206
Turkey Waldorf Salad 22
Warm Spinach Salad with Smoked Duck 204
Wedding Reception Punch 121

BREADS

Aunt Min's Swedish Rye 97
Biscuits 149
Blueberry Bran Muffins 15
Blueberry Grents 6
Blueberry Muffins - Queen Victoria 75
Blueberry Scones 9
Brown Breakfast Bread 140
California Orange Raisin Loaf 195
Cheese-Filled Apricot Bread 7
Chocolate Bread with Vanilla Butter 193
Corn Meal Muffins 138
Daniels Family Waffles 196
Daniel's Pumpkin Bread 49
Datenut Bread 103
Famous Awahnee Pancakes 185
Flat Top Orange Date Muffins 66
Fresh Lemon-Nut Bread 191
German Apple Pancake 181
Hot Cakes 104
Irish Soda Bread 96
Jared's Cranberry Nut Bread 48
Lemon Yogurt Bread 230
Oatmeal Bread 27
Prune Bread 131
Pumpkin Bread 33
Pumpkin Gingerbread 190

Raisin Bran Muffins 154
Rolled Oats Molasses Bread 2
Scottish Oatcakes. 237
Sea Chambers Lemon Tea Bread 80
Sheila's Cranberry Almond Bread 69
Sour Cream - Cinnamon Loaves 151
Spoonbread 18
Stone Ground Wheat Cakes 61
Strawberry Nut Bread 202
Victorian House Granola 157
Whole Wheat Raisin - Nut Bread. 199
Wienerbrod 162
Yankee Cornsticks 74

DESSERTS

Apple and Banana Fritters 117
Apple Butter 153
Apple Cake - Captain Whidbey 203
Apple Cake - Fairfield Inn 32
Apple Cake - West Virginia Blackwalnut 109
Apple Crisp 91
Bamboo Peach. 221
Best Ever Coffee Cake. 47
Black Bottom Pie. 128
Blackberry Jam Cake. 134
Blueberry Gems. 63
Brandy Alexander Pie - Chocolate Crumb Crust 56
Bread Pudding - Homestead Inn 45
Bread Pudding - Inn at Pleasant Hill 145
Bread Pudding - Old Fashioned 209
Bread Pudding - Salmen-Fritchie House 180
Bread Pudding - The Pelican Inn 197
Breakfast Cake 168
Burnt Creme 85
Buttermilk Pie. 122
Cabinet Pudding 62
Caramel Walnut Pie 229
Carrot Mousse 76
Chocolate Antlers and Chocolate Cups 223
Chocolate Raspberry Cake. 212
Chocolate Treat 161
Chocolate Walnut Pie 89
Coconut Pound Cake 86
Cocoa Kisses 184
Cranberry Torte 25
Creamy Berry Royal 187
Divinity Candy 167
Fresh Muselix 82
Frozen Lemon Pie 73
Fruit Cocktail Torte 225
Fruit Cream Pie 124
Galatoboureko 213
Gingerbread Muffins 171

Grandma's Cake . . . . 13?
Honey Apple Crisp 139
Hummingbird Cake . . . . 5?
Indian Pudding - Curtis House. . . . . 2?
Indian Pudding - Red Lion. . . . . 7?
Key Lime Pie . . . . 7?
Lemon Cheese Cake 68
Mamita's Key Lime Pie 135
Mocha Mousse 105
Molasses Breakfast Pie 88
Morning Cake Delight with Hawthorne Inn Topping 42
Old-Fashioned Maple Frango. 224
Overnight Coffee Cake 164
Peanut Butter Custard 136
Pearl Tapioca Pudding. 136
Pecan Pralines 83
Poached Pears with Almond Raisin Stuffing and Raspberry Sauce. 183
Pound Cake 112
Raisin and Walnut Pie 239
Raspberry Cheese Pie 39
Raspberry Chevre Cheese Cake 144
Raspberry Cream Cheese Coffee Cake. 188
Raspberry Gem Tarts. 215
Rhubarb Pie. 54
Sam Hill Breakfast Cake 226
Southern Peanut Cream Pie 44
Southern Pecan Pie 107
Stage Puffs 37
Steamboat Coffee Cake 210
Sterling Inn Coffee Cake 90
Strawberry Consomme. 228
Tart Linzer. 16
Tia Maria Cake 81
Vanilla Yogurt - Granola Dish 230
Welsh Cakes 98
White Chocolate Coeur A La Creme 11
White Chocolate Mousse 222

DRESSING, SAUCES AND RELISHES

Brown Sugar Sauce 145
Celery Seed Dressing - a la Weathervane. 95
Celery Seed Dressing - Golden Lamb 220
Cheese Sauce. 14
Chocolate Sauce 87
Chutney. 214
Honey Dressing. 130
Honey Mustard Dressing 159
Hot Bacon Dressing. 232
Lemon Syrup. 213
Mint Sauce for Lamb. 114
Mornay Sauce 150
Newburg Sauce 208
Nut-Raisin-Cinnamon-Sugar Mixture. 168

Orange Sauce 209
Raspberry Barbeque Sauce 223
Red Eye Gravy 132
Roquefort Dressing 175
Strawberry Butter 237
Sundried Tomato Pesto Sauce 51
Sweet and Sour Sauce 118

ENTREES

Arroz con Langostinos. 155
Artichoke Frittata. 211
Baked French Toast Almondine 182
Baked Goat Cheese, Rochambeau 23
Baked Stuffed Shrimp 21
Beef Stroganoff 94
Breakfast Log 12
Buffalo Stew 219
Chicken and Andouille Gumbo 177
Chicken Cilantro 173
Chicken and Dumplings. 147
Chicken Breasts with Pistachio Nut Dressing. 240
Chicken Enchilada Pie. 198
Chicken Logan au Peche 52
Chicken Middletown 59
Chicken Nonie. 100
Chicken Saute with Cheese Sauce 14
Chicken with Garlic Sauce. 207
Clams Genesee Falls Style. 35
Country Ham with Red Eye Gravy 132
Country Ham Quiche. 119
Crab Bisque, Evermay-on-the-Delaware 29
Crab Bisque, Maryland Inn 137
Crab Imperial 156
Cranberry Baked Chicken 92
Crawfish Etouffe 179
Creamed Ham and Mushrooms 40
Curried Lamb and Apricots 53
Duck at Gristmill Square 125
Easy, Elegant Brunch Casserole. 67
Escalloped Oysters 156
Fine Fowl with Shrimp 26
Fish Boil 234
Gravad Lax 163
Grilled Duck Breast with Raspberry Barbeque Sauce. 223
Halibut and Rice Casserole 205
Hazelnut Chicken with Orange Thyme Creme 84
Hickory Smoked Beef Brisket 201
Hominy Grits Cheese Casserole. 184
Hot Brown with Mornay Sauce 150
How to Cook a Country Ham 143
Mastery Key-Ch of Baldpate 186
Medallions of Pork 79
Must-Go-Quiche 1

Osso Busso Milanaise 238
Pepper Steak 113
Porcupine Meat Balls. 178
Rainbow Trout Almondine. 54
Ravioles De Homard 30-31
Rillete of Goose in White Wine 236
Roasted Sea Scallops with Pistachio Nut and Cognac Butter 8
Rotolo 65
Russian Chicken 159
Salmon 50
Salmon Papillote 208
Sausage-Egg Souffle 176
Sausage Strata 58
Scallops Pernod 146
Scallops Steamed with Spinach and Red Peppers. 70
Scallops with Garlic and Tomatoes 116
Shaker Ham with Red Geranium Glaze 227
Shrimp Scampi 10
Smoked Pork with Braised Red Cabbage. 46
Southwestern Brunch Eggs 170
Spicy New England Pot Roast 20
Spicy Shrimp. 19
Strawberry Buttered Omelet. 110
Stuffed French Toast 165
Sweetbreads, Balsam House 5
Veal Maison 72
Veal Normandy 101

SOUPS

Black Bean Soup. 55
British Cream of Carrot Soup 71
Chicken Corn Chowder. 4
Chilled Strawberry Soup 60
Crab Corn Soup. 166
Cream of Pimiento Soup 108
Cucumber Soup - Glen Iris Inn 36
Cucumber Soup - Westmoor Inn 99
Leek and Potato Soup 189
Melon Soup. 233
Mountain Apple and Vidalia Onion Soup. 148
Peanut Soup. 160
Philadelphia Pepper Pot Soup 93
Split Pea Soup 216
Sweet Potato and Pumpkin Bisque. 102
Tomato-Basil Soup 192
Yogurt and Cucumber Soup. 34

VEGETABLES

Baked Beans 141
Beaumont Corn Pudding 106
Beets in Orange Sauce. 172
Broccoli and Rice Casserole 152

Candied Sweet Potatoes with Peanuts 123
Cauliflower Rinaldi 111
Corn Pudding - Hilda Crockett's 112
Cornwallis Yams 115
Eggplant St. Claire. 169
Indian Corn Pudding 17
Jane's Potatoes. 200
Maple Squash 64
Mexican Eggplant 194
Mushrooms en Croute 3
Squash Casserole. 120
Squash Casserole, Skoglund Farm 231
Stuffed Eggplant 142
Tomato Florentine Strata 13

Index of Inns and Lodges

Northeast

The Abbey 1
Adirondak Loj 2
Andover Inn 3
Asa Ransom House 4
The Balsam House 5
Barnard-Good House 6
Bishopsgate Inn 7
Black Bass Hotel 8
Blueberry Hill 9
The Bradley Inn 10
The Bramble Inn 11
The Brass-Bed 12
Breakwater 13
The Cameron Estate Inn 14
The Captain Lord Mansion 15
The Inn at Castle Hill 16
Century Inn 17
Chalfonte 18
Charles Hinckley House 19
The Churchill House Inn 20
The Claremont 21
Colligan's Stockton Inn 22
Country Inn at Princeton 23
Curtis House 24
Dana Place Inn 25
Dobbin House Tavern 26
The Edgartown Inn 27
1811 House 28
Ever-May On the Delaware 29
Exeter Inn 30-31
Fairfield Inn and Guest House 32
Fitzwilliam Inn 33
Garnet Hill 34
The Genesee Falls Inn 35
Glen Iris Inn 36
The Golden Stage Inn 37
Greenhurst Inn 38
Greenville Arms 39
Griswold Inn 40
Harbour Inne & Cottage 41
Hawthorne Inn 42
Hickory Bridge Farm 43
The Holloway House 44
The Homestead Inn 45
The Hotel Hershey 46
Howard House 47
Jared Coffin House 48
The John Hancock Inn 49
The Kedron Valley Inn 50
Lincklaen House 51
Logan Inn 52

The Londonderry Inn. 53
Longfellow's Wayside Inn 54
Lovett's 55
Lyme Inn. 56
Maine Stay 58
The Mainstay. 57
Middlebury Inn 60
Middletown Springs Inn 59
Mill House Inn 61
Mohonk Mountain House 62
Moose Mountain Lodge. 63
Morrill Place 64
Mountain View Inn 65
The Nauset House Inn 66
The Okemo Inn 67
Old Drovers Inn. 68
Old Fort Inn. 69
Old Lyme Inn 70
The Old Red Inn & Cottages 71
Old Riverton Inn 72
Philbrook Farm Inn 73
Publick House 74
The Queen Victoria 75
Rabbit Hill Inn 76
The Red Lion Inn 77
The Redcoat's Return 78
The Inn at Sawmill Farm 79
Scarlett House 82
Sea Chambers 80
1740 House 81
Shartlesville Hotel. 83
Shelter Harbor Inn. 84
The Sherwood Inn 85
Snow Den Inn 86
Springside Inn 87
The Squire Tarbox Inn 88
The Inn at Starlight Lake 89
The Sterling Inn. 90
Three Village Inn. 91
The Village Inn 92
The Inn at Lake Waramaug 93
The Waterford Inne 94
The Weathervane Inn 95
The Wedgwood Inn 96
West Mountain Inn 97
West River Lodge 98
The Westmoor Inn 99
The Inn at Weston 100
The Winter's Inn 101
Yankee Pedlar Inn 102

Southeast

The Bailey House 103

....am Mountain Inn 104
.... Banyan 105
....aumont Inn 106
....he Boar's Head Inn 107
....oone Tavern Hotel 108
....he Inn at Buckeystown 109
....uttonwood Inn 110
Casa de Solana 155
Chalet Suzanne 111
Hilda Crockett's Chesapeake House 112
The Clewiston Inn 113
The Cloister 114
Colonial Inn 115
The Corner Cupboard Inn 116
The Country Inn 117
Doe Run Inn 118
Dudley's Restaurant 119
DuPont Lodge 120
Elmwood Inn 121
Fryemont Inn 122
General Lewis Inn 123
Graves' Mountain Lodge 124
The Inn at Gristmill Square 125
The Haslam - Fort House 126
Herndon J. Evans Lodge 127
High Hampton Inn 128
Hotel Hilltop House 129
Hound Ears Lodge 130
Indigo Inn 131
The Jarrett House 132
The Kenwood Inn 133
Loder House 134
Maple Lodge 135
The Martha Washington Inn 136
Maryland Inn 137
Meadow Lane Lodge 138
Mentone Inn 139
Mill Farm Inn 140
The Nu-Wray Inn 141
Old Stone Inn 142
Old Talbott Tavern 143
Planters Inn 144
Shaker Village of Pleasant Hill 145
The Red Fox Tavern 146
Renfro Valley Lodge 147
Richmond Hill Inn 148
Rokeby Hall 149
Science Hill Inn 150
The 1735 House 151
Smith House 152
St. Francis Inn 153
The Strawberry Inn 154
The Tidewater Inn 156
Victorian House 157

Vine Cottage Inn . . . .
Von-Bryan Inn 1
Wayside Inn 16
Wells Inn 16
Westcott House 16
Williamsburg Lodge 163

Southcentral

Anchuca 164
Annie's 165
Asphodel Plantation 166
Borgman's Bed & Breakfast 167
The Burn 168
The Columns 169
Crystal River Inn 170
Dairy Hollow House 171
Excelsior House 172
Laborde House 173
Lamothe House 174
Le Richelieu 175
Linden 176
Oak Alley Plantation 177
Oak Square 178
The Pontchartrain Hotel 179
Salmen-Fritchie House 180
The Schwegmann House 181
Williams House Bed & Breakfast Inn 182

Southwest

The Apple Blossom Inn 184
Arizona Biltmore 183
The Awahnee 185
The Baldpate Inn 186
Benbow Inn 187
Campbell Ranch Inn 188
Hotel del Coronado 189
The Gingerbread Mansion 190
The Grey Whale Inn 191
Harbor House 192
The Hearthstone Inn 193
Meadeau View Lodge 194
The Old Milano Hotel 195
The Old Miner's Lodge 196
The Pelican Inn 197
Rancho de los Caballeros 198
The Seal Beach Inn 199
Sutter Creek Inn 200
Tanque Verde Ranch 201
The Wine Country Inn 202

Northwest

The Captain Whidbey 203
Columbia Gorge Hotel. 204
Favorite Bay Inn 205
Lake Quinault Lodge 208
Lone Mountain Ranch 206
Paradise Ranch Inn 207
Shoshone Lodge 209
Steamboat Inn 210
Inn of the White Salmon 211
The Winchester Inn 212

Northcentral

The Archer House 213
The Blackfork Inn 214
Botsford Inn 215
Cascade Lodge 216
The Cider Mill. 217
Duneland Beach Inn 218
Fort Robinson State Park 219
The Golden Lamb 220
Grand Hotel. 221
The Heritage House 222-223
Lowell Inn. 224
Michillinda Beach Lodge. 225
The National House Inn. 226
The New Harmony Inn 227
Old Rittenhouse Inn. 228
The Pine Edge Inn 229
Sherwood Forest 230
Skoglund Farm 231
Stafford's Bay View Inn. 232
Welshfield Inn 233
The White Gull Inn 234
Wickwood Inn 235

Canada

Auberge Handfield Inn 236
Blomidon Inn 237
Gray Rocks 238
Marathon Inn. 239
The Oban Inn 240

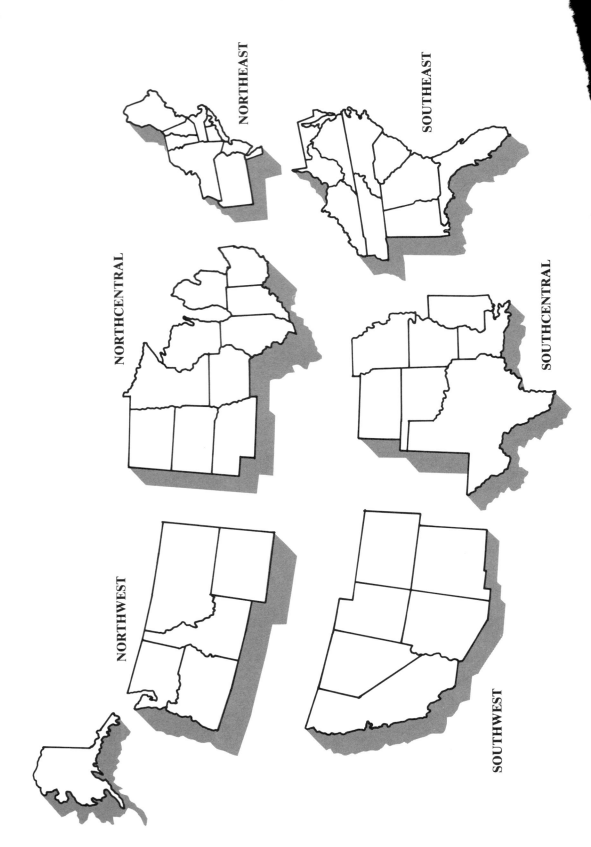

NORTHEAST

SOUTHEAST

NORTHCENTRAL

SOUTHCENTRAL

NORTHWEST

SOUTHWEST